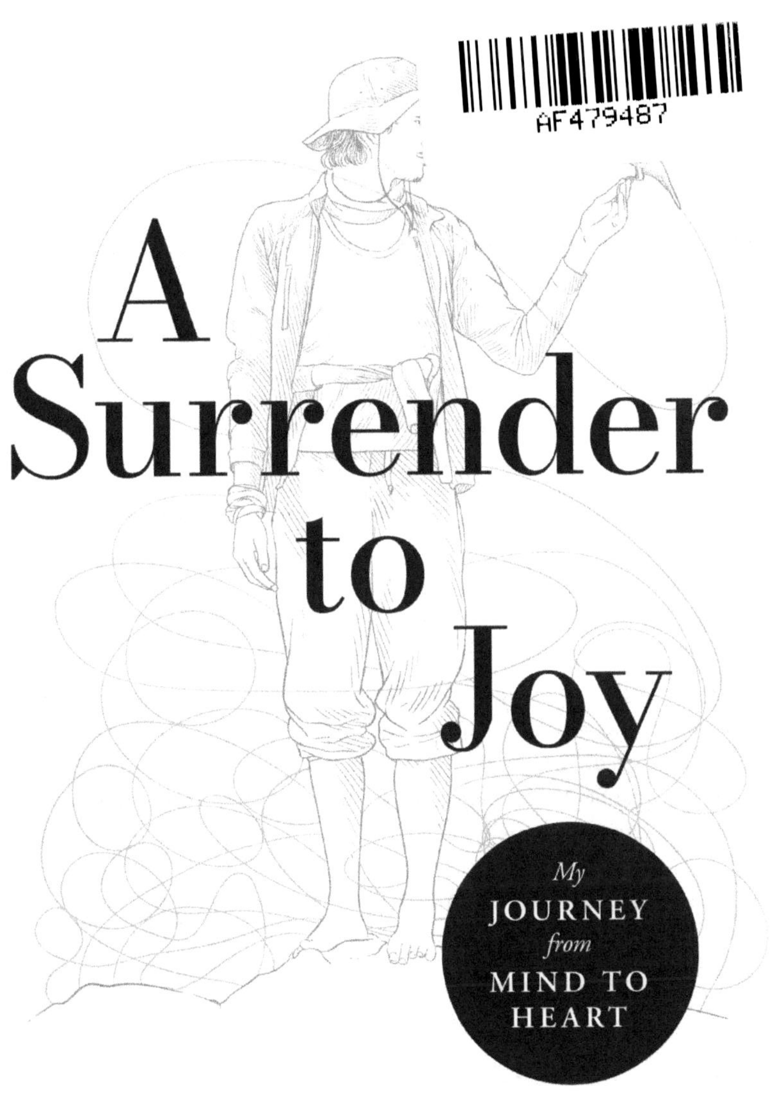

A Surrender to Joy

My JOURNEY *from* MIND TO HEART

DANIEL CAMERON BECKER

CONTENTS

To my mother,
for taking her life,
so that many may find theirs.

To my aunt,
For buying the typewriter which started this journey.

To God,
for everlasting, unchanging, unconditional,
Love.

FOREWORD

I can't take credit for this book.
This is Life's story.
I have put pen to paper only what Life has gifted me.
In this case I lovingly received chronic illness, depression, anxiety, death, burnout, and a return to joy.
A meeting with the miraculous.
A surrender to Heart.

I count my blessings that I have many friends and family who journeyed with me during this time. They can vouch for the tales which painted this season of my life.
The true credit goes to the Master Painter.
May Divinity's intention reach out to you as you look upon it.
I pray I have portrayed it with the very finest, detailed brush strokes.

May you look at this canvas and find what is yours.
May you see what needs to be seen.

Let us journey together into the story of our lives.

WHEN I FIRST HEARD THE MUSIC

I was living the dream. But soundtracks change. I was in my mid-twenties, working in the advertising industry. I had my dream car, dream job, dream house, and dream girlfriend. I lived a life I was grateful for daily. I had reached the top of my career aspirations and yet didn't feel complete. Every day I would wake up and go to work in this amazing life—yet something was missing. I felt hollow, empty, yearning.

Is this it?

I wanted more, but what more was, I couldn't imagine.

This hunger for "more" wasn't always present, so I ignored it and carried on. I buried any fear that came up to indicate I may need a lifestyle change. The 'empty feeling' came and went on its own accord. Sometimes it was sudden and strong. Sometimes it was subtle. It came in many forms. I often dreamt of traveling or holidaying "somewhere else". Sometimes this unsettling feeling lingered after a nice weekend break. It would grab at me on a Monday morning as I stared out my office toward the mountains. A desire would float within me for freedom, nature, or both.

Anywhere but here.

It was a voice that popped its head up, whispering in my inner ears, *something is missing.*

What is missing? I would continuously ask myself.

I could not figure it out.

As the months passed, I forged on, but the voice became louder and more frequent.

You're destined for greater things, the voice would say.

Immediately my mind would reply, *No Daniel, be happy and content with what you have. You live an awesome life, and you have everything you need, be grateful.*

I chose to listen to my mind.

It made the most sense.

I pressed on.

I tried my best to enjoy myself.

To escape the unsettling voice I filled my life with as much as possible. I frequented parties, social gatherings, yoga studios, festivals, and outdoor activities. I pursued international travel. I chose the on-the-go, on-the-run, looking-for-fun attitude to life. Eating, drinking, experiencing, absorbing. Sometimes the hollow feeling left for a little while as I filled it with activities. But when I returned to my job, it came back to greet me.

My fulfillment cup would drain quickly again, the voice would return, *Daniel, are you born to be just another sheep, following the flock of 'normal society' into a life of planned mediocrity?*

Something deeper was trying to make itself known but I didn't want to hear it. I didn't want to change. I knew I wasn't destined for the life of an "office keyboard warrior" slaving for someone else's dream, but I didn't know any other way.

I didn't know how to change track.

Months went by, and to keep the passion, I tried changing my role in the company. It helped for a while. The new position increased my learning curve and the initial excitement of new challenges kept me busy. However, after I was through the honeymoon phase the familiar feeling of emptiness returned. I started to feel an even deeper hollowness on the inside.

Now what?

I should be happy.

My closest friends started noticing I was losing my glow, remarking something about missing my "Daniel spirit". I knew it. I could feel it. I appeared on the outside as my normal shiny, happy-go-lucky self, but on the inside my joy was slowly sliding out of reach. I was a boy in man's clothing, too terrified to ask myself, *Is this really it, Daniel? Is this really the greatest version of yourself you can be?*

As the inner battle raged, I continued to work harder and harder. Up to this point, I had really loved my work. The problem was, it was getting harder and harder to love. I was in the same industry, same clients, having the same fun, but something was changing inside me. Something I couldn't control.

My very own soul seemed to have its timing, and it did not suit me.

You are supposed to love this Daniel. It is everything you ever wanted.

As my inner world changed, I worked harder. Any distraction was more welcome than the *There is more* voice. When the heat was on, in the fast-paced, deadline-driven advertising work, I forgot about this other life and was happy for a moment. Well, what I thought was happy. Going at a million miles an hour, the adrenaline made me happy, yet this kind of rocket fuel didn't last forever.

Eventually, I would have to face the music.

Maybe this is what everyone else is also going through, I thought to comfort myself.

I looked at the people around me. Everyone seemed so happy and content, getting on with their day-to-day office fist pumping, high fives, client meetings, and broad smiles.

It can't be true.

There must be something wrong with me.

Why am I not able to do this?

No one else ever spoke about their unhappiness in the workplace, which made me think I was alone.

Why am I not happy? Don't I have everything?

The cycle continued – eat, sleep, work, weekend, repeat. The addictiveness of a monthly salary made it nearly impossible to exit the trap.

The harder I worked, the more I received praise—so I began working extra hard. This moved me further away from the inner whispers and drew me closer to burn out. Pleasing others is a dangerous game. I crafted my identity to the personality of the workplace. Bow ties and suspenders were the costumes of my daily office party. All the while, my soul quietly returned to its inner cubicle to suffocate.

I was beginning to hear the music, but when would I listen?

THIS SHIP IS SAILING

THEN IT HAPPENED. I was sidelined from my fast-paced life. One day I was playing soccer and tore the ligaments in my ankle. I had to stop. No more always-on-the-go as my mobility was restricted by a "moon boot" I had to wear for recovery. I was forced to lie down. Reclining on the couch, I had enough time for perspective to rear its head. The "There's something more" voice returned. This time I couldn't escape. I lay there and had to decipher it. I made this observation; At work, I was *busy, busy, busy... energyless.* Outside of work, I was *activities, activities, activities... energy full!* Inside the office, my spirit and lifeforce seeped from me. Outside the office, where I could make decisions for myself, I was alive and happy. When left to the flexibility of my own schedule, I experienced freedom, joy and fulfillment.

Why can't I live my whole life like this? I said to myself.

Why must I sell my soul in a 9 - 5 job?

The thought chewed at me as I lay on the couch and watched my friends living their joyous lives. Work hadn't always been like this for me, but something was changing. The joy outside of work was a cherry on top of an otherwise melting ice cream. Spending 9 hours a day in an office upset my whole applecart. Overcommitting to corporate spilled negatively into all areas of my life.

Why can't my entire life feel like the one when I'm not at work? Must I watch the work clock before I can be freed into fulfillment?

I observed the lives of my two housemates and close friends, Sebastian and Grant. Sebastian had never been to university and didn't have a full-time job. He didn't "work hard in the corporation to get ahead," yet he was enjoying exactly the same lifestyle as me. Same house. Same beach. Same fruit. Same friends. Everything was the same except for the whole working-9-hours-a-day part. It irked me I was working myself to death for a lifestyle he appeared to achieve effortlessly.

How did this happen? No school, no job, no worries?!

His "being" in the world was attractive to me. He appeared to ooze a level of freedom and "aliveness," which permeated all environments and attracted people around him. Whilst I was toiling for most of my day, losing my spark for life, he was living in what he called "the flow", believing "life will provide". No medical aid, no full-time employment, no insurance. He was living and trusting it would all workout. And it did. Repeatedly. Life constantly provided for him. Don't get me wrong, he had his own concerns, but it worked out for him time and again. A bit of work here. A contract there. A favor here. Friend support there. He didn't resist opportunities, no matter how small or big. He simply flowed like a turtle on a warm Indian ocean current. It further unsettled me that I had to live with this man who was walking proof this style of existence worked. It didn't always look easy, but he was free. Often receiving gifts from life that those of us with the "work hard" mentality could only dream of. One day he returned home in a new 4x4 the size of an army truck and simply said, "We've got this for a month!" Someone had given it to him to create awareness for a sports drink company. We cruised around showing off, chatting with girls, and having fun.

In my "hard-working" mentality, I would have to suffer for decades to enjoy this kind of lifestyle. For Sebastian, it was commonplace. Receiving all life wanted to give him. Minor miracles continuously presented themselves. Gifts appeared in times of need because he had chosen to live this way.

This manner of living gnawed at the strings of my conditioned self. It defied what I had been taught. *Could I really live like this?* Not knowing where a salary would come from. Not spending time in an office. Not knowing where life was carrying me. I had a degree, an income, and a plan. Sebastian niggled at my comfort zone. My other close friend didn't support my nine-to-five job prospects either. He spent more time running in the mountains than in an office. He was an outdoor sporting events manager. He would often be in the mountains for days, marking new trail routes for races or setting up festival tents to accommodate incoming adventure athletes. He appeared to have a lot of time to do what he loved. My inner voice grew louder. *Why can't I live like this? Why am I stuck with these two housemates who are living their dreams? Why can't I do what I really love?*

I didn't realize my life was calling for a shift.

My heart was downloading a new program.

There was certainly a time when I loved the advertising world and thrived in it, but my heart was beginning a fresh journey, ready to be set adrift on a new ocean of life.

I was soon to start writing a chapter marked with one simple desire: to make a difference in the world whilst having fun.

NO DANGER BEGINS

I HAD TO rest for weeks because my ankle was sprained badly. Instead of participating in physical activities, another activity emerged for me. It happened the first evening of my rest day. I was lying on the front porch when my best buddies arrived home. Happiness oozed from them with their post-adventure and activities glow. "Howzit Dan man!" They greeted me. I could feel their sympathy that I'd missed out on the fun-ventures.

"You guys are so lucky," I said, "in fact, I have realized *we* are so lucky."

I expressed my reflections on our quality of life. The mountains. The beach. The frisbee games, skateboarding, surfing, paddling, swimming, running. Every day we were peaking in joy. I explained my revelations as I observed the aliveness of our lifestyle. I told stories of the people I had seen in corporate, looking like war survivors shuffling past desks to eke out a living. We were lucky not to be fighting for our souls' survival in the deep corporation. I wanted to share our lifestyle and joy with others. My friends agreed. I wanted to encourage all people to a life of freedom and happiness. I shared my yearning about how I wanted to make a difference in the world.

I commented on the "there's more" feeling within me. I wanted to help others.

The boys were in total agreement.

We all felt the same.

If we could do that, we said, *it would truly be a successful living.*

We need to make a difference in this world.

Since the porch was the perfect place for percolating ideas, the brainstorm came alive immediately. Travis lit a cigarette, Grant picked up a guitar, Sebastian grabbed a beer and excitedly paced back and forth whilst sharing incoming ideas. He showed us video clips of other people positively impacting the world.

We were sparking like fireworks.

THE JOY LIST

AND SO OUR project and mission called *No Danger Diaries* was born.

We brainstormed a list of tasks, each one designed to bring joy or make a difference in the world. Examples were: "Take a blind person hiking up Table mountain, put on a puppet show at an orphanage, and paddle to an island with underprivileged kids". We had discovered our mission: "Share joy with as many people as possible and have fun doing it". As my friends returned to work the following day, I picked up my laptop and brought our mission to life. On a simple blog, I captured our list of 100 tasks and ensured every third task made a tangible social impact in our community. Our motto in bold read: *Not scared to make a difference.* I thought about all the impactful fun ahead of us; this was meaningful work to me. When the guys arrived home, they were stunned. Our brainstorm had already made it to the real world. We were all excited. A feeling of passion and adventure entered us. I had a purpose and drive again. Something to aim at.

Sebastian excitedly paced the porch with his usual vigor, "Boys, what task are we gonna do first?"

The premise was simple. We would try to do as many tasks on the list as possible and invite people to join us. We would film each task and post it on the blog as evidence and inspiration for people to attend. We unanimously decided which task would start our joy rollercoaster— "Take a homeless man to a sit-down dinner". Sebastian ensured we picked a soon-approaching day, we agreed to a time, and No Danger was born. On some idle weekday we gathered outside the porch for the first time as "No Danger". We armed ourselves with a GoPro camera for evidence, hopped in a car, and headed off to find someone who looked like they needed a good meal. Within 15 minutes we had our first joy recipient. We brazenly introduced ourselves as *No Danger Diaries* and told him we wanted to have dinner with him. We asked him to choose any restaurant in the city. He chose a very simple local chicken diner around the corner. We didn't just buy him food; we got to know him. We sat with him and asked him questions about his life. We shared our lives, ate, and connected over the dinner table.

We left as friends.

After this first No Danger encounter, I was profoundly touched. We had slowed down to see the world through the eyes of someone who lived at a very different pace. It broadened my understanding of people. It helped me to see we are all alike, no matter our differences. No Danger had already grown us after one task, and there were still 99 more to do.

We didn't slow down.

Next task—"take chocolates to elderly ladies on Valentine's day".

We dressed up in suits and headed to an old age home nearby. Supplied with chocolates, Turkish delights, bowties, and suspenders, we brought a certain level of 1960s charm to the old gray building. We played some golden oldie songs, danced with the ladies and men, shared our chocolates with anyone we could find, and were touched by a visit through the frail care center. Our energy compared to those men and women lying in bed provided a huge perspective for us. Some of these folk were the opposite of us. We were alive, boisterous, brimming with energy—they were lying in bed, with no one to visit them, forgotten by society and slowly fading away. We tried to bring as many good vibes and "joy points" as possible. After the chocolate handouts, the swing moves on the dining hall dance floor, and the conversations, we felt we had made a small difference in these people's lives.

"Yeah sure, why not? I'm a chocoholic!" was our favorite, memorable quote from the task. It was said by one of the ladies as we offered another round of Valentine's sweets. We were finally making meaningful memories. We were touching people's lives.

Also, we were having the time of our lives. Tasks were being ticked off, and the people of the city wanted to join our infectious good vibes. We became known as the "No Danger Boys" simply because the 4 of us did everything together. You can still see the videos online of those days. Young, full of passion, with a desire to make a difference. Some more of the tasks included; "Share roses with strangers on Valentine's Day, Do a beach clean up in speedos, Perform a song for charity."

No Danger was an important start to unconditioning me from the system. Each time we completed a task, I grew as a person. I will never forget when we put on a fashion show in the city with homeless people as models. The funds raised were directly beneficial to the people on the street. Working with the richest in the city (for clothing and donations) whilst simultaneously coordinating heroin addicts (as the models) certainly gave us unforgettable experiences. We saw the essence of being human; A need to be loved, to give and receive. A need to be wanted and feel valued.

These tasks slowly became the focus of my life.

While my office job brought in the money, No Danger Diaries gave me life. It was the fuel my soul had been missing. Giving back and receiving so much. Making a difference whilst having fun. We weren't just another Non-Profit organization. We were living the dream. It was the liquid of life filling the empty cup inside of me. The press and news soon got onboard. We had some videos and pictures which went viral, and some tasks became bigger events. One of our tasks—"Dress as superheroes and abseil off the Red Cross Children's Hospital (to surprise sick kids)," became an annual event. Charities and social workers got involved in the spectacle to watch Scooby Doo and Superman pop up at children's bedsides. I remember Sebastian dressed like Spiderman dangling ten stories off the ground, hanging upside down outside a hospital bedroom window smiling at the sick waving children inside. It was magic out there, and we were following our hearts to new levels of sharing joy.

After a year or so of doing this, my office work started getting in the way of sharing joy. It felt like I had two jobs. I would go on road trips to share joy all over the country, only to rush back and pitch multi-million dollar marketing strategies to alcohol brands. The contrast between my two lives grew. On one hand I was selling consumable products, on the other hand, I was selling joy. The one life would take me down the path of traditional success; money, leadership, status, and respect. The other path offered joy, love, goodwill, and the opportunity to make a tangible difference in the world. This path was a journey into the complete unknown.

My inner tension increased as I struggled to balance the two.

Everything I had worked and studied for seemed to be exiting the building. I often thought, *You've worked so hard to get this corporate advertising job, don't give up now!*

The tipping point came when the company elected me to join an elite leadership program. An expensive, fully paid course to groom us as the next wave of CEO's or business leaders.

I quit.

It came after a day I witnessed my own CEO show up at a client pitch meeting 24 hours after his son was born. Something changed in me. I could see the amount of stress he had to deal with.

I never want to be in a situation like this, I said internally.

I never want to ask for permission to be at my son's birth.

Quitting was hard.

A big part of me didn't want to leave. My identity was in advertising.

Who would I become without advertising?

I broke the news to my bosses. I expected backlash and counter offers. Neither happened. They supported me wholeheartedly in my decision. My pride was a little hurt by no one fighting to keep me around. I think they saw something I hadn't fully accepted yet—being a 'desktop ninja' for the company was not my highest calling. I was born for other things.

With no clue where money would come from or what exactly I would be doing—I left.

I only knew I wanted to share the joy.

This was the calling in my heart.

I went into No Danger Diaries full-time. Before I knew it, the two fellows I lived with quickly transformed from being my best friends to my business partners in joy. We registered an official non-profit company under the name No Danger Diaries. We created an office in the back room of our Camps Bay cottage and proudly named it *The Rocket Ship.* We planned to take off into new heights of joy. We dived right in, clueless, full of passion, and brimming with goodwill.

It quickly shattered everything I knew about business.

What were our products? How would people support us? What were our cashflow strategies and plans? How would I convince people that sharing joy is where they should spend their money? My mind often said "no," but my heart shouted "go."

I was finally beginning to listen to the calling in my heart. I said, "Don't worry. If all this fails, you can always go back to advertising."

I never did.

LEADING WITH HEART

LEAVING THE WORK cubicles forced me into the flow of my own life. I didn't have rules, structures, regulations, or systems. I didn't know where my monthly salary would come from. I had to trust in the flow of life that it would all work out. It did. People showed up to support us in the most interesting ways. Props, clothing, supplies for our house, and resources for tasks. In desperate times money appeared. The miracles somehow kept us afloat, and No Danger Diaries kept gaining momentum.

When I looked up from the day-to-day of this new life, I realized I was finally beginning to live like my friend Sebastian (on hope and a shoestring). I remember a particularly big miracle in my life during this time. My mother came to visit me down in Cape Town, and as we were having lunch together, she looked at me with tears in her eyes and said she would give me her car because she was so proud of what I was doing. She was so proud of who I had become in the world. She wanted to offer all her support for our *Mission to Joy*. I cried. I was touched so deeply by this. Never in my wildest dreams could I have imagined the support I was receiving. I felt life was rooting for me. By trusting and following my heart, the magic, and support came to meet me. Our community was rooting for us. They believed in our mission. It was as if life itself was supporting our mission to make a difference in the world.

I was forced to trust my heart daily, and it was working. The monster of hollowness which crept up on me in corporate had disappeared entirely. The taste of depression and meaninglessness I had in the cubicles departed from me like a ship in the night. The emptiness was replaced by pure daily joy.

The joy of simply being alive.

It was a joy to wake up in the morning. It was a joy to hang out with my best friends. It was a joy to share joy with the world.

Living "hand-to-mouth" wasn't always easy, but for the first time in my life, I was truly free. I didn't need to ask for permission to go on holiday or work from home. I didn't have to ask if I could share joy with the world. I was already home. Every single day. Not only a physical home, a coming home to a more fully expressed version of myself. Stepping into the home inside of me. Exploring some new inner rooms in my personal mansion.

I was finally walking closer to my truth.

SEASON 2

INTO THE BURN

NO MONEY, NO WORRIES

THE AMOUNT OF money I previously needed to survive became a lot less. I didn't need to spend cash on meditation classes, wellness massages, yoga or fitness classes, nutritional supplements, or expensive holidays. Life was a holiday every single day. All the things which used to be mandatory expenses to keep me in-balance, de-stressed, or in-check were no longer necessary. My monthly budget more than halved. I realized the money I had worked for in my previous jobs had been used to bring back the happiness the nine-to-five lifestyle drained from me. Looking back at my old lifestyle, it was clear my corporate days were a giant mousetrap—I had narrowly missed taking the cheese to be stuck in a repetitive cycle for more years. Now I was able to achieve what I considered a real work-life balance. There were still sometimes 12-hour workdays, but it didn't feel like work. It was exciting. There were also some days that started with no work. It was a walk on the beach in the morning, SUP boarding during lunch, and a sunset run on the mountain, with three hours of work dotted throughout the day. Life flowed according to my needs, not the needs of the corporation.

No Danger Diaries was part of a unique movement in which

our entire business was not driven by profit, but by a simple need to share joy. Money was not the motivation, it was a byproduct of joy. Joy was our bottom line. This defied everything I had been taught as a business and brand strategist. All my years of strategic training were conditioned to increase the bottom line. This was being undone by one giant joy experiment. I could hardly practice any skills I was trained to use because we were building a business without a business plan or a strategy. Our strategy was to have no strategy, to build a business on good intentions, and keep following the desire in our hearts for what felt right. We believed the rest would appear whilst we held onto our *no-fear* approach to living. We were driven by love. We were creating a heart-led business instead of a mind-led business. We had no idea where it would lead us. Little did I know it would grow to become a worldwide movement under a different name. At the time it didn't matter. All that mattered was living in complete fulfillment every single day.

Waking up was a gift.

THE FALL OF FREEDOM

INEVITABLY, THE SYSTEM started to sneak up on us. First it started with an intern. Then two interns. Then we moved our "Rocket Ship" from our home by the seaside and acquired office space in the city. "Rocket Ship 2" was born. It was an upgrade for the business but a downgrade from the beach-house lifestyle. We got a few more people in "Rocket Ship 2" which fueled our next dilemma: *How do we pay salaries?*

And the next: *How do we split cash flow fairly for the four of us when we are contributing different time and skills?*

Before I knew it, I was back. Back in an office. One I had created.

How did this happen? I thought. I got out of the corporate stress trap only to recreate my own trap and a trap for others. I felt like a monster ensnaring the innocent.

"The work could be worse," I told myself, "At least we are trying to change the world for the better."

I felt the need for a healthier business environment, better work processes, or a fresher way of doing business, yet we didn't seem to have any other options. We didn't know a better way. My heart whispered—*this isn't serving us.* On the surface, our new office was vibey, fun, daring, loving, and exciting. On paper, it was the same as all other offices. Businesses, employees, agreements, contracts, deliverables, tax, and a nine-to-five work schedule. Because of my business experience, I put myself in the position of being responsible for most of the decision-making. I felt everything rested on my shoulders to make it a success. *If I don't do it, we will all fail*, I told myself.

It was a dangerous thing to believe.

TENSE FAMILY SYSTEMS

I DIDN'T HAVE much of a functioning family unit at this time. My mother had split from my stepfather a few years prior, and both were focused on their personal challenges. I also didn't have any relationship with my biological father. My family was No Danger Diaries. I was somewhat unconcerned about this, and the people I lived with were family to me. This provided a more precarious situation than I realized. Because the people I lived with had become my business partners overnight, all the love, joy, and support I received was slowly replaced by spreadsheets, strategies, brainstorms, and deadlines. Although we were a posse of outlaws—cowboys gone rogue against the system—I was losing the support of an actual family.

And things were really starting to heat up.

Not only was I trying to lead the posse on the business front but I was also leading on my dysfunctional family front. My mother was severely depressed. It wasn't unusual for me to receive a phone call from her at work and have to step out of the office to help her make simple decisions or stop her from jumping off a bridge. I spent more hours than I would care to admit trying to convince her not to take her life. She was suicidal.

I was also there to listen to my stepfather. He would speak end-lessly about his business problems, complaining about employees and looking for solutions. I was a sounding board for him regularly. I was a listening ear for both. Forever the platform for them to express their woes about life and each other.

This was creating an inner build-up. My cup was filling with a kind of liquid which wasn't good for me. I didn't understand at the time what personal boundaries might be. I thought it was my job as their child to always be available for them. I continued to listen.

I recall exiting the office one sunny day as my mother threatened to jump out her apartment window, twenty stories high. I calmly reassured her, went through the usual mind games, put my phone back in my pocket, and returned to the Rocket Ship. Another day when I was visiting, I had to run across a roof to rescue her. She had a tie around her neck and her legs were dangling off the top of a 40-story building. I grabbed her shirt and pulled her back.

I handled it all and brushed these incidents aside.

Or so I thought.

The incidents were piling up inside me. Hiding in closets I did not know existed. By not talking about them, they were festering somewhere, like a rotten apple fallen behind a stove.

I allowed my relationships to continue like this for years.

I thought I could convince my mother out of her slumps.

I thought my stepfather would one day ask how I was doing.

With the waning support of my substitute go-to family in Travis, Grant, and Sebastian, I was entering dangerous territory.

I needed to talk but instead increased the activity load in my life.

Distractions were a breath of fresh air, and I didn't even know I wasn't facing my problems.

To me, this was normal.

And professional help was not for cowboys.

I didn't recognize the invisible baggage added to my emotional burden and caused stress my central nervous system couldn't handle.

I didn't know my nervous system could break.

I thought I was invincible.

I'll handle it all, I said to myself.

I'm strong enough.

It's my duty.

I'm sharing joy.

I have broad shoulders for a reason.

I am so strong.

These were dangerous beliefs.

The more control and responsibility I took without adequate support, the more stress burned inside me. Without this and the financial support to de-stress, I was a caged animal trapped in my own self-built systems.

It became harder to answer the phone calls.

Simple work problems seemed insurmountable.

I couldn't handle the load like before.

We were getting nowhere but I was working harder than ever.

Resentment began to ooze within me at the people around me.

I decided to work harder. I thought the harder I worked, the faster we would all get to success and financial freedom, and then I could rest.

I never got there.

I burned out along the way.

BEGINNING TO BREAK

I WAS TIRED, a lot. It was the kind of tiredness that never cleared. Not after a sleep. Not after a weekend. Not after a holiday. It covered me like a silent, invisible cloud. I didn't have the energy to be who I thought I was. I couldn't live up to the expectations of my usual lifestyle. It became harder to get up from the couch. I couldn't keep up with the people around me. I couldn't concentrate as I used to. My sharp wit became a foggy quagmire. I forced myself to go out, hoping the energy would return. It didn't. My desire to party, see friends, or be social after work dissolved. I wanted solitude and downtime. I thought that was strange. That this reclusiveness "wasn't me", so I didn't make an effort to listen to this voice. I didn't make space for myself.

At this point I couldn't seem to get away from the business at all. My friends (whom I lived with) had become my business partners. *No Danger Diaries* was our lifestyle. There was no time out.

When the opportunity came to take a trip to Thailand, I jumped at it. I met a lady who had grabbed my attention and traveled there, so it seemed like a good idea to visit. I was desperate so I sold my car to pay for the vacation. I didn't have money because

I had over-invested in the business. I figured Life would somehow provide for me when I returned. It was my rest and escape strategy to try to regain some balance from the burnout tipping point. *Rest, or breakdown,* I remember thinking. I said to a friend at the time, "Something has to snap soon—I can't carry on like this."

Traversing the airport's international terminals, I remember a few final phone calls before boarding. I was wrapping up, trying to make sure everything was perfectly in place. I called my step father to tell him I would be offline for a while. I was beyond exhausted.

He was proud I was working so hard. It felt good to be able to share the battle of stress and success together. I didn't realize the danger of this game—work hard to impress. My nervous system wasn't built for constant "always on" work like he could handle. I was killing myself for attention.

I had been running at maximum capacity for months on end. There was no stopping, I couldn't stop. This is why I was desperate to get on the plane and be out of signal—so no one could call me. I didn't have boundaries. I didn't say no. I gave and gave.

I didn't know I was creating this poisonous lifestyle for myself. I felt I *had to* do it. I *had* to keep everyone happy. I was choosing the pressure for myself. I didn't *need* to be so busy; I had created a world where busyness was normal, and constant manic days fuelled my pride.

The need to impress my stepfather, business partners, and society would nearly be the death of me.

RETREAT TO THE ISLANDS

I TOUCHED DOWN in Thailand after a long flight. My mind was in la-la land. My brain was stretched beyond its capacity. The thin airplane sleep and my hyperactive nervous system were already cooking up an illness. Instead of arriving with shiny eyes and a fresh floral shirt, I had washed ashore in Thailand like a shipwreck victim. I couldn't care what I was wearing. I only cared for rest. To make matters worse, I still had multiple transport connections on planes and boats to my final destination.

As we flew over streaks of beautiful turquoise-blue water, I looked at the island, the beaches, and the beauty. I was hollow. Whilst my eyes absorbed the treasures of the picturesque paradise, it had little to no effect on my inner wellbeing. My joy levels were not rising.

"Aren't you supposed to be excited, happy, relaxed?" my mind said. I didn't have the energy.

I hungered only for sleep.

To hibernate.

To say goodbye.

I felt empty, drained, and fatigued, like a weary bear who had delayed his hibernation season. These feelings traveled along with me like unwanted companions. I hadn't left them at the airport back in South Africa. Being excited required energy, and I had none left to fuel it.

I boarded the ferry and slid into a chair. In an uncomfortable position, I fell asleep on the hard plastic bucket seating. I didn't need an island adventure—I needed seclusion.

As my ferry arrived at its final destination, a remote island beach, I roused myself to witness fellow travelers disembarking in hurried anticipation. I unglued myself from my seat, stood up, and looked around. I felt like a piece of cardboard—dry, emotionless, drifting with the wind. I looked toward the jetty and spotted my lady standing on the pier like a loyal wife at a navy homecoming. I was happy to see her. A small ray of positivity in the gray island of my life. I walked onto the wooden deck toward her and hugged her. My smile hid my internal zombie-ness, the secret third wheel on our journey.

After a quick dip in the ocean, we hopped on her scooter and dropped off my luggage.

It was time to explore.

ONE LAST SHOT

WE WENT STRAIGHT to a bar.

I didn't listen to my body or my feelings. I didn't know how to communicate I needed rest. My motto was "activities first". My philosophy was "push through". My mantra was "never scared". I ignored the voice which said, "slow down, sleep." I didn't know how to give my mind or body a break. I didn't know these things needed rest. I didn't know that if I didn't give my mind a break, it could break down. I didn't know how to sit and relax. I thought engaging in more adventures was resting.

We ordered our first round of alcoholic beverages at the bar. Something inside me was strongly averse to the incoming drinks. I didn't want to be there. I didn't want a drink. I didn't want to be social. I was there because I didn't know what else to do. Drinking for the sake of drinking. I was craving quiet, quality time to build a meaningful relationship with my partner. Instead I pushed through—my mind drunk and my body poisoned.

The evening continued. More drinks flowed. This was our generational culture. Bars, binge, party, repeat. Even though I was craving something more, I didn't know where to start. While my soul searched for meaning, I was a passenger in the party scene.

My body and mind gave up around 2 am. I hit the wall. I couldn't keep standing. I was out of gas.

I wasn't particularly drunk or intoxicated, I simply could not squeeze any more words out of my mouth or take one more sip.

We returned to the small, hot island room.

I passed out.

Fourteen hours later, I awoke from a deep sleep.

I was still exhausted.

Fourteen hours was not going to cure a lifestyle of exertion.

Little did I know I would continue to face this fatigue for many many months to come.

This was only the beginning, where the chronic fatigue seeped in like an unwelcome guest in the honeymoon suite of my life.

BATTLE FOR PEACE

THE HOLIDAY DID not turn out to be the relaxing break I had anticipated. I found my lady partially involved in the Thai drug scene. She was helping traffic illegal substances for an island syndicate. I didn't know what to do or say. I felt like I was in a drug cartel movie in someone else's life. It made me angry. My mind kept asking, "How could this loving, kind, nurturing woman choose to be involved in this?" To add more salt to the wound, I witnessed her disappearing into bathrooms with men I didn't know to partake in substances I didn't approve. She worked at a bar, so this was normal for her, but it didn't sit well with me.

Why is she treating herself like this? I kept asking.

I heard the way men at the bar jostled and degraded her—it fueled my anger. It was torture to sit and watch them belittle her. *Why would anyone allow themselves to be talked to like this? Why doesn't she choose to work at a more upmarket place where she would be treated better?*

I was furious.

Does she not see her value? Does she not know she's better than this?

Ironically I was in the same boat. She was my perfect reflection.

Could I not see my value? Was I not in the same situation? Why was I sitting at bars with unhealthy men, watching my girlfriend sniffing away her well-being? Why was I using my energy to fix someone who didn't want or need to be fixed?

It was clear I also needed help, but I couldn't see it at the time.

When she came out of the restrooms, I had had enough. I told her I was leaving to find something more uplifting. I walked around the island looking for something more peaceful. It was hard to find. There were parties, music and drunk people littering the beautiful beaches. I was losing energy with each hour spent in the island party atmosphere.

When my girlfriend finished her shift, she came to find me. I was sitting on the steps of a bar talking to two girls about yoga and meditation. They stayed on the other side of the island and remarked it was much more peaceful. I longed for it. For peace. I longed for their description of the natural silence and beauty. They soon left. I was faced with the conversation at hand. I asked my partner about the bathrooms. She told me honestly what she was doing. I gave her my point of view. She saw the pain and anger it was causing.

Right then and there, she decided to quit.

A glimmer of hope.

For her.

For us.

Things may actually improve, I told myself.

This island might actually turn out ok.

The next day, things got worse.

The happy-go-lucky person I once knew in my partner, the one I had come to visit, had transformed into a moody, angry Thailand Tigress.

Bursts of anger and snappiness created a whirlwind of razor blades that appeared unexpectedly in the slightest conversation. The sharpness cut us both.

The next few days were torturously tense. The tightrope between us wobbled at the slightest provocation.

I was juggling a short stick of dynamite.

Anger erupted for seemingly no reason.

I guessed this anger was withdrawal symptoms. My arrival ignited lifestyle changes. I expected my partner to be different, this was a problem for both of us. I had forced change upon her. Her world was now turned upside down. The tension between us manifested in verbal attacks. Triggers for outbursts included; clouds of mosquitoes, big barking blue-headed lizards, talk of exploring different parts of the country, waves and wind on the ocean, and anything that involved spending money. What were normal traveling situations became fireworks.

I am no saint. As the fire burned, I often threw petrol on it by holding up a mirror to her inner flaws. The quickest way to extinguish a fire is not to throw gasoline on it. We were both wobbling like punching bags in a Muay Thai gym, receiving blows with nowhere to go.

I tried to challenge her with my own return fire but lost the battle. She had more intense anger so I quickly learned it wasn't a game I could win. Instead, I decided to shift strategies. I aimed not to meet her in her anger and would try to respond in peace. The peace the two girls had told me about at the bar. I wanted this. Natural peace.

Instead of being a tiger, I tried to be the "perfect boyfriend" keeping my cool. Instead of standing up for myself and creating more turmoil, I adopted what I thought was a more "mindful" approach. I had been in tumultuous relationships before and decided I wouldn't repeat past patterns.

I adopted a non-reactive approach. My idea was to be as calm as possible with "The Tigress" no matter what the situation. When she got angry, I now chose to be quiet. Her anger often triggered anger inside me, yet I repressed my own feelings. I took the hits and didn't respond.

One day we decided to paddle across to a small adjacent island. I needed a change of scenery from the bar life. We'd hired a stand-up paddle board, and she was sitting at the front directing our procession. I was paddling, keeping my eye on our destination, a smaller island off in the distance. The Tigress, now getting slightly wet from the ocean, was growling orders, telling me to do this and that, watch out for the wind and waves. At this moment, a small wave chose to splash up the side of the board. The tiny wave lit up a list of cusses and verbal abuse from The Tigress. As I tried to enjoy the sun, the picturesque island, the moored boats, and the paddling—the Tigress fumed. She hissed, "Boats are too close, the lapping waves will tip us, the currents are pushing us in the wrong direction". I had long since been a SUP boarder and was calm in these conditions, yet I couldn't control the wind or the waves inside the lashing Tigress.

I kept quiet.

I bottled up my emotions like a note in a glass bottle floating on the ocean.

The cycle continued.

I kept paddling.

She kept cussing.

I kept paddling.

My own anger brewed and stewed.

I tried to keep my eyes on the island to ensure we were timing our crossing correctly. I tried to tune out the tension, but I couldn't. Eventually, her words penetrated my defenses. I snapped internally. I joined The Tigress' anger party. Her anger was contagious and I'd caught it. I didn't blow out verbally. I simply turned the SUP board around and headed back. The Tigress, confused, began to bellow fire and confusion. I maintained my silence. There was nothing mindful or peaceful inside me about the resentment boiling away. She had gotten to me. My day was ruined. This gave me double anger—I was subject to her moods and couldn't maintain my own inner sanctuary. She affected me. I could not escape a tumultuous tigress.

I kept paddling back to shore.

How can she have this power over me? Why is she affecting me so much? Why can't I be calm? How can I claim to be a peaceful meditator if I can't find peace?

It fueled my inner flames. Self-judgment turned up the heat within me.

I paddled back to the island we had just come from.

I asked her to get off the SUP.

She did.

She lit up a cigarette on the beach and glared at me.

I turned the board around and paddled straight back out into the ocean.

"When will you come back?" she said.

"Later," I said.

I secretly wondered how I would find her later.

Did I even want to find her?

Would she be back in the restrooms?

I gave a few short strokes on the water, back toward our previously planned destination.

The beautiful island.

Alone.

Peaceful.

I paddled, finally finding my groove.

Enjoying nature at its finest.

The fight hung around like a foul odor in my clean, inner garden. It annoyed me. I wanted to feel like I was on holiday, yet I was in the boxing ring of a relationship.

It bothered me that bouts with The Tigress would leave me simmering for hours after the match. My mind told me stories about how I ought to be, how it should've gone. "You shouldn't be so angry. You don't deserve this kind of treatment. Leave. It's better on your own." My dear mind always opting for separation and judgment.

In reality, The Tigress was probably equally as confused.

I wasn't speaking about my anger. I was changing my actions. This can be confusing for any person. Action without communication can cause a lot of pain for both parties. I didn't know how to deal with it.

The entire holiday was not meeting my expectations, and neither was my newfound lady Tiger. This double layer of constant anger meant I experienced tension, frustration, resentment, and pain, building within me day after day. Instead of sitting on an island sipping cocktails, I was sipping emotional poison. If I wasn't drinking Tigress poison, it was the lack of expression creating its own toxic brew.

The quieter I became, the less joy I had.

The less joy I had, the less energy I had.

I was creating the perfect conditions for getting sick.

Nothing is more welcoming to disease than an angry heart.

My island dream became an island nightmare.

NORTH WITH THE TIGRESS

WE DECIDED TO leave the island and travel north together. I said I wanted to explore other areas of Thailand. More truthfully, I wanted to run away. I blamed the island and its unhealthy party scene for what I was experiencing. At the time, it was easier to blame things outside of me than look at my inner world to see how I created this reality. I had made the decisions that led me there. I had ignored warning signs previously. I was not able to state my needs and stand up for myself. I was confused. *How has all this happened?* I looked for the clues and signs which carried me into this situation. Instead of heading away from burnout I was heading faster toward it. With each adventure we went on, I felt more "floppy", like a tired puppet being dragged along a sightseeing expedition. Even though I had the will, I had less stamina. The adventure race of life continued to set a sturdy pace which I silently struggled to keep up with. The question; *What is wrong?* continually tried to surface as I pushed it down again and again.

I didn't speak up about my fatigue because I kept thinking, *One more night's rest, then I'll be better.* It never happened. Each morning

I could've continued sleeping for many more hours. There was no pulse inside me to seize the day. My batteries were flat.

We tried the scooter tours, the sightseeing, the change of location—the hollow monster still didn't leave.

Along the way, I discovered my wallet was missing… maybe lost, maybe stolen. It could've happened on the ferry, the bus, the taxi, or the train. Either way, another few cents were added to the relationship stress wallet. Now neither of us had money.

I put on a brave face pretending everything was okay, but none of it was okay. This trip wasn't ok. My unsustainable life in Cape Town was not ok. My relationship with the Tigress was not ok. My pursuit of peace was not ok. I couldn't figure out what I was doing wrong.

In hindsight, I should have been looking for peace in my own heart. I wouldn't discover peace in another country, another relationship, or another adventure. I was running from the exact thing I needed to face—my very own life.

The more I pushed, the more I got knocked down.

It was a game of less-rest-more-depressed, coupled with less-expression-more-depression.

A one-way ticket to joylessness.

THE SIDEWALK CALLS

WHEN WE ARRIVED at our final destination in the northern jungles, we sorted out our financial situation by making emergency calls to our family. Our parents graciously supported us with a Western Union international money transfer. I had one more week before returning to South Africa, and she had one more week before returning to the island. We had just enough money to lick our wounds before taking our separate paths.

Having avoided the cash-less nightmare and still desperately needing rest, I suggested we go for a massage. I said I would pay to alleviate the stress of her having to spend money. I thought it might help us relax and provide much-needed self-care.

We agreed and headed off to a massage center.

It was then it finally happened to me.

The end of my adventure race.

The massage was over and we were walking down a street. My head started to spin. I felt like I was slipping off the back of a moving car.

I collapsed onto the street.

My body gave up.

It was as if someone had cut the puppet strings holding me up. Like a limp rag doll, I dropped to the ground. My energy disappeared as I lay awkwardly on the sidewalk. I couldn't get up. I could hear the Tigress calling to me with concern. Her voice sounded far away. It took an enormous amount of effort to stay conscious and fight my way to formulate some thoughts. I looked at the Tigress through hazy vision. She was full of care. I tried to drag myself up, but I couldn't. My life force had been leeched. It was as if my energy had oozed into the gutter.

I was stuck.

Sitting on the dirty sidewalk, I was aware of what was happening but could not do much about it.

Speaking was a challenge.

All I wanted to do was close my eyes and sleep. To dissolve from the world. To enter a cocoon and hibernate.

I had no idea where this lack of mobility had come from.

Panic rose in me.

Is this a brain stroke? Am I having an epileptic fit?

I looked at the Tigress. I was hopeless and weak. I felt I was dying. Fear and confusion overwhelmed me. Something was giving up inside of me.

The Tigress hailed a passing taxi. She helped pick me up and guided me onto the seat.

I slumped immediately into the chair with heavy limbs. Any words I wanted to speak were thick molasses in my mouth. I was melted butter on a back seat.

The Tigress turned on her nourishing mode and helped us back to our accommodation in the forest.

I flopped onto the bed.

I didn't know what was wrong.

I lay there.

Hate bubbled inside of me.

I despised this holiday. This place. These experiences. This relationship. This disease. I detested the never-ending tiredness. I simply could not win. I hated feeling trapped.

Hate is death to the body.

Resentment is poison to the blood.

My love had dissolved and I was sick spiritually, mentally, physically, and in my heart. I hadn't yet discovered the power of forgiveness and love, and the healing it could bring.

As I wallowed in my own drama, I realized The Tigress' holiday was also spoiled by my mysterious disease. Hours and days passed in a haze as she spent hard-earned money on me—a sick patient in a sad jungle. I lay in the hammock and at best spent a few hours on the communal couch. We had to cancel our planned tours. Guilt was the icing on my drama cake.

Maybe I have some kind of incurable jungle disease? I told myself.

Maybe I'm going to die in this place.

My mind wasn't making life any easier for me. Lying in a hammock one evening, more waves of panic surged within me. I didn't know how to deal with it. I was frightened. I swung gently from side to side, consoling myself as the terror harassed me silently.

This cannot be a simple flu, I said to myself.

Without any more energy to hold back my feelings, I turned to face the Tigress. Tears began to form, "I feel like I'm dying. I'm really scared." I gazed with hollow eyes into the jungle, wondering how my suffering would end.

She consoled me.

I had gone from Tigress prey to being nursed like a cub.

We both agreed a trip to the hospital was in order.

The following day we headed off, our planned jungle adventure replaced by a hospital waiting room.

After a long wait in the reception, a Thai doctor finally prescribed some antibiotics for my stomach. I knew there was nothing wrong with my stomach. *I'm not another weak tourist,* I fumed to myself. I knew this illness was something more. The doctor triggered more anger as the diagnosis we had waited for gave us little hope. My inner confusion increased.

I need to get home.

The trip to the hospital didn't end well.

In my moment of weakness, The Tigress turned on me and verbally attacked me for lying on some reserved hospital seats. She told me they were for more needy people, probably for monks. I couldn't believe it. I was lying down because I did not have the energy to sit or stand. In what felt like the weakest moment of my life—I received a lecture about respect and humility.

Maybe she was right.

Her comments broke me down further.

I asked if she could get me food. We argued more. As she walked away, I threw my last bit of energy at her, my money bag.

It scattered across the floor.

I had no idea how to get out of this jungle boogie.

PEACE OUT

AFTER WE COOLED off and she returned with a sandwich, we drove back to our accommodation and I beelined for the couch.

My decisions were leading me to the land of the sick. I was beginning to dwell in a place where I was never well enough to feel alive but never sick enough to stay in hospital. My sick inner world had become my physical reality.

Two more slow days passed on the jungle couch until I was well enough to move about. I could lift my arms without feeling I was moving through sticky molasses. I could walk to the kitchen and see what was cooking. I was getting well enough in the nick of time, as I had a farewell flight to catch.

On my last day, I mustered enough energy for a small scooter tour to see some sad elephants. They were chained and stuck, a stark contrast to animals in my native South African wilderness.

The elephants looked how I felt.

The following day I said a painful goodbye to The Tigress as I boarded the minibus for Bangkok. There was so much unsaid between us, and it was largely my fault for not being more open with my feelings.

It would be a long time before I learned the skill of being vulnerable—to speak my truth in a more healthy way. It would be an even longer time to speak it in a non-attacking, non-threatening, non-judgmental way. I'm still learning.

The Tigress was the nudge I needed to begin my learning curve in the art of expression.

I stared at her through the minibus window. She looked sad. She too, had very little money, limited direction, and hardly a clue what to do.

We were both lost, looking for the same thing, but finding it not.

Where was the peace?

Wrestling with rest

TICKET TO PEACE

As the minibus wound through the jungle and mountain passes, I finally felt the slightest sense of peace. I was heading home. Heading back to routine. Heading to food I was used to eating. Heading out of the dance with The Tigress.

Maybe I can finally get better?

I felt hope.

I couldn't wait to board the airplane.

I reminisced about what had happened on my 'holiday'.

Although I was suntanned on the outside, I felt lower inside than when I left Cape Town. My joy meter was virtually zero. *Never again,* I said. *Next time I need rest, I will ensure I'm going to a restful place. This trip was too risky.*

I arrived at a town where I needed to switch buses to the airport. I asked for a ticket. "Too late," the lady said in broken English. I would have to stay the night. My finances weren't exactly peaking so I found a cheap motel. I spent a restless feverish night in a damp room, tossing and turning, burning up and burning out.

I took the first bus the next morning.

I was already worried.

If the bus arrived exactly on schedule, I would only be 2.5 hours before my international flight. This was only enough time to catch a taxi to the airport and check-in. If the bus were any later, it would be a sprint for me.

I hoped for the best.

After a few hours we neared Bangkok. A thunderstorm rolled in right then.

The thunderstorm produced an overwhelming amount of traffic on the highway. Cars were bumper to bumper for miles as the lightning flashed and the thunder boomed. I was stuck in my seat, watching the minutes go by. I wanted to get off the bus, start running, or find a scooter. As we inched slowly along, the very plane I needed to be on inched slowly to take off.

The traffic made me miss my international flight by mere minutes.

I came skidding into the airport at full sprint.

I arrived at the counter with hope-filled eyes, pleading I could still make it to the gate.

"Sorry sir," came the reply from the desk attendant.

"I need to be on that flight," I fired back. "I have no wallet. I have no money. I have to get home."

I was watching my ticket-to-peace disappear.

"Sorry sir, the baggage collection is closed."

"I can run fast," I said. "This is all I have," motioning to my one backpack.

I looked to the left, and I saw people who had checked in for the same flight only minutes ago walking through security. I knew I could make it on time.

"Sorry, sir," she said again.

That lady was the first in a long line of people who stopped me from running any further.

The race was over.

I couldn't run toward peace.

It was time to slow down.

I was the elephant in chains.

I had spent my last pennies on an expensive taxi from the bus stop to the airport.

I had no more resources.

I looked at the desk attendant, "My wallet has been stolen. I have no money".

I was desperate. Panic rose in me.

I didn't have the energy to not have the energy.

She gave me some coins and motioned to a nearby payphone.

It was a nightmare situation.

I had only enough pennies to make one call to the airline office to see if I could be on the next flight.

I dialed the number she had scribbled on a piece of paper.

She looked concerned for me.

A man answered the call. I thought he might be an angel. He reserved a seat for me on the next flight. It was leaving at 17h00 ish the next day. My flight would be reserved on one condition, I had to pay the change of flight costs before 14h00 the following day.

"Ok," I said to him.

No money, I thought to myself.

I dragged my bags across the floor to a secluded place behind steel airport chairs. I messaged my parents. I was embarrassed. I was the small child again needing their care, protection, and provision. It wasn't their fault I had missed my plane, now I was dumping my admin on them from across the ocean.

To my surprise, my mother said, "Ask your father." It was unusual for her not to rush to my assistance. I figured she was in some troubling times of her own.

Fortunately, after a few messages with my stepfather, he was up for the adventure. As busy as he always was, he said he would help. One problem, the banks were closed in South Africa, and the deadline for my flight payment was the following day at 14h00 Thailand timezone. The time in South Africa would be 8 am Monday. This meant the South African banks were only opening when my payment was due.

I was scared.

No way. I CANNOT SPEND ONE MORE DAY HERE.

My stepfather promised he would do what he could and I trusted him to be there first thing in the morning. There was nothing more he or anyone else could do.

I thought about the following day.

Stress rattled me.

Thirsty, my voice said.

I decided to focus on my current problems.

I didn't have enough money for drinking water.

Next problem—where would I rest for 18 hours?

It was getting late, I was exhausted, and I was penniless. I figured the worst-case scenario would be a thirst-induced sleepless night on the airport floor. *Would I even make it home?*

I started piecing together a plan. *Maybe I can beg at the bathrooms? Maybe I can approach a businessman at a restaurant for a meal?*

Who should I ask for help?

The answer came to me, and I headed for the Airport Information help desk. Seeing two happy, smiling people behind the desk was a lighthouse in my sea of turmoil. *Please help,* I thought. I told them my situation. I was hopeless. I wondered if they would suggest I spend the night at a homeless shelter and organize a free taxi to drop me off.

Instead, the man asked if I knew my credit card numbers. My fatigued brain churned like an overweight hamster on a rusty wheel. I remembered I backed up my credit card with a picture I had saved in the digital cloud. This was new stuff back then—access to pictures on digital clouds. I showed him the card. Luckily I hadn't canceled it when the wallet went missing.

He phoned a specific hotel.

Breakthrough.

The hotel was able to process my payment with the card numbers without a physical card. They would send a shuttle to fetch me.

A glimmer of hope for rest. After weeks of pushing through mud, this was some kind of silver lining.

I was so relieved.

I could eat breakfast in the morning and be brought back to the airport to wait at the Western Union for my money (if it came on time).

The shuttle picked me up at the airport and carried me to the hotel reception. I wandered toward the desk, lightheaded and in a twilight zone. I was running on thin air. No food, no water, just a will to survive and make it home.

Someone guided me through carpeted walls until I reached my room. My head was spinning, and I wondered if I would be able to find my way back to the desk in the morning.

The concierge opened the door.

A clean room with air conditioning!

It was heaven.

I sent some last messages on my phone, then crashed into the pillows.

My alarm went off only a few hours later.

Must. Get. Home.

I ate a quick hotel breakfast and returned to the airport.

I headed straight to the Western Union office.

I kept watching the time in South Africa. 07h00am.

I messaged my stepdad.

He was already en route.

Time passed slowly. My body was jittering nervously.

Message from my stepdad: *The Western Union office is closed. I will have to find another.*

My heart sank. My stepfather had driven to a branch that was no longer operating.

Every 15 minutes felt like a full hour.

My stress levels rose like a flooding dam.

I've made the payment, came his next text message.

My spirit leapt with joy.

How long does it take the cash to clear on my side? I replied.

He didn't know.

They couldn't say.

My stepfather had done his job, now I was in the hands of the money transfer system. The people in Western Union were watching me through the glass. They all knew my situation.

I waited 5 minutes.

I asked the supervisor again.

Nothing.

I looked at my watch.

I was in a time squeeze to make the booking for my flight.

Five more minutes.

I asked again.

Nothing.

I thought my foot was going to fall off from furious nervous tapping.

I wasn't even sitting anymore, I couldn't bear it.

Will I or won't I get home today?

Five more minutes.

The panic monster was sliding in for a look at its prey.

The Western Union cubicle person called my name.

I jumped up.

The printer was printing.

The money had come through!

Hallelujah!

He printed more receipts and gave me the cash.

Forgetting about my lack of energy, I jetted off across the terminal like a bat after an insect, back to the counter who had refused my entry the night before.

I paid.

They printed my boarding pass.

It was like receiving Willy Wonka's golden ticket.

All was confirmed.

"Are you sure this takes me all the way home," I said.

"Yes, sir, everything is confirmed".

I was elated.

I was finally on my way to rest.

The tickets I held were the way out of the land of the sick.

Or so I thought.

THE LAST STRAW HAT

Rest was calling to me like sweet, green grass to a flock of sheep.

I got onto the plane and sank into my seat. I was sleeping within minutes.

I didn't wake even when the food trolleys moved down the aisle.

When I landed in South Africa, I collected my luggage and checked in for my domestic flight.

At passport control in Johannesburg, the surge of people around the official's desk swarmed like ants. There didn't appear to be much of a line or process, and multiple passports were collected and given to the desk. When it was my turn to receive my passport, I was handed a maroon color passport. *Strange, my passport is supposed to be green.* I flipped it open. A picture of an older lady stared back at me. My brain struggled to comprehend what was happening. It hit me—the lady standing in front of me moments before—I was holding her British passport. She had left, probably with my passport. I panicked. *Lord, don't let me be stuck here. I've made it this far.* Ideas of getting rest were slipping away quickly. I wondered if the lady was out of the terminal, probably getting into some private shuttle on the way to an exclusive game reserve. I wondered if I would ever see my passport again. I prayed. It was probably the first time I prayed during my entire trip to Thailand. Probably the first time in years. I was at my wit's end. I couldn't rely on myself anymore. I had to rely on some kind of supernatural intervention. Any help was welcome. I pleaded for help in my heart.

Suddenly, I had the urge to run.

I rounded some officials asking to check my passport and dashed passed into the arrivals foyer. I stood there. I imagined a huge angel standing above the crowd. I prayed for a miracle. Something had got to give. *My passport, please.* Suddenly, with the police still coming up behind me, the crowd seemed to part like the red sea as a lady walked toward me. Not any lady, the lady whose passport I had. I looked down at the open passport, I looked up at her. It was definitely the same person. She had a confused look on her face as she stared down at the open green passport in her hand.

"Is this mine?" I asked. She looked up at me, still bewildered.

I semi-snatched the passport from her hand. It was mine. I handed her hers. I didn't say another word. I simply turned around, sidestepped the incoming rotund police officers, and headed back through the swarm of ants at the passport control.

Did I just encounter a miracle?

I didn't have time or energy to dwell on it. I had to keep going to make it to my flight. I wasn't sure whether to be relieved or scared the police might continue to chase after me.

I had no more energy for drama.

I was trying my best to avoid further confrontations, conversations, or explanations.

No more challenges please.

I simply wanted to get home.

I headed to the counter for my connecting flight. In Thailand they said I'd need a new boarding pass on arrival in Johannesburg.

I handed over the boarding ticket to the lady at the counter.

She tapped a few buttons on her keyboard.

A pause.

"Sorry sir, the flight is full," she replied.

My mind flopped like a pancake.

I stared blankly at her.

"Sorry sir, the flight is full, it's a long weekend and it's also the school holidays. Unfortunately you will have to buy a new ticket with another carrier if you want to fly today, or you can wait until tomorrow afternoon".

No money.

I wanted to scream-run-cry-throw-a-tantrum or break down.

How could so many things go wrong?

This entire journey was like barbed wire, an endless supply of sharp, pointy edges to test me.

Maybe I should write a story about this one day. I felt like I actually might.

Considering I didn't have a wallet, my mind started churning.

At least I can drink the water here.

Must. Get. Home.

I didn't feel like I could call my parents again—I had cashed those tickets already.

I sat on the floor next to the counter.

Grant, maybe Grant can help?

I dialed him, hoping he was available.

He answered after a few rings.

"Dan," he said.

"Hey bro, I need your help. I'm in Joburg airport and don't have enough money to book a flight to Cape Town. Sorry to dump this on you. Can you help?"

"Now?" He replied, clearly a bit taken aback by my urgency.

"Yes, now, it's a long weekend, and all the flights are fully booked. I'm in transit".

I stayed on the phone as he searched online for available flights.

"Only three tickets available on a last flight today", he said, "but it's pretty expensive."

"Book it, please." My dreams of getting home were fading.

He fetched his credit card and plugged in the details. I stayed on the line in anticipation.

"Failed," he said.

I started crumbling in my inner world.

Two flights left.

"Why Grant? Just book me a flight!" I said rather sharply. I think he could hear the fear in my heart.

"Only one seat left," he said.

In the time it had taken him to fetch his credit card, someone had booked it.

Help me.

He tried again.

Flights were easily triple their normal price.

"Booking confirmed," he said. "I can send through your flight details now."

"Are you sure?"

It sounded too good to be true.

The last ticket-to-peace.

Confirmed.

We ended the call and he messaged me the details.

I went to a new airline counter with my freshly purchased travel details. They confirmed everything was ok and printed my tickets.

There is no price I won't pay to get home, I thought. I was desperate.

I messaged Grant a big thanks and said I would see him soon. As I safely tucked the boarding passes into an impenetrable pouch in my moonbag, I wanted to crumple to the floor. I couldn't explain the adventure I had been on for weeks. It wasn't only about today. It was a never-ending grind up a mountain. Everything was difficult.

The smooth life I was living a year or so ago seemed to have faded with the Thai sunsets. Incessant pressure and mishaps seemed to be waiting at every corner. Nothing went my way.

What now? I said to myself as I had time to kill at the airport. I thought of searching for a row of extended airport seats – the metal chair oasis in a desert of sleep—but I was worried if I closed my eyes I might fall asleep and miss my plane.

I simply stretched out where I was, right on the floor by the airport counters.

I'd seen travelers before, looking like shipwreck victims piled with their last belongings, washing wearily about airport terminals. I had now become one. In fact, I was already one when I left the country those weeks ago. Now I was returning in worse condition. I had gone beyond being a shipwreck victim. I was in the twilight zone, soon to enter the death zone. Too many nights of not sleeping, too many days of stress. I needed oxygen. Something to boost me to complete the last summit of my disastrous life adventure.

After a few minutes of floor recovery (which no one gave much attention to), I decided to be the first person on the airplane. No more opportunities for mishaps.

Heading toward the boarding gate, I slipped into the airport bathroom to take some long deep drinks of tap water (which I was elated was now free, clean, and drinkable). As I entered the bathroom I pulled in next to a man wearing a big straw hat. I looked at the hat. Memories came flooding back—a piece of Thailand waiting for me in the bathroom.

I tried to escape but here it was, right next to me. I bent down to sip some water, a little fear flickering in my heart. *Is this some kind of sign?* I hoped this traveler had an amazing time in Asia. I didn't want to engage in conversation for fear of being rude about my adventures. I was still processing everything that had happened. As I tried to ignore his presence and sip the clean, free water, I suddenly heard a retching sound. I looked up. His straw hat was tipped low. He was holding the rim of the basin. He vomited again. I stared horrified. Blood was running down the white ceramic basin.

"I'm so sorry," he said, bending over to hurl more red liquid into the basin. "I'm so sorry."

Sorry for what? I thought. *How is this guy sorry when he is the one vomiting in the basin?*

I couldn't drink any more water.

I looked at him. He was in a bad way. I thought my inner reserves were wearing thin, but as I watched him, I realized my problems were small.

I looked at myself in the mirror. I was healthy compared to what was next to me.

He wretched again.

"Thailand?" I asked as he came up for air.

He nodded feebly.

I gained perspective instantly. I was in a much better situation than this man. I didn't think he could complete the last leg of his journey.

I felt better, I suddenly had hope.

It gave me perspective—no matter how dire you think your straits are, there is always someone in a deeper hardship than you.

As I watched with pity, I guessed he had picked up some illness in the jungles or islands. I imagined some virus or bacteria ravaging his intestines or airways.

I suddenly had an appreciation for my situation. Grant had helped me. My stepdad helped me. I got to sleep in a hotel. I was not vomiting blood. A little voice whispered to me, *appreciate what you have, life can always get harder.*

I remembered the antibiotics I had been given in the jungle for my "stomach issues". I had never taken them. I ruffled in my rucksack and put them on the counter next to him.

"Antibiotics for your stomach," I told him, "use them if you want."

I stooped to have a final awkward sip of water.

Joy simmered within me for the first time in weeks. I was nearly home free. With joy giving me extra internal fuel, I decided to find help for the man in the straw hat. I exited the bathroom and drifted over to some airport personnel. As I was about to speak, I spotted some medical staff already on the way. A team of two or three was carrying a small, square, white plastic box with a red cross logo.

At least he has some help, I thought, *but I doubt he will make it where he is hoping to go.*

I felt lucky.

I hope you make it, brother, I said in my heart.

I turned from the bathroom entrance to face security. It was time to resume my mission.

I did not want to miss my plane.

I had just enough energy to wait in line and get to my seat, and then I would collapse.

What I didn't realize as I left the bathroom, I was also sick. Sicker than eyes could see. I wasn't vomiting in the basin, but my blood carried a virus that would haunt me long after I made it to my seaside home.

One which would gnaw at me for years.

One which would change me.

It wasn't an external disease for all to see, it was an internal disease.

I hadn't contracted an illness in Thailand, I had created it.

It was the beginning of a real-life adventure.

Entering zombie mode.

BOTH ENDS BURNING

I **FINALLY RETURNED** to my seaside home in Cape Town later the same day. I was far beyond fatigued. I slept about fifteen hours that first night back in my own bed. It was a restless sleep filled with night sweats, fevers, and wild dreams. I woke up tired.

I figured I needed to eat a good breakfast cereal with plenty of nutrients and vitamins to regain my stamina.

This will make me better, I thought as I piled my breakfast bowl full. Yet, no amount of breakfast cereal brought my energy back.

As the first few days passed, I worried I had caught a more serious illness during my travels. Something maybe a tropical disease center needed to assess.

Two weeks later, I was still waking up with the bed sheets completely drenched. I went to the doctor to get tested for malaria or dengue fever. The tests were negative.

I must be fine, I said to reassure myself.

I didn't know how to listen to my body, so I threw myself back into work. No Danger Diaries was thriving. I needed to support it.

Very quickly a panic in my heart returned. The discomfort inside me was best summed up by—*I can't handle it.* Even the simplest tasks. I tried going to the office, I tried dealing with business problems, I tried sending emails, I tried doing what used to be day-to-day straightforward jobs. I simply couldn't handle it. I couldn't understand why. I had no resilience. I was so sensitive to everything. The smallest problems were now the biggest mountains.

I blamed the unknown disease which no medical professional could diagnose. In hindsight, this "panicky" sensation was actually a call for change. It was burnout. My burnout was not only a tiredness, it was a constant call for rest, even if I didn't want to. It showed itself by not allowing me to do any of the things I used to do. Whatever form of disease it took, it was never about the disease in the first place. It taught me to *feel* what I should be doing. Perhaps I should have asked myself—*Why is my immunity so low in the first place? Why is my body continuously struggling to overcome this virus? Why am I so sensitive? Why is my health in a chronic state of fatigue?*

I was looking for a quick fix for a 'patience problem'.

I didn't know how to slow down and truly rest. I didn't know some healing took time. I lived in a place of *isn't there a magic pill for this?* I didn't know what burnout was or why it happened. I kept looking for a cause. I looked for physical symptoms so I could have a solution. I didn't really stop and identify the emotional symptoms. Panic should have been a red flag. To me, it was a green light to push through.

The only solution for burnout is change.

Take the time to incubate and rest, so a new version of yourself can break through. A version who can handle stress again. The tasks. The emails. Burnout is the slowing down so the new can emerge, like a seed in the soil. It is a waiting game. I thought the new thing in my life was No Danger Diaries, but there was newer to come.

The knife edge was cutting a new path.

THE KNIFE EDGE

As simple and as difficult as burnout is to explain, I was unconsciously in it.

The more I continued to push, the more I wanted to crumble to the sidewalk again.

My weights-for-arms came back, and it was getting harder to move.

I tried to convince myself I would get better with time and routine.

More good breakfast cereals, more night's sleep.

Instead, my sleep got worse. I struggled to fall asleep at night. If and when I eventually drifted off, my sleep was light and restless. Any small sound would wake me. Sometimes I wondered if I had slept at all. After a night of no sleep, days passed in a haze. My brain was neither fully awake nor asleep.

More zombie than human.

My lovely seaside bedroom became a nightmare for me. People's voices, cars, the ocean, partygoers—all of it hindered my sleep. Sounds that never bothered me before started stressing me out—I blamed them for my insomnia. The happiness from work disappeared with my non-existent energy. My joy for life fled like a robber in the night. I couldn't recharge my battery no matter how long I rested.

Burnout isn't only about rest. Burnout holds the seeds of a new beginning. We're called to let who we once were metaphorically pass away, so new sprouts can bloom in the garden of our lives.

You don't have to be working hard to burn out.

Is a flame working hard when it burns the candle?

Or is the flame effortlessly burning?

Either way, it reaches the end of the wick, it burns out, and a new light must come to start a new flame.

This is burnout.

A changing of the candle.

It can creep up on you at any time.

It crept up on me when I least wanted it to.

I was so focused and committed to sharing joy I forgot about my own joy.

I could not share joy from an empty joy cup.

My life as I knew it slipped away from me.

I fought until the end.

I didn't face it sooner because it was too scary to acknowledge this "perfect life" wasn't all I was meant to be or have.

One day, standing wearily outside my house, leaning on the wall, a friend walked up the road. We chatted for a brief moment passing pleasantries. He commented trivially, but it cut me to the core: "Life is like a knife edge," he said, "you never know it's there until you're on it."

How did he know?

I am on a knife edge.

The doctors were trying to figure out what was wrong with me. I was constantly in and out of hospitals for more inconclusive blood results. I was wasting my energy. My arm was becoming a medical pin cushion. As trips to the hospital drained me, I waited for the verdict and continued to pretend I was still normal. I remember rushing from the hospital to the Rocket Ship office to host a meeting. The electrodes were still attached to my chest from the cardiac tests only an hour before. As I led the meeting's agenda, I could feel my heart beating irregularly. I ignored it. The doctor told me the virus might be causing inflammation in my heart. He said I should return immediately if my pulse got dangerously high. I never bothered checking it.

I didn't want to slow down. I believed if I stopped then everything around me would stop too. I believed that all the things we had painstakingly built would come crashing down, our joy mission would stop, and our momentum would die.

My life would be a failure.

I believed if I crashed, the whole system would crash.

This was my ego talking.

I was fighting against my ego.

The frustrating part was that this invisible virus was forcing me to do the thing I least wanted—Slow down, relax, and rest. The virus was forging a new life for me. It was demanding change. I was fighting with everything I had to hang on. Whilst the virus called me to the patience of healing—to let go of certain responsibilities and relationships, to let others in to support, to discover new fields of interest, to stop taking control of everything—I tried my hardest to keep a handle on it all. I couldn't let go. I couldn't surrender.

The virus was trying to whisper new plans for me—plans to bring fulfillment and happiness into my life. I had to stop resisting. I held on to the very end. To surrender to healing is to lay down ones life to the unknown. A death of what once was. Giving space for a new version to emerge. A software upgrade. Same same but different. A butterfly from the cocoon.

I didn't want to cocoon.

I wanted to share joy with the world.

Shine my light.

Be bright and confident, and happy.

I was too hard-headed to let the flow of Life carry my own personal life and desires. I didn't realize I couldn't keep sprinting through life without consequences. I started paying the price of forever speeding.

Patience wanted to partner with me.

This virus and I were about to become best friends.

It was not a friend I wanted.

MY SISTER VISITS: NO STOPPING NOW

I WAS SITTING in my kitchen one afternoon when my sister showed up. She lived around the corner from me so it wasn't completely out of the ordinary, but considering it was a work day for her, the timing was a surprise. She entered the house, chatting animatedly.

Something is amiss. Warning bells inside me started tinkling.

Listening to her, she seemed out of character. I had this ominous feeling that the sister I had grown up with wasn't the same person sitting on the counter. To my housemates she was normal, but I felt something was out of place. She was acting giddy and unusually passionate about some topics she was discussing. At first I thought they might be revelations for her, but as the day wore on, her actions became more unsafe. Later in the day she threw my clothes into the ocean and started swimming in the rough sea. I panicked.

She was having a psychotic episode.

I didn't know what to do. None of us did. The fear monster gripped me in a panic. *How can I help her? What is she capable of right now? I'm her big brother. I'm supposed to help. What does someone do for a person who has disconnected from material reality?*

Caring for her at the time was like walking with my worst fear.

I witnessed a mind who had temporarily lost its sense of normal reality. It was one of my own worst fears coming true through my sister.

How did it end?

With Sebastian and I using all our strength to carry her through a hospital foyer, naked, writhing and screaming words of hate. Each word pierced me to my core. I felt I had lost someone I loved.

I was broken.

It was heart-shattering seeing my sister in this wild state without being able to help. As the obscenities and confusion continued to pour out, I doubted whether I had done the right thing. My parents were en route on the first available flights. I felt deeply alone.

As I lay on the hospital floor waiting for daybreak, it occurred to me, my sister had finally cracked for us all.

The pressure of our unhealthy family system had broken through her.

She drifted in and out of rational consciousness, and eventually, praise be to God, she returned.

It took her two weeks to fully recover.

The hospital visits, traumatic conversations, night sweats, and psychiatric meetings with various doctors left me broken inside. I was shattered and yet I couldn't escape what life was bringing me. I couldn't find rest. Real life kept marching toward me. I couldn't handle anymore and yet I could not stop it.

The meetings, office responsibilities, employees, volunteers, family burdens, social image upkeep, financial stress—all of it layered itself like an ice cream burnout cake. I ate too much.

I melted down.

Not in a particular blowout or manic episode.

I quietly broke apart inside.

As I did this, so too did my body and mind shut down completely.

There were obviously many warning signs before this, but since I had never burned out before, I didn't know what to look out for or obey the signs for rest.

My body didn't heal.

My heart couldn't heal.

I couldn't handle the tiniest of stressors.

And then my mind became too tired to sleep.

My central nervous system was beyond overloaded.

The slightest sounds kept me awake at night. I couldn't nap in the afternoon because I had too much anxiety about not being able to sleep at night. I spiraled into a constant panic about not being able to sleep, not being able to cope with life. My anxiety meter was on full volume.

I no longer had it all figured out.

I was no longer the "master of my own destiny".

I was no longer Fantastic Mr Fox.

I was a bird set free in the world but hadn't learned to fly safely.

I realized I had never been taught to live with heart, so I didn't have guidelines for a heart-led lifestyle. I didn't truly know how to look after myself. I didn't truly know how to love myself.

I didn't know what to do next.

Without guidance from anyone, I disappeared into disease.

I sunk deep into burnout.

The candle went out.

No more light.

In the dark, I had to look for the signs.

SEASON 4

WATCH FOR THE SIGNS

BIRDMAN

BEFORE DISEASE, I noticed I had a special connection with birds or them with me. We joked about it as friends—all the ways in which they showed up in my life. They seemed to have an attraction to me which was unusual. The connections intensified whilst I was in the grip of disease.

An example of a pre-illness feathered encounter happened one day at the barber. I was sitting in the chair, listening to the scissors go snip, snip, snip. I watched a pigeon gliding around my feet as the hair fell to the floor. It was bobbing in and out whilst contently shuffling around. I was curious. I imagined pigeon nests made from all the different people's hair gathered in the barbershop. *Whose hair makes the best nest according to a pigeon?* I chuckled internally to myself.

As I watched it doing the pigeon dance between my feet, I asked the barber, "Doesn't it bother you the birds come into your salon?"

"It's never happened before," he replied.

I was taken aback. The pigeon looked naturally at home. The barber appeared naturally calm. We were all doing the haircut dance. I thought this was an everyday occurrence, a symbiosis of hair chopping and pigeon gathering.

I was touched.

On another occasion, I was on a romantic getaway. We were being shuttled around on a guided tour when we gathered on the floor of an upmarket hotel.

As the tour guide told a story, a tour group member exclaimed excitedly, "Look! Look at his foot!"

I looked around at people's feet wondering what the hype was about, but no one was moving about.

Then I realized the people were looking at me. They were beginning to point.

The cameras came out like paparazzi.

I tipped my gaze downward and perched quite comfortably on top of my loafer shoe was a small, yellowish bird with a white eye.

It looked completely at home like it had been there the whole tour.

I stood still.

The cameras snapped.

Whilst my date cooed with feminine adoration at the little ball of feathers perched on my foot, I wasn't so sure about the situation. *Where has this bird come from? Why did that bird choose me? Why do they come for me? How was it possible it got into this room?*

I played it cool. But I was secretly touched.

The encounters continued.

Running down a lower section of Table Mountain, I stopped on the trail. It was the last section of the footpath before the road and was covered with small, crunchy acorn shells. As my feet touched the crunch, I slowed to wait for my running partner and friend, Marina. I listened for the crunch of her footsteps behind me. Nothing yet. I was a little further ahead than I thought. I absent-mindedly surveyed the surrounding trees.

A quick, jerky movement in a large tree caught my eye.

I focused my gaze.

As the movement settled, I realized we were looking eye to eye.

A big brown owl and me.

It's daytime, I thought, *aren't you supposed to be sleeping?*

Curiosity filled me.

Crunch-crunch-crunch, came Marina's steps behind me.

She bumped into me with a playful gesture.

"Shhh," I said, pointing upward to the trees.

Her eyes scanned the branches.

"Ooooh Danny!" she cooed as she spotted the owl and clung to my arm.

The owl moved its head from side to side and gave us both a full once-over.

It was an uncommon meeting of two curious species decidedly interested in each other.

Whilst Owlie was figuring out who we were, we were looking back at it figuring out how we were having this chance encounter.

Side to side went its head again.

It was as if we were communicating with each other. It felt intimate. Marina grabbed onto my right arm even tighter and continued to quietly 'ooh' and 'aah' in her childlike manner.

As a joke, I held my left arm straight out as an invitation for our feathered friend to land on me.

The owl flapped its wings once or twice as if preparing to take flight toward us.

No way, I thought, *this can't really happen.*

The owl launched from its perch.

Marina grabbed my arm tighter.

In total disbelief we watched it drop from its perch and fly toward us. My arm was frozen in outer space. In the final meters of the descent, as our emotions were at their climax, a dog leapt from below with a loud bark and scared the owl. The owl swerved sharply to its left and flapped clumsily around a tree looking for a perch. The dog barked some more. The owl finally settled on a new branch above our heads. The dog hopped energetically about, barking at its airy intruder. My heart was beating.

DID THAT OWL JUST TRY TO LAND ON ME?! My mind screamed.

Or was it trying to attack us?

Marina was squeezing my arm like a stress ball.

"Danny! Danny!" she exclaimed, her eyes wide with amazement.

"Did that owl just try to land on us?" I asked.

Her eyes filled with wonder.

"Let's go," I said. I didn't want to hang around in crazy owl land.

We moved off down the path. I glanced back over my shoulder. The owl was still watching us intently.

As we continued into a run, the owl hopped from branch to branch to keep up. It followed us to the edge of the forest.

Why is this owl following us? Where did the dog come from? Thoughts circulated in my head. *What if the dog hadn't shown up? What was that owl about to do?*

I was embarrassed. I had only lifted my arm as a joke. The joke backfired.

It had created a remarkable moment for both of us.

SICK HAWKS

THE BIRDS DIDN'T only show up physically but also came to meet me in conversations. When I was ill, a series of conversations really drew my attention. The birds found me, even during my illness.

My friend Jenny visited and filled me in on her recent move to the Cape Point Peninsula. Her tone changed as she told me a story about a hawk she found walking on her front lawn. It appeared sick, and she guessed it was likely poisoned by a farmer in the area. Her heart was tender. She described its suffering with great compassion. I considered the unusualness of having this majestic bird ambling around her front lawn. The bird was grounded. No leaving the airport.

The story touched me.

Next, my stepfather called me. While wrapping up our conversation, he flippantly mentioned an incident with a hawk. It had landed on the balcony of his apartment and was simply sitting there. When he approached it didn't fly away. It appeared dazed or confused or resting. He got within feet of the hawk and guessed it might be tired or sick. He was in amazement at the majestic encounter, being so close to this winged predator. It was unusual. Something touched me about this story. I felt his words tugging at something deeper inside me.

My heart went out to the bird.

It was strangely familiar to Jenny's story. The hawk was still grounded, unusually close to humans, out of the ordinary.

Are the birds reaching out to me through my friends and family?

The thought was too crazy to bear.

The finale came when Solveig, a dear longtime friend, visited me. Sitting on the couch chatting, she explained with wonder a story that happened only a few days before. Outside her apartment window, in the middle of the city, a hawk hovered and landed briefly right on her window ledge. I felt the wonder and surprise in the story. An unusual encounter. Same as my stepfather, same as Jenny. Three stories, three hawks, three unusual encounters.

"Now that's weird, Sol," I said, a little uneasy. "This is the third time someone has recently told me about an unusually close encounter with a hawk."

She smiled in her kind, gentle, and knowing way.

"Maybe you should look into that," she said.

I didn't know what she meant.

"Look into what?"

"Hawk meanings," she said.

It hadn't occurred to me that maybe, just maybe, the hawks were bringing me a message.

PICNICS WITH OWLS

WHEN I THOUGHT about those hawks, I noticed one thing in common—all the hawks were acting strangely. They may or may not have been sick, but one thing was certain… they were behaving out of the ordinary. In my illness, this is how I felt. I was out of the ordinary. My normal life and normal behavior were no longer. I was grounded and sick. Walking around confused.

The bird stories were an accurate reflection of my life. A mirror.

They had found me even though I was trapped indoors and diseased.

They found me through my friends and family. They brought me a message from beyond.

I didn't want to accept it, but The Deep inside me vibrated with the chords of knowing.

I noted it, but my mind played it down.

I spoke to some friends about the stories and some of my previous encounters. The general consensus—"random" experiences without much meaning. "It doesn't mean anything if a hawk killed a pigeon in the air above your head," a friend said when I shared another interesting encounter.

"But", I offered, "I heard the hawk whack right into the pigeon meters above me. Surely this doesn't happen often. It seems too strange to be a coincidence when all this other bird stuff is happening".

I was confused. I didn't know what to make of it.

They must be right, I thought. *I'm making meaning out of nothing.*

"Maybe you're the birdman," they jokingly teased.

The encounters didn't fit into my understanding, so I dismissed them. The thought that beneath my advertising suspenders and bow ties also lived "the birdman" worried me. I had no desire to follow in my grandfather's footsteps of raising wild animals or looking after nature conservation areas. I didn't want to change.

I didn't have a choice. The birds were coming for me.

Ross and I were sitting on Camps Bay Beach.

It was moments before twilight, and we were enjoying the last rays of the setting sun.

It flew in fast.

A flash of feathers interrupted our sunset experience.

It landed in front of us.

It stared at me.

A large owl.

Perched on the white beach sand, with the waves breaking behind it, its gaze was still and transfixed.

Ross slowly backed away.

I was stunned to stillness.

This wasn't an encounter, it was an interruption.

TAKE NOTE OF ME, the owl said by its positioning and demeanor.

This was no place for an owl.

It was a popular tourist destination where we played frisbee, volleyball, beach bats—we lounged with friends under sun umbrellas. This was not a forest or hospitable place for such a nocturnal creature. Yet, nestled in the sand in front of me at sunset was a large, brown owl.

It was rather shocking to see.

I looked at it.

It stared back, unblinking.

Something deeply uncomfortable stirred within me.

I felt fear, foreboding, and a sense of tragedy. I felt shocked, terrified, horrified.

It was not pleasant.

This encounter wasn't like the bird encounters of before. This one moved me in a disturbing manner.

I looked for Ross, he'd moved to a grassy embankment behind me.

I looked at the owl again.

With one last deep soul gaze, it flew over to a nearby palm tree at the roadside.

I followed.

It launched from the tree and disappeared.

Ross walked over to me.

I was standing there, riding waves of emotion. The other bird incidences had sparked surprise, joy, or curiosity. The meeting with this feathered friend rattled the dangling chains of my inner spirit.

"Why did you leave me, Ross?" I asked as he approached.

"That one was for you," he said nonchalantly.

I felt truth in his comment.

We knew something special had happened on that beach.

I was beginning to believe.

The owl was for me.

It brought a message.

I was petrified.

Who was speaking to me?

My mind started asking questions I didn't want answers for.

Who sent the owl? Has it come to tell me something? Could I communicate with birds? Why me?

I didn't want these encounters, but I couldn't stop them.

Owls on beaches, what next?

I didn't like the unexplainable because it forced me to confront a reality that I didn't know everything and I wasn't in control. This was not lovely for my ego to face.

I shuddered—I had to start listening to the incoming messages.

I knew I had to pay closer attention.

I knew life was speaking to me.

I knew this owl came to tell me about death.

I knew something important would happen.

Months later, my mother killed herself.

When I received the news, I remembered that owl.

BURNING OUT

MY TEACHERS

DURING THIS PERIOD of time, I had been going from doctor to doctor taking blood test after blood test. I knew I was sick but the doctors couldn't figure out why. After weeks of frustration, I finally tested positive for a diagnosable illness: Epstein-Barr virus.

EBV is known as the cause of mononucleosis or glandular fever. The virus is a common malady; most symptoms disappear after a few days or weeks. Mine lingered. The doctor who diagnosed me explained that extreme fatigue and fever, along with swollen lymph glands, are the common symptoms. *No surprises there,* I thought, reflecting on the wet bed sheets from midnight sweats and the constant feeling of slowly moving through mud at the simplest tasks. The doctor warned me if I left it unchecked, the glandular fever could turn chronic, meaning it could linger for much longer.

I didn't realize the seriousness of this statement at the time. I was only happy to receive some medical direction.

The doctor recommended I take some supplements and two weeks of full bed rest. Before this period, rest meant working on my laptop and having meetings when my business partners got home.

The "backpacker beach house" never rested, with a constant slew of people coming in and out. It was a highway for high-energy people.

To try and honor the two weeks of proper rest, I decided to fly to my stepfather's house, where I could have a little more privacy and downtime. I figured being at his apartment away from the always-on culture would do me good.

It didn't work out as planned.

I was creating the stress. It didn't matter if I went to Timbuktu or lived in a campervan in Alaska. As long as I kept creating stress, I would take it with me wherever I went. It wasn't only the physical environment causing a lack of rest. It was my internal environment. I chose to throw myself back into work. I allowed myself to be reachable when I had nothing to give. I tried to share joy when I had none. I was busy, busy, busy inside… all the time. My internal world was constantly thinking-about-this, planning-that, worrying-about-this, trying-to-solve-that. Even though I had left the office and Cape Town, I was still attending online meetings, returning urgent emails, and participating in creative concept sessions. I was using the digital world to create my demise.

I simply couldn't let go.

It was unfathomable to me to stop completely.

The *business of joy* was everything to me.

It *was* me. I believed I put the "Dan" in "No Danger".

This dangerous belief was killing me. I thought letting go of this world was letting go of myself. It was too hard.

As the disease tried to slow me down, I danced dangerously around it. At times I managed to blank it out and carry on.

"This is my mission," I repeatedly told myself. "I will share joy or die trying."

This attitude fed the virus, and as the doctors warned, it became chronic. I never gave myself a break for long enough to heal. The EBV transformed into chronic fatigue syndrome. The sick hawks were right. I was poisoning myself. It was now me, standing dazed on the front lawn outside someone else's life. It was me lying on the deck of my stepfather's apartment, too tired to fly away on my own journey.

I continued to push. I still didn't listen to the M.E messenger.

As soon as I had any energy, I turned it toward my businesses. As soon as I had any wellness, I invested it into relationships outside of myself.

I gave myself to everyone but me.

LESSONS IN ME

SINCE I PUSHED through the chronic fatigue with coping mechanisms and strategies, Life gave me an upgrade. Then I got sent to the headmaster's office for being extra naughty. The headmaster gave me a new teacher – M.E. (*myalgic encephalomyelitis*). This disease was mainly characterized as a neurological condition, notably for high levels of inflammation concerning the nervous system and spinal cord.

I was no match for M.E.

The naughty corner quickly silenced me.

I don't even remember the doctor who diagnosed me with M.E.. My life was too much of a haze at the time. M.E. does that to you. It takes the ocean of your mind and applies a mist so thick you can't see which way is left, right, up, or down. I mostly resembled a three-toed sloth in the Amazon jungle, moving slowly from tree to tree, never really sure what was going on, wondering what happened to the agile monkey I used to be. Life had sent me something which forced me to change track, to change my tune, and to start listening to the new music.

The funny thing about M.E. is that some days feel almost normal, while others feel like it takes everything from you. You never know the time or the day, or the reason. It just happens.

Some days I couldn't get up to get water from the kitchen. Some days I couldn't lift my arms or my legs. Some days I couldn't get out of bed and even the thought of picking up my phone was impossible. On other days, I felt nearly fine. M.E. makes it difficult for the people around you to understand what you are going through. The inconsistency means at some moments you're the friend or partner they remember, whilst at others, you are a floppy mess on the couch or bed. On the bad days, it was like being in a coma, somewhat trapped in my body, yet aware that life was moving by. Then I would be up again. Laughing and joking with my friends. I was very supported for the most part, and yet it was inevitable some people thought I was seeking attention, or being lazy, or needed to just "get on with it."

If you are suffering with M.E., I bless you right now with so much love. I pray everyone around has grace and understanding for your journey. May you be filled with direction and healing. May the right people show up to support you. May the M.E. teacher's lessons land in you with incredible love.

I know how difficult this pit is. I know how relentless this teacher makes you change.

The brain fog on some days was so incapacitating I would do circles around my room, forget what I was doing and climb back into bed. On other days, I was able to complete basic business tasks, but as soon as the clouds lifted for a moment—giving the people around me enough time to think I was okay— I was quickly reduced to lying in bed again. The agile, smart, witty, energetic go-getter who used to be "Daniel" was more often than not a 90-year-old man moving slowly around a nursing ward at an old-age home.

DYING TO SLEEP

ONE NIGHT LYING in bed, all the energy I once had was completely gone.

I am totally lifeless, I thought.

Not only my metabolic energy—which used to fuel my zest for life—it was deeper than this. I was missing the energy I needed to be alive. To be human. I remember thinking, *This must be what it feels like to die. I wonder if I will feel like this at 90 years old, about to cross over.* I was tasting the end right in the middle. The dessert before the mains. I had no life force in me at all. The sustaining energy to maintain my body and functioning had slipped away. I was unplugged.

I wasn't particularly worried either, worrying took energy—I didn't have enough to care. Not able to move, I focused on my breathing. In and out. I turned my thoughts from dying to my breath. In and out, in and out. Watching. Observing. In and out. I lay for ages inhaling and exhaling. Totally at peace, wondering if I was about to pass on. At only 30 years of age, I felt I was retiring from life, and I could do nothing about it.

This new teacher called M.E. was giving me a real lesson. It took me to the very edge. I wasn't afraid, I knew I would more than likely recover, but I did think, *Why am I experiencing what it feels like to die?*

I woke up the next morning resenting M.E. It was as if it kept me alive so it could feed off my energy. It wouldn't completely end me, it would drain me to the last drop, let me recover slightly, then feed again. It was as if M.E. waited to see what I would do with those drops before it was feeding. If I didn't use my energy-drops correctly, the teacher would take the drops away again. Back to square one where vitality and life force were non-existent. It was a constant struggle. I wondered what the point of being alive was. Life was no fun. Lying in bed incapacitated was not the "alive" I wanted or was used to.

If I do not have health, I have nothing, I thought to myself.

I promised if I could get out of this mess I would always look after myself.

If my cup is empty, I have nothing to give.

M.E. took everything and gave me everything I needed to know at the same time.

HOMELESS

To add some extra spice to my life, due to "technical difficulties" living together, my stepfather asked me to leave his apartment where I was recovering. I don't think he knew his apartment was secretly my last hope of getting better. I had hedged everything on being able to turn around my health there. Now I had to leave.

And go where?

I had rented out my room in Cape Town to try and make some extra money to live off whilst I could hardly work. I was out of options. I couldn't handle the fast-paced lives of friends or noisy, "normal life" living quarters. I knew it would make me sicker.

I decided to fly back to Cape Town anyway. Something would turn up. Cape Town was more like home since I didn't have a family home anymore.

I packed my bags and off I went. Back to Camps Bay. Back to the beachside cottage, which was more like a backpackers than a private house. I was worried. I knew this would be difficult and dangerous territory to navigate with my health. I was fortunate one of our housemates was out of town and I could stay in her room. It would give me a few days to plan for the next roof over my head.

I felt hopeless.

Even if I could stay somewhere, what would I do?

Where would money come from?

How would I get better?

I remember walking out of the house onto the beach. I felt like a foreigner. I was a tourist in my own life—totally unsettled and unsure of what was coming next. It wasn't a holiday. I was visiting a nightmare. I was desperate. As I walked aimlessly across the beach sand, my heart cried out in despair. I awkwardly entered into a prayer. I think it was the first time I prayed since I was a child. As I walked along the beach, my heart was reaching out to something much bigger than myself. I felt my heart crying, "Please help me, just help me. I don't know where to go or what to do. I need somewhere to sleep tonight." My heart was reaching for the stars.

I finished my sunset walk and headed hopelessly home. As I walked back into my housemate's room, my phone beeped. It was a friend in a nearby suburb called Hout Bay. She welcomed me to spend the night as I searched for a resting stop.

My heart leapt with hope.

Was the subtle prayer in my heart immediately answered? I pondered this with a mixture of confidence and doubt.

Was this another coincidence?

I was backpacking through my life with no clue where to go or what to do. I had to say yes to this invitation.

It was nearly time to pick up my backpack and go on a journey that would take me to the deepest parts of myself.

A STRATEGIC BREAKDOWN

AFTER SPENDING THE night at my friend's house, it finally happened.

A complete breakdown.

My internal world crumbled quickly and completely.

No one knew except for my entire soul, heart, mind, and body.

After all the moving from place to place, not having a home, not having answers, never getting better, and never getting sick enough to be permanently in hospital, I spiraled into the abyss.

Existing, but not living.

It was midmorning and I had woken up from yet another night of broken and shallow sleep. My host had headed to her office job to continue with normal life (something I was constantly aspiring to do, yet never attaining), and I was left floating in her loft apartment seeking purpose.

Lost and confused, I turned to the same thing I always did —work.

At this point, while I was falling apart, our business was thriving. We recently launched a new project called Secret Sunrise, which was attracting a lot of public attention. A Secret Sunrise was a 60-minute facilitated session, combining music, movement, play and dance, to help people unleash themselves and express joy and freedom. It was a lot of fun. It helped people connect to each other, to themselves, to wellness, and to the joy of those around them. It was my personal corporate weak spot, I couldn't resist working on this business to help it reach its potential. As hundreds of people were showing up to dance at sunrises in beautiful locations all over the city, I was facilitating dances and tapping away on my keyboard at all the moments I could. It was as if years of joy work had resulted in this product.

I couldn't stand by and watch it take off without me.

It needs me.

On this particular morning, I knew I needed to write a strategy to help change our business model to scale the movement globally.

I set my laptop at a desk and tried to push on. I tried to get through the brain fog.

I was midway through the strategic presentation when it happened.

The words on the screen became blurry.

My mind stopped.

I was aware I was staring at the computer, but my brain had become entirely blank.

Nothing.

I was no longer able to process anything or do anything. I was looking through my eyes, yet the world seemed incomprehensible.

I tried to recall what day or time it was.

I could not.

I tried to remember where I was.

I could not.

I started to panic.

I knew who I was, yet I could not fathom what I was doing.

I'm losing my mind, came a thought from a faraway land.

My breathing became labored and heavy whilst anxiety gripped me.

"My worst fear is coming true—My mind is going to snap," said a voice far away.

I braced myself for the moment between sanity and insanity.

I wonder if I will remember this, I knew this day would come.

Too much pushing.

I looked absentmindedly around the room.

Blank.

A question suddenly arose from my depths and hovered in my mind.

"Daniel, what are you even doing right now?"

I knew exactly what it meant.

It wasn't about what I was doing at that moment in the room. It was about what I was doing in the entire landscape of my life. I could actually *feel* the question more than interpret it mentally.

It was a call for perspective.

I realized I was a complete mess.

The truths landed like bombs on a battlefield:

I have no place I can call home.

I have no feeling of family support.

I have no health.

I have no bed I can call my own to sleep in.

I have no idea what I should be doing.

I have no feeling of friendship because I can't keep up with the pace of a normal, active life.

I have no energy, direction, vitality, or salary.

I feel like I have absolutely nothing.

I realized in those few brief moments this had been going on for months.

I was slapped in the face by the reality of my own life.

I had been constantly fighting for normality, yet finally, something had woken to realize my never-ending struggle. The cords holding me to my old life were beginning to break. Like a hot-air balloon trying to take flight, the sandbags of my life were dropping. Due to some miraculous inspiration, I pierced the shell of darkness and received a light of sudden perspective.

What had become visible wasn't pretty.

I got off my chair and sat on the floor. I tried breathing, meditation, and stretching to clear my mind.

None of it helped.

My mind was churning, and panic was pulsating.

I have to get out, I thought.

I opened the door of the loft apartment and headed into the street. I thought about my sister and how she had wandered the streets on the day of her mental fallout.

I wonder if the same thing is happening to me? I wonder if I'll even find my way back here? My mind was at the end of its tether, ready to leave and never return.

Total mental burnout.

I meandered aimlessly through the streets. Walking to keep sane. I wanted to run but knew if I did, it might deplete my energy for days.

I was desperate. I needed something to help me feel like I was escaping.

I started to pick up my pace.

I allowed myself to start jogging.

It was the first moment of freedom I had felt in months.

FIRST SIGNS OF VULNERABILITY

MONTHS OF BEING cooped up with my laptop, working, and stressing, whilst holding myself back from exercise (because of my illness) finally came to a halt.

I let go.

I ran and ran and ran.

I let my legs stretch and opened up my stride. The wind moved through my hair. My body was moving in rhythm. Energy pulsed through me. I was coming alive. The love of mountain trails and warm invitation of the open road swept back in. I missed it all so much. I missed being this version of myself. I was free for the first time in ages.

I ran until I got to the beach.

I slowed down to walking speed and finally stopped.

I gazed over the horizon.

Staring into the distance of the great Atlantic Ocean, I felt so small.

I didn't know how this had all happened or who I had become, but I finally knew I needed serious help. I knew something important had happened to me, and I couldn't ignore it anymore.

No more pushing on.

I reached for my phone to message three of my closest friends.

It was a big deal for me.

I had a "never say die" attitude and certainly never admitted defeat, especially to my closest friends. I typed something along the lines of: "Guys, I need help right now, I am not getting any better, and I just don't know what to do anymore".

The message was simple, and yet at the same time, it was momentous for me. I admitted I couldn't carry on and couldn't do it alone. I had very seldom asked for help before. It was hard to admit and own that I didn't know what to do. I always knew what to do. I was the guy people came to when they didn't know what to do.

It was my first step in the direction of vulnerability.

I got quick responses from everyone, saying they would be there for me. It brought tears to my eyes that the three of them dropped their plans to come to my aid.

One of my friends was staying right up the road from my current spot. We decided to meet there that very evening.

There happened to be a spare room next to his.

We huddled in a corner of it.

They listened to my story.

"You need to take a break," they agreed, "the business will be fine. Take a month or two or as much time as you need."

I nodded in agreement, letting their words sink in.

I knew it was time to shift into a different, slower gear.

"Ok, let me take two full months off to get better," I said.

"Dan, two months, three months, six months, as long as it takes," replied Grant.

I was still goal-setting and giving myself timeframes (and stress) to complete things according to my agenda.

It would be a hard beast to kill.

The advertising industry had conditioned my mind to work according to fast-paced deadlines and deliverables.

Grant was right. It would be a lot longer than two months. The road to recovering my life had begun.

BEGINNING TO LISTEN

ROOM TO FACE THE MUSIC

THROUGH FORTUITOUS CIRCUMSTANCES, the very same room we huddled in was for rent.

"I'll take it right now," I told the landlord.

"There isn't even a pillow on the bed," she replied, slightly amused.

"It doesn't matter," I said.

She had no idea how desperate I was.

I was a backpacker and needed a place to land—this was it—it was perfect.

I had a friend next door for support.

I had a small stream at the bottom of the garden for nature time. The area was leafy, green, quiet, and on the side of a mountain.

It had a view of the ocean.

It had everything I knew I needed for total wellness.

I returned to my backpack where I had left it during my earlier meltdown. I looked around my friend's place. She wasn't even home and would have no idea what I had been through in my day whilst she was tapping away in the office.

I sent her a message and returned to my new room. I knew this was finally the beginning of my real journey to recovery. I sensed the gravity of the commitment I was making. Life had given me this space, and it was time to use it wisely.

Stop ignoring the signs and start facing the music.

I went to sleep that night and woke up to a new tune.

A tune of surrender.

With my business partner's blessing and encouragement, I knew stopping was okay for now.

Surrendering was okay.

What was required of me was to shift the focus of my energy from everything and everyone else to my own needs. To my healing. To my wellness.

What are you going to do? Where will you start? My mind was searching for ideas. I hadn't a clue. As I woke up that first morning in my new healing spot, I decided the best thing was to communicate with my family about the seriousness of the timeout I was taking. Not your average holiday timeout, more like a "life out". A break from my own life whilst I was living in it. A tricky thing to communicate, indeed. I figured I would type an email and attempt to explain what I was going through. I couldn't handle a phone call due to the frazzled state of my nervous system.

Here is the actual email I sent to my family:

Subject: Family Matters

...

I'm going through extreme challenges and changes in my life at the moment.

I've been sick now for six months. I relapsed badly again a couple of days ago (third time) and I simply cannot carry on living any semblance of a life I used to. Let me put this in perspective… I cannot run, surf, swim, play frisbee, go out with friends, play tennis, clown around, go to boxing, do yoga, or now… even do work. Life, and Daniel as you know him… is simply no longer… It is just that I, and you, need to accept that the version of me on the other side of this will be very different and may not include anything I've built this far.

It is interesting how I knew that the Daniel who would pop out on the other side would be very different. It was foreboding because little did I know how much I was to change on the inside.

I also remember how incredibly hard it was to write this email. The warrior who thought he was always looking after the family and was forging a path to success was finally admitting defeat. I felt like I had failed. Failed to support my depressed mother. Failed to support my family. Failed to support my friends, my business, and myself. Failed to get better. I was overwhelmed with guilt.

I knew no doctor could offer me a "magic cure" or "quick fix" to get me out of the pit. I knew in my heart that to discover a way out meant I would have to do things I had never done before. I was going to have to change. I knew I would have to go beyond my comfort zones and face my fears. I knew beyond my fears was my place of healing. Sending the email was my commitment to healing. Becoming accountable for my healing was a very important step in my journey. This contract made that promise to myself and others.

An inner and outer commitment to my wellness.

Time to write a new song.

THE SLOW-DOWN EXPERIMENT

THE FIRST TWO weeks in my room were torture. Nothing inside me wanted to be still. My inner being was wired for go, go, go. Even in these confined living quarters I invented ways to keep myself busy. Wellness to-do lists, coloring in books, craft projects, juggling, and making things out of bamboo in the garden. I didn't believe I was born with an off switch or a stop button.

One day I felt well enough to walk to a nearby shopping center. I prepared a backpack of supplies: water, snacks, and warm clothing. It was a big adventure for me as I never knew when my energy or brain fog might set in, so I had to be prepared for all situations. The walk was less than 2 kilometers, but I set off with the mindset of climbing Kilimanjaro. About midway I discovered a bench in the middle of a park. I paused for rest and saw dozens of people hopping on and off buses, crossing the busy street, and cars honking their horns impatiently. I thought about how that used to be me. Now I felt like a retired person let loose from their old age home, looking at a world that moved too quickly to notice me. *Does a cheetah at full sprint notice a snail?* I thought.

I was the snail.

I rested a few more minutes, rehydrated, ate some snacks, and pressed on to the ominous mall experience. As I arrived at the entrance of the shops, I walked slowly inside, floating in my bubble in a foreign landscape. I was present in body but not fully present in mind. Too much fog. I drifted up and down the aisles, not knowing what I really needed, struggling to concentrate with the overwhelming stimuli this commercial environment presented. I was moving Zimmer frame pace up the aisles. *Where has all this extra time come from to be so slow?* I thought. I noticed different things the slower I moved. I noticed the old man reaching his shaky hand out for some beans. I noticed the old lady struggling to find the right cash in her handbag. I noticed the state of a poor person forking out his pennies for a packet of crisps. Slow people tend to absorb the surroundings like a sponge. Before, when I was a cheetah, I saw in a straight line. Now that I was the tortoise, my view had opened to life happening around me. The mall was the watering hole of the Serengeti. As I changed figurative animals, I realized I had a lot more time to choose: To choose groceries, to think about life, to observe the world around me. I used to be like a busy mom whisking her children through the isles at breakneck speed, picking up the essentials to rush home and make a meal for the family. Now I was a tortoise on the edge of society's norms. The extra time was torture because I preferred to be running at high speed. It deeply bothered me that I was in the middle of a normal work week and was only a passenger on the global economy contribution bus. I tried to calm down by reminding myself of my current focus—keep alive. Once I was better, then I could pick up speed again.

The contrast in my life was startling. Only months before, I was dashing around a city dancing a straight 67 hours for Mandela Day. I was also juggling contractual work and web development projects, running No Danger Diaries tasks and interns. Now here I was, a few months later, standing in a shopping aisle with one core mission—get groceries and get home alive. Overdoing it could cost me three days lying in bed.

I exited the shops with some bare essentials as I couldn't carry too much weight. A shortcut led me through a small garden nursery. I rested on a bench and looked around, tuning into my 80-year-old self. Absorbing. Watching. Resting. The plants soothed me. I looked out into the parking lot at the busy people everywhere. I looked at the nursery. Even the garden caretakers didn't pay attention to me as they moved quickly from one pot to another. I felt rejected from society—no longer a contributor—now a watcher. Like a beggar on a bench, I was unnoticeable to people traveling at speed.

"Shouldn't I be doing *SOMETHING?*" the voice in my mind cried out, "Anything?!"

I can't believe this is even real. Sidelined from society.

My mind judged me further, "You are literally drifting about your day with absolutely nothing to do, useless."

I knew the consequences could be big if I tried to exert or apply myself to anything. It didn't stop my mind from torturing me. *"Aren't you supposed to be DOING something?"* it asked.

I couldn't.

I didn't know if I ever would have the capacity to *do do do* again.

I wallowed in hopelessness.

I imagined what it was like to be ninety years old, trying to buy groceries but barely being able to complete the task. No one to phone. No one to speak to. No one to really understand how close I was to the tipping point of being alive. Unable to keep up with the pace of normal society, discarded like an old sack of potatoes in a forgotten pantry.

I purchased an ice cream.

I found a little bench to park on.

I stared up at the trees and watched some birds above me.

"Even they are *doing something*", I thought.

It was incredibly challenging to break through the rat race culture of "doing" into a state of "being".

My healing depended on it.

A NEW HOME

After I returned from the store, I was mainly confined to bed rest for a few days. This cycle would repeat itself. I spent most of my time in bed or lying on my wooden deck outside my room. If I was beginning to get mentally anxious, I would slowly walk down a small bank to a nearby stream, sit on the rocks, and listen to the running water. It had a calming effect on me. My friend Travis, who had been my neighbor, left soon after I moved in. I felt very much alone, yet I knew there was no other way. My main companion became a cat called Sheila. I didn't even like cats at the time, but Grandmaster Life had sent me Sheila, so what else could I do?

I accepted that Sheila, trips to the grocery store, and watching the birds were my new lot in life. I needed to surrender to "not-doing" so the tight knot of "doing" could unwind itself and my central nervous system could return to a normal state of being—whatever that felt like. I wouldn't know. Stressful jobs changed that a long time ago. My mind zoomed like a racing car on steroids. It never stopped. In the first two weeks of facing myself, I felt I was going cold turkey from some kind of drug.

It was the too-much-work drug.

The night sweats were still there and the dodgy sleep patterns were still there. I went from states of universal insights to anxiousness, to unbelief, to depression, to being back on top of the world. I would sometimes cry for no reason. The sobs would blub themselves out of me at a time they wished. It freaked me out. I didn't know what was happening. Then M.E. would rear its head again, and I would return to a state of lethargy. Hopelessness would come to say hello, depression revisited, and stress would swing by. I was constantly walking into the unknown, beginning to live life in a way I never knew existed. "Being" was very difficult because I had never been taught how to "be". I had only learned how to "do". Now I was facing the effect of my burnout. By slowing down, I was speeding up my healing. I would only learn this later. For the time being, I was allowing it all to unfold for me. I was allowing my breakdown to break through. The cycles repeated for the first couple of weeks. Highs. Lows. Manic states with thoughts of "YES, I'm overcoming this!" to "HELP ME, someone, I'm nowhere".

Perspective crawled in after a couple of weeks.

"What do you really want from life, Daniel?" I asked myself.

"How do you really want to live?"

I wrote it down.

The answer was simple.

I want to live in harmony with nature. I want to live in a community, I want to experience the freedom of being fully alive. I want to contribute to the world not only financially but in a way that brings life, healing, joy, and more.

As the stormy seas of my life tossed and turned, I was beginning to navigate the vessel and reposition myself for a brighter future. A position that was more true to who I was inside.

In the new spaciousness of my life, I started to hear my inner world which was crying to be set free. I started the process of unlearning. Releasing myself from expectations that were not really my own, setting down things I thought I needed to be. Slowly, as I went into this state of hibernation, I was tentatively visiting the first chambers of my inner castle.

BEST QUESTION EVER

I REMEMBER ASKING myself, "What do *you* want right now?"

I was so wrapped up in saving the world, in society's voice of success, and in patterns developed by an unhealthy culture, the question took me some time to truthfully assess.

My answer, "I want to be the healthiest I have ever been in my life by the end of the year!"

I knew without my health, I couldn't do anything.

I looked at the date—it was March, which gave me nine more months to increase my wellness levels.

It seemed reasonable to me.

I wrote the following question in thick letters on a piece of paper and stuck it on my door:

"IS THIS GOING TO MAKE YOU MORE HEALTHY?"

It would be the new question I would ask myself about everything.

It was my new target.

To get completely well.

I would measure all my actions against this question.

Everything became centered around this.

I still attended a work meeting here and there and engaged in obligations I felt I had to, but the important change was that my priority had finally shifted. The business wasn't the center of my life anymore. I was. This question helped to focus on me. I realized every decision I made carried me toward my recovery or away from it. I watched everything I did to see if it aligned with my health goal.

I started letting go of things that did not support my healing. People. Places. Projects. The slow exit from my life ensued. I created space in my life so something new could take its place.

I faced my own music.

Everything I had been running from came to meet me.

As I lay in bed and tried to rest, lessons came to meet me one by one.

The revelations were marching toward me.

I was turning down the volume of the old music and inviting in the new.

THE SMALL GREEN HAMMOCK

ONE DAY MY friend Sarah came for a visit and brought some groceries and a small green hammock. This was very helpful. The groceries saved me a dreaded shopping trip, and the hammock supported my undying need for rest. The hammock became an excuse to get out of my bedroom. I now had somewhere else to lie down. I set it up near a stream where I could look up into the treetops and hear the running mountain water below. My landlords would not look to find me here, and so it was my little sanctuary—free from any worldly human engagements.

I decided I would make it mandatory to go down to this private semi-secluded spot every day and lie down for at least 30 to 60 minutes of rest.

It was torture.

If I had energy, I would allow myself a small amount of reading aligned with my question, "Is this supporting your health?"

Otherwise, the green hammock was strictly for nothing but lying down. I was learning the hard way that life wasn't always about me *doing,* and sometimes I just had to *be.*

It was so difficult to be with myself.

I was extremely uncomfortable.

My mind didn't seem to have an off switch and it told me what it thought I should be doing.

"What about work?" it would say.

"Shouldn't you be doing something *useful* right now?"

"You are so useless you have burned out, and now you are going to do nothing *forever*."

This voice was harsh, critical, and lacking compassion.

After a week or so of lying in the hammock, I invented a game. It entailed trying to stay actively focused on the natural sounds around me. The goal was to try to tune out Mr. Negative Voice, which I could hear most of the time, by rather focusing on the present tune of nature. I would lie in my green hammock in a cocoon and focus on the sounds of the babbling brook, the birds as they chirped in the trees, the frogs in the foliage, and the distant rumble of the ocean.

It was a lot harder than I thought.

Sometimes I lasted only a few seconds before the music in my mind whisked me into some dramatic story about the future or past. The sweet sound of the birds was forgotten as I became consumed by drama. My body would respond with clenched fists as the stress set in.

It would dawn on me, "Where have the birds gone?"

With great self-determination, I would try to turn my thoughts back to the harmony of nature. To tune into the joy of the birds as they flitted in the treetops.

Chirp, chirp, tweet, tweet.

A smile would return to my lips.

There they are, I noted. *They haven't left. It's just I can't hear them when my mind is a raging bull.*

I fought my mind to remain present with the sound of the birds tweeting.

Again and again.

When I connected to them long enough, harmony entered me. It was as if I could sense the perfect design of the world, and I could be a part of it.

The only barrier to entry was my wild, untamed mind. At this point, it could not focus on anything beautiful for more than a few seconds or minutes at best. It was completely wrapped up in its own agenda. Work. Stress. Unhealthy relationships. Drama. Extreme situations. The future.

Are all people's minds this busy? I wondered to myself, *Or is it only mine?*

HEARING MY MIND

As I became more familiar with the voice of my mind, I was surprised at how shocking it could sound. Sometimes my thoughts were like intruders, ready to rob me of my happiness. The voice of my mind could interrupt my day at any moment with a harsh critical judgment, a shocking thought of hurting myself, suicide, or some wild idea that would radically change my life. It might also be thoughts of what else I could do instead of where I was. Anything to take me out of the present moment and displace me to a better or worse place. Anywhere but here. My mind at this time was not the kind of friend I wanted to have around. The mind voice assumed the worst and bossed me around constantly.

Sometimes I thought my mind was damaged or broken. I learned later it was stuck in the "negative program". It was like only having the bad late-night news channel available when I wanted happy nature documentaries. I knew the channel I wanted existed somewhere but couldn't find it. I was losing hope before the small green hammock. Now I had the determination to return it. To return to that childlike state of happiness I remembered from decades before.

I've been poisoning my mind all these years, I thought. *Now it is time to be kind and win back my friend Mr. Positive mind.* I had created a mind which was not at ease. My mental health was in dis-ease.

Now I was in my season of replacing the batteries of my mind remote. A fresh charge gave my mind the time and space to rest and heal. My mind didn't actually like it, it resisted the idea, but a part of me knew it was the right thing to do. As my mind hurled reasons not to rest or spend alone time, I simply treated the thoughts clouds that would pass by. I saw my mind as less of "me" and more of "my mind's thoughts", two friends living under one roof trying to get along.

It was no easy feat having this flatmate.

On a bad day, my mind was so busy it was nearly impossible to focus. It didn't want to upgrade. It liked the old, rusty, defunct batteries it was operating on.

I invented a game to help me regain control over my wild, distracted thoughts.

As I lay in my green hammock, I would wiggle my toes or feet and bring my attention to these specific body parts. I would focus on the sensations of only this area of my body. The sensations in my feet would help me focus all my attention precisely there. For a moment, my thoughts would be fixed on this point, and all the problems of my world would dissolve as my attention was in the present. Simply focused on my feet. Everything was ok. Then, as the attention was rooted, I would take another step. I would shift my attention one part up. I would hold my awareness on my ankles. By rotating both ankles it would help keep my mind concentrated. Round and round I'd go, like a curious child experiencing his body for the first time. I would then shift my attention one body part higher, slowly resting my awareness on my shins. I would repeat the process slowly to my knees, quad muscles, etc. If I could reach my head, my whole central nervous system relaxed. Internally, I felt a change.

Oftentimes my mind would drift long before I got to my quads or hips. I'd then have to start again. I was determined to focus my mind. I was determined to be able to shift from 'problem churning' to being present. Sometimes I would start again many times.

Eventually I would prosper.

Hips. Stomach. Chest. Hands. Elbows.

I could feel my weight sinking into the hammock.

Shoulders.

Neck.

Face.

Ears.

Forehead.

Top of my head.

A small window of peace opened at this point—it flowed into me like a light mountain stream.

I would then try listening to the birds again.

I would hear them and my peace would expand. Sometimes light smatterings of joy would accompany this connection.

My breathing returned to normal.

Everything was ok again.

I was ok!

Training my mind to focus was like taming a wild horse.

It would gallop wildly until I put a rope on it. I would have to try again and again, walk around the pen again and again patiently as it ran and ran and ran. Eventually it would finally slow. It would halt the stomping. When it stopped bucking, the sound of birds returned to my ears. As I heard the chirping, for a brief moment, I recognized no matter what was happening to me, birds around the world were joyously going about their day, and all was in perfect harmony.

It gave me a great sense of peace, and a sliver of joy seeped back into my heart for a moment.

Then poof.

The good sensations and positive mind disappeared again.

The wild-stallion-mind would pull me away, and I'd be dragged back into some dramatic story.

I realized not all the mind stories were true or real, but they were still consuming my energy. My mind generated intrusive thoughts without my permission. On its own accord it played loud dominating stories. Sometimes it was all I could hear whilst the thoughts and moving pictures took me away from my precious present moment with the forest sounds and birds.

I would repeat this process every day. Forcing myself to lie down in the hammock. Forcing myself to try and focus on the birds. Listening, being pulled away, listening, being pulled away. I didn't realize I was in training, taming the muscle of my mind.

Over weeks and months of repetitive practice, I slowly got pulled away by my mind less and less. It gave me space to tune into the sounds of the birds and nature more and more.

The more space I had to listen, the more I heard the voices within me. The moods of my inner world. The patterns of my mind. The impulses. The intuitions. The emotions.

The hammock was my listening teacher, and it was guiding me to the sound of my own inner music.

TRIP TO THE HOMEOPATH

OUT OF THE blue, a friend of mine booked an appointment with a homeopath for me. She called me, told me, and gave me the date. It was a rather sudden shock as I spent so much time at home that I had mostly lost contact with the outside world.

Now I was forced to head out.

I was nervous, yet her kind gesture also touched me. I knew I had to try new things and get out of my comfort zone; this was the perfect opportunity. The idea of seeing a homeopath was uncomfortable. It felt very alternative and against the norm. At the same time, I was also aware of my greater context. I was in a deep place of letting go and I needed to try new things. I put my judgments and resistance aside and decided to try it. After all, it was booked and paid for, and I knew my small, green hammock wasn't going to save my entire life.

I thought, *worst case scenario, this person could give me an opinion I don't like or a medication I won't take.* This took the stress off my mind.

The day of the appointment arrived and I was nervous. I was scared of the unknown. The plants, the medicine, the alternatives.

My name was called and I headed into his room.

As I entered, I immediately experienced something different from the doctors' rooms I was conditioned to. My memories of doctors were sterile, clinical, practical-factories-of-health—yet this atmosphere was different. It was warm, kind, and loving. Care permeated the atmosphere. He greeted me with a genuine smile of interest and compassion. I could immediately sense his kindness and genuine interest in my well-being. I wasn't another number or medical case. He wanted me to be well. This approach made a world of difference to me.

He listened to my story.

My battles.

My struggle.

This was a part of my healing. To be heard by someone who could understand.

I sensed his heartache at my heartache. He was writing notes. When I had finished pouring out my cup of sorry, he filled me with information I had never heard before. This new liquid life force gave me hope. It lit me up. This homeopath understood my problems weren't only related to my body. He asked me about my emotions, my life journey, my relationships.

I left his room with hope, something miraculous I hadn't found anywhere else. He helped me understand my journey of healing was completely unique to me. It wasn't a "one cure heals all" or "one Band-Aid fits all" scenario. I had to start tuning into what I thought and felt I needed.

He asked, "What do *you* feel like *you* need to do to get better?"

No one had asked me that before.

HEARING MY BODY

He invited me to start listening to the different parts of myself. It wasn't about what others thought I should do or what my mind thought I should do. It was more about what I felt I should do for myself.

It was an open invitation into my own intuition. My body knew what it needed, I simply had to listen.

My mind needed to get out of the way.

"What are you eating?" the homeopath asked. "Do you have any cravings?"

I was embarrassed to admit it, but replied honestly, "When I can walk to the shops, I love buying myself a pepper steak pie."

I expected a lecture from him as I knew pies weren't the healthiest option—especially for someone in my condition. He smiled and said, "Follow your intuition Daniel and eat what you feel you should eat. If you need to eat a pie, eat it. If you need to eat a burger, eat it. You will know what is an unhealthy craving and what is not. Eat what you *feel*."

This stunned me. I'd never asked myself what I *felt* like eating. Usually, I would shop with my mind—I purchased things that I thought were healthy for me, not things I felt like eating. Up until this point I had mostly been eating with my mind, using my mind's intelligence to consume things based on research or information. If I knew it was supposed to be healthy, I often forced myself to eat things I didn't want to. My homeopath challenged this belief by explaining that if I ate what I felt, I would be in tune with my body's own intelligence. He said, "What is good for you now may not be good for you next month. Ask your body what it wants".

LISTENING ON THE INSIDE

BEETROOT OR CHOPS?

ARMED WITH THIS piece of strange advice, I decided to give it a try.

On my next visit to the shopping mall, my usual shopping list stayed in my pocket while I asked myself, "Okay, Body, if you could choose anything here, what would you have?"

I paused in the veggie section waiting for some kind of response. I scanned my body for any direction or sensations. Then, as if on their own accord, my feet shuffled over to the veggie section. I scanned my body some more, resting my mind in the process. My body hovered over the broccoli section. "Is this what you want?" I asked. My hand, as if being tugged by a small invisible magnet, reached out and grabbed some broccoli. I vibrated with a subtle sense of joy and satisfaction. My body had chosen this for its health, without my mind dictating what was right for me. My body was driving the ship.

Woah, I thought as I put it in the trolley, I really do want to eat these greens. *It just feels right.*

I asked again, "Okay, Body, what more do *you* want to eat?"

I looked around.

My eyes landed on some nice yellow bananas.

I shuffled over as my hands joyfully reached out for a bunch, and I put them in the trolley. I was shopping with my eyes, following instructions from my body.

It wasn't my usual kind of pre-planned linear shopping-from-a-list, it was a moment-to-moment shop, allowing my eyes to feast and my body to respond with a yes or no.

I asked my body again, "What's next for you?!"

I witnessed a strong craving for red meat arising within me. *Where did that just come from*, I thought. *My Body is really talking to me!*

The strange thing was aside from an occasional pie as comfort food. I ate very little meat. I very seldomly would choose to cook raw meat and had no desire to purchase any. I didn't like the blood or the texture of it, and I didn't think I needed to eat meat. Nonetheless, I couldn't deny what I had heard. I could still taste the Body's desire for the juiciness of a steak.

I headed to the meat section and hovered in front of the fridge.

"Surely not," I said as my eyes fell to meet the desires of my body, "I never eat lamb chops!"

In terms of meat, lamb chops were last on the list. I disliked the fatty parts of chops and the marrow, oh no, not the marrow! With its yellow pussy and slimy texture, it reminded me of something which comes out of a person's nose. I used to wince at dinner when I watched my mother sucking the marrow out of bones like a calf on an udder. *Savage!* I would think to myself. I was far more cultured than this!

I was still hesitating in front of the chop section. *Are you sure?* I asked my body.

My hand again, as if pulled by a thin invisible force, happily opened the fridge and reached out for a packet of lamb. My mind had a mutiny. "I do not want to cook these?!" it said. "You will get worms! They are disgusting! We don't eat lamb chops!" Overcoming my personal resistance, I spoke gently to myself, "Let me not get in your way then, Body," and I lifted the lamb chops and placed them in the trolley.

"What will the vegans think?!" my mind cried.

"Hush hush", I said to myself, feeling a bit guilty, "hopefully there will be no vegans at the checkout counter".

During the shopping experience, I didn't try to read the ingredients on the packaging, count calories or worry about what others thought. I looked around at the abundance on the shelves and let my body choose. I felt into my body's intuition—it knew what it needed. My arm reached out for items that would nourish me. I was conscious not to let any unhealthy cravings disguise themselves as "needs". I didn't linger in the sweets and chips aisle, but I did remain flexible enough for a treat once in a while. After all, an ice cream wouldn't kill me, and I needed some small joy victories when I could get them.

I arrived home the first evening after the 'Body Shop' and placed the dreaded lamb chops on the counter. I would eat them right away. I reluctantly took them out of the packaging. It was like handling a raw living creature. I winced. I couldn't stand the smell or the blood. My thoughts haggled me with concerns it was still partially alive. I imagined it was a little baby sheep jumping around in a field at a very recent time.

I had no idea how to cook the meat either. Most of the meat I ate resulted from someone else having purchased and prepared it on a fire—now I was faced with the gruesome task. I embarrassingly searched online for instructions. It was pretty straightforward. I put some olive oil in a pan, the pan got hot, I threw the lamb chops in, they sprayed oil and fat onto my white shirt, and the spray burnt my arms. I prodded them around until they were more on the charcoal side of cooked, then I turned off the heat. As I poured them from the pan onto my plate, my body shivered with excitement. I could *feel* how much my body needed the nourishment of these chops. What was in this little sheep? Iron, protein? I didn't know, but as I poured my tomato sauce onto the chop (to cover the meaty flavor), I devoured them. My body inhaled them. There was something in them my body was desperate for. I licked the fat off my fingers at the end and sat in my dimly lit kitchen, wondering who I had become. I wished I had bought more! I was astounded. I felt nourished. Happy. Completely satisfied. With my mind aside, my body had won a victory for its own well-being.

I returned to the shops two days later and followed the same procedure— lamb chops a la carte. I think I ate lamb chops every night for about three weeks. Sometimes with spinach, sometimes with sweet potato, and sometimes by themselves, fried in olive oil. I was worried it might continue forever. *Would I become the lamb chops man?*

Then one day, the craving stopped. I went to the shops and joyously asked, "Body, what do you *feel* like eating today?" I expected the land chop craving to arise. It didn't. As suddenly as it had come, it was gone. My food craving was not the least bit interested in having any meat. *What?!* I thought. *This is so weird! Where has the lamb chop fetish gone?* I tuned in deeper to be certain about "no chops" and asked my body again what it needed. I suddenly felt like walking over to the vegetable section. I paused to feel *the feeling.* Listening. Waiting. BINGO! I looked at the beetroot, and I craved it immediately. My body wanted beetroot. I could feel it. I didn't much like beetroot or know how to cook it, but there was no doubt my body wanted it. Beetroot season began.

Trusting my body's intuition for its needs was liberating. I was finally learning to *feel,* and I was becoming healthier for it.

I researched beetroot and learned it was particularly good for my blood. *Of course my body knew it before my mind,* I thought to myself, *My body is so wonderfully clever!* I also regularly craved broccoli – and found out it was particularly good for my brain. My body knew what it was doing to combat this virus without any lists. It already had the built-in intelligence for wellness. All I had to do was give it space to talk and me to listen.

BODY'S INTELLIGENCE: THE LOVE DIET

ALSO, DURING THIS time of tuning into my body's intelligence, I noticed the powerful effects of sugar. If I ate sugar after a meal, I would develop an ongoing craving for it. This I deemed an unhealthy craving. It was a drug for my body. I probably wouldn't have minded if I was physically active, but lying down with nothing to do, the sugar invited anxiety. The sugar rush had nowhere to go, so my body would become electric jitters. Lying in my hammock after eating sugar was like asking a wild cat to relax beside a mouse. Impossible. I writhed and turned. I kicked my legs. I could not focus on the sound of birds for more than a few seconds. My mind bucked like an untamed stallion. I had never noticed this strong effect before. It felt like a drug in my system whose purpose was distraction and confusion.

If I decided to have some late-night chocolates, I would wake up tired, dehydrated, and my brain fog would be worse than usual. I quickly experienced the highs were not worth the lows. Before, when my body was healthy, I hadn't noticed the effects of sugar. Since my health was compromised and I was observing myself closely, I finally knew what sugar was really doing inside me.

I noticed the same thing with wheat. Not all wheat, but particularly low-cost bread. If I had a slice of normal brown bread, it would have a similar effect with brain fog, confusion, spin-out, and lack of concentration. It was like eating ADHD. It turned my listening sessions in the green hammock into torture sessions. I decided wheat and sugar both had to go.

After seven days of cutting out sugar and wheat, I noticed a remarkable difference in my body and mind. My mind became clearer, and the little energy I did have felt much more stable. No more wild cravings. No more big ups and big downs. It helped me distinguish the difference between healthy and unhealthy cravings. The unhealthy voice had an "extreme" nature. Ice cream, peanut butter, chocolates, sweets! These cravings would come in hard and fast and say, "Eat me now!" I would have little control over them. I noticed I would often crave foodstuffs according to my emotional needs. The more difficult the day – the more my hand reached for the chocolate wrapper. The comfort foods filled a void my life was unable to meet. The-sweeter-the-better was my motto. I looked for the sweetness in food because the sweetness was missing from my life. The problem with filling the gap with the sugar-plum-fairy was my body and mind suffered at the hands of my emotional eating habits.

Healthy cravings on the other hand were not really cravings at all. They were more like desires which could be fulfilled with ample time. They didn't demand attention right away and allowed me to wait until I could acquire them. These cravings were like a mature person who knew what they wanted, could look at the menu, order calmly, and wait to be served. Browsing through the shops, I could hear the voice say, "Sauerkraut, kombucha, bone broth, please." This was very different to "Get the corn chips right now!" Sometimes my hand would open the packet of crisps as soon as I grabbed it. Crunch, crunch, crunch. In went the chips as soon as possible.

The voice of a healthy craving was a confident and quiet "yes, please" when I checked in with my body's nutritional needs. "Do you feel like you need this now?" I would ask, then I would listen as best as I could.

I no longer looked at recipes or thought about what I needed. I felt my way through the whole process. Sometimes my meals were extremely simple. Sometimes after smelling or tasting a spice, I knew my body needed it. I didn't force myself to eat anything I didn't want to. I felt great before, during, and after my meals. I was cooking with love.

As my gut healed, so too did my mental health. A healthy body and healthy gut were directly proportional to having a healthier mind. If I ate things that did not resonate with me, like what I called "sad meat", my mind would spin out with the same effect sugar and wheat had on me. My definition of "Sad meat" was the by-product and result of maltreated and mistreated animals. My entire being reacted to this poisoning. This did not contribute to my health. This stole from it. I was not ingesting love. I was ingesting abuse. I remember one out-of-the-norm night when I was tired of cooking for myself. I went into the village to order something to eat. I sat down for a change of scenery and chose the chicken. When it arrived, I could see it was a sad chicken. Hormone-fed, full of anti-biotics, not the free-range type I imagined had been running around happily before landing on my plate. I ate it. Ten minutes later, I felt dizzy and a strange emotional tension hung over me. I was anxious. I left the restaurant with a drunk sensation, my head and my mind were slightly spinning, and my thoughts were scattered. I felt uneasy in my body. I wanted to wash my insides with soap. My being was not happy. I sat quietly on the deck of my home, bearing witness to the effect the sad animal meat had on my mind. Ingesting suffering caused me to suffer.

What I put in, I got out.

Unhappy in, unhappy out.

I was momentarily separated from purity and love.

During this stage in my life I was extremely "pure" in the sense of what I was eating and drinking. This allowed me to experience the subtle sensations that came from what I ate. Before this time I had no idea of the effect. Even now, I would not experience the effect of sad chicken or alcohol as I did back then.

I will never forget the sensation which vibrated in my being: *You are what you eat, Daniel, so eat food that has been loved.*

I decided my new diet was the love diet.

Not vegan, vegetarian, fruitarian or carnivore.

I would eat what I loved and what was loved I would eat.

WHAT IS MY MIND EATING?

I ALSO CHANGED the food I was putting into my mind. What I mind-consumed had a direct effect on my well-being. If I consumed negative media, intense docu-series or books with overt violence or untoward sexual activity—they would leave their imprint on me for hours or days. Let's say I stayed up late watching scary or violent movies—a simple bump on my security gate would make me jump. My nerves would be on edge. My thoughts would turn to moments of battle and violence. Instead of seeking peace, I'd seek the sword as a solution. If I listened to calm, nature-based documentaries or sounds in the evening, I would fall asleep with awe and appreciation. The following days I would have a deeper understanding of the natural world and would gravitate to harmony. Any input through my mind or body affected my entire system. Healthy mind, healthy body. Healthy body, healthy mind. I guess it would be the same as putting diesel into a petrol car—the whole car is affected, not only the engine. I paid close attention to what I was ingesting with my mind because my mind is the fuel tank for my body.

I decided that to get better—mind-snacking on any form of violence, negative emotions, fear-mongering, explicit sex, drugs, rock n' roll media—it all had to go. This was not the foundation for building a pure mind capable of healing. Even though I wasn't participating in any of these things, if I was mentally exercising these concepts, they were equally as harmful. They all had to go. I stopped watching unhealthy documentary series, pornography, negative media, or reading disgusting jokes in my men's chat groups. The reshaping of my mind and well-being required letting go—all that was not serving my mental health—which I now realized made up a large part of my overall health.

By letting go, I could now choose what I wanted to *put in*. I was able to choose the kind of mind I wanted to build. Like an athlete training for a sport, I could decide if I was going to be fit for javelin, swimming, or shot put. I decided I would start exercising the muscle of my mind daily toward the goal of a "positive mind".

I drew up a mind-exercise routine.

My training schedule included a minimum of 30 minutes of quiet time and stillness per day. This was different from rest as this was happening already with an after-lunch siesta. This quiet time was "active stillness". No matter what I thought I had to do, I would sit on a rock, a chair, a towel, or even in a bathroom cubicle and practice the 30 minutes of quiet time. I couldn't always do 30 minutes in a row, so sometimes I would do five minutes in the morning, five minutes around lunch, and 20 minutes in the evening. On a good day I could quietly sit for 45 minutes to an hour. It was mandatory for my mental training and I noticed how it calmed my central nervous system. More often than not, it wasn't easy to sit still. My mind could not comprehend the value and did not want to move into calmness. It wanted a fast-paced action thriller. It was addicted to the adrenaline ride. When I sat to begin my practice, my mind would be protesting in the build-up with shouts of, "No, I will not be quiet!" Sometimes days would pass and I could not achieve a resting state. Even though my body was still, my mind was worked up. Hyperactive. Playing fast-paced movies. As I sat in the morning, my mind was busy from start to finish. My 20-minute sit down could disappear quickly amidst a drama of stories.

It didn't matter.

I kept going.

I knew I would win out over my mind. I eventually did. The mind-muscle slowly became trained. Like breaking in a new horse, it stopped running wildly around the pen and was slightly more willing to come toward me when I stretched out my hand. Not always. But more often than before.

Eventually, I could sit for five minutes and disappear into a sense of peace and quietness. This time was recalibration time. My reset time. Me time. Pruning my inner gardens created a safe, still room inside myself to which I could always return.

It was the home I always wanted.

LET GO OF THE LABEL

Taking the time to focus on my mind helped me realize I was not my thoughts. My "self" was not necessarily "my thoughts". I noticed the thoughts could pop up when they wanted to. I had little to no control over who and when would arrive, but it was better to treat them as a guest in my home than as myself. The same applied to the physical. I could soon distinguish between "me" and "my body". My body wasn't me either. It was my body. My mind wasn't me, it was my mind. This helped greatly in having compassion for both of these important parts of my whole being. Treating them as guests helped me treat them with kindness. They were friends who were on this life journey with me and needed taking care of. The still time also helped me apply the same approach to my emotions. Instead of saying to myself, "I am depressed" or "I am anxious", I could now experience this discomfort as a passing moment. I reframed the experience as, "I am *feeling* anxious right now" or "I am experiencing depression *at this time*". This perspective allowed me not to become this discomfort but to recognize it as a ship on the ocean, simply sailing by. I realized these states of being were not "me", but rather a state of being which would pass.

This gave me hope. If they weren't me, then nothing was wrong with me. They weren't my identity, and I didn't need them.

My identity was a whole, healthy person who at the moment was moving through the shadow of the valley of sickness.

Negative thoughts were not me, and there was nothing wrong with me. It was a state I was in, and each negative thought was waiting to be transformed into positive thoughts.

That's how I looked at it.

It was very different from the notion of "I have anxiety" or "I am my anxiety". When I heard my mother speaking of her anxiety or depression, it seemed like she had come to a place of acceptance. Like her anxiety was part of her, how she was born. To me, this was admitting defeat. I thought bringing it into the light was a good thing (instead of pretending to be healthy and well), because at least she could talk openly about what she had been concealing for years—but I also felt sorry because I did not share the opinion that this was a "state for life".

This I believed is what the doctors wanted her to believe. Not because they are malicious, but simply because there is yet to be a new way.

In my mother's case, I had seen too many photos of her in her youth with her eyes alight at the joy of being alive. She had a glow and excitement about her. This was very different from the mother sitting with me explaining there was something horribly wrong with her brain and "this is how it is". Creating this belief was dangerous, and I did not want to go down the same road. I was in a more fortunate position to realize I didn't want to create a label that allowed "dis-ease" in my mind and body to hang around forever. I wanted them to go and I believed they would.

By witnessing the short-term coming and going of emotions and feelings, I believed I could create a canvas where chronic disease and negative thoughts would be able to pass by too. It was only a matter of time.

The canvas of my life changed daily.

One unavoidable essences of life became clear to me—everything is ever-changing. The environment, the seasons, the creatures, the people, the projects. At this moment I am not the same person I was the moment before. Each moment presents change. There is a season for everything. For crying, for laughing, for birthing, for dying, for being sick, for being well—nothing lasts forever. This too shall pass.

Trust in the change.

By knowing this, I became less worried about being in a state of disease forever. As long as I changed, things would change. Worst case: I died. Best case: I came fully alive. I knew it could pass if I was willing to embrace and fully experience the seasons, so new growth could materialize. I could also be a bit less judgmental when the voices in my inner world were cruel or unkind. I knew they would pass, and they were there to teach me a lesson. I knew all I had to do was make some changes, and they would change too. If I could tidy up my inner home and welcome fresh new guests, the party would get a better vibe. As I replaced the label of society, "I am an anxious person", with "I am currently suffering from anxiety", it reminded me I could return to the state of perfection I knew existed inside myself and my mind.

I knew it was only the years of work stress, drinking, deadlines, and dangerous behavior which had created a brain state I was now slowly undoing.

It was time to exercise the mind-muscle.

THE MIND-MUSCLE

No one said rewiring my mind was easy. The green hammock was my constant teacher and reminder of this. One particular day I was lying in the hammock trying to hear the birds. I was really struggling to remain focused on the positive.

It was a battle of willpower. My mind's will, telling me dramatic stories, versus my own will to hear the sweet sound of the birds. My mind was on a rampage.

All I could experience was the playing of mind-movie after dramatic mind-movie. Saga after saga. I was lost in the over-animated version of work issues, family faults, friendship faux pas, and deadly diseases. No sooner would I catch a shimmering of peace for a brief second, my mind would whisk me back to some dramatic detail or uncomfortable thought, and the sound of the birds would dissolve into drama.

Eventually, I gave up.

My focus game in the hammock was too difficult at this time.

It was too hard to tame my mind and tune into the natural perfection happening around me. I was stuck in the alley of a dirty, downtown city subway station whilst above the ground, the sun was shining and birds chirping. I couldn't see it, hear it, or feel it. Even though I knew it was there.

In a burst of frustrated energy, I loudly proclaimed to my mind, "You know what, I think your busyness is using up all of my energy. I've had it with you!"

It was a revelation.

I was right.

This big muscle in my head consumed kilojoules at a rate I couldn't keep up with. The constant berating, worrying, planning, judging, criticizing, strategizing, stressing, drama telling… it took up my precious life force. It was a busy factory that never shut down. No public holidays. No rest days. No Christmas. I was on a treadmill I couldn't get off.

It was exhausting. Even my body was becoming tired from the busyness.

This rampaging bull-of-a-mind was dominating me and kicking up so much fuss, and I had been listening to it for years.

I had given this particular voice too much priority in my life. Too much say and too much sway in directing the course of my life. Too much weightiness in running my affairs. Too much logic. Too many boxes.

It was draining the life out of me.

LIFTING THE NEEDLE

I noticed the voice of my new mind-friend sometimes told me the same thing three times in a row, sometimes more. It repeated the story, morning, noon, and night. Sometimes for multiple days in a row. It was as if my mind-thoughts felt like they hadn't been heard the first two times and needed to repeat itself. If I became aware of this record loop, I would try to stop the thought with a response of, "I heard you!". It would leave me feeling frustrated. I was aware of the voice, but I couldn't quiet it. I could hear the distasteful music, but I couldn't switch tracks. *Why can I not stop the song?* Some days I could lift the needle, and the story would stop spinning, yet on others it was simply unstoppable. I remember finishing a "quiet time" session by the stream one morning. Walking up the embankment back to my room, I was chatting to myself…

"I would never let a real friend tell me the same negative story five times in a row, so why should I let you, mind?"

It was a good point.

I knew I needed to change the dialogue and get out of the negative narrative.

I experimented with ways to "lift the needle" of my scratchy record player.

At first, I tried the interruption technique…

Mind: *Repeats a story for the third time*

Me: "Yes, I heard you."

Mind: *Same story again*

Me: "That's enough. I get your point. Calm down."

I would speak back to my mind when I realized its story-telling was repetitive. I wanted to interrupt it, to stop it. I was sometimes a little forceful. This helped, but I wasn't always left with a good feeling in my heart. I was becoming a policeman, always on the lookout and ready to discipline.

Me: "Mr Mind, I've heard enough. What you are saying is not true. Be quiet and stop it."

I felt guilty for shouting at myself. I was forever disciplining a naughty child, it felt like a never-ending battle.

It was exhausting.

Seeking a way to stop the constant record playing, I decided to change my own tune. I figured if discipline wasn't working, I would try the loving approach. In my understanding of this, I tried forgiving my mind instead. I hadn't really considered forgiving people or myself or "practicing forgiveness" in general, but with little else helping, I went for it. My inner dialogue changed tune…

My mind: *Dramatic story-telling*

Me: "Thank you for this story, mind. I have heard you clearly. I appreciate your concern for us".

My mind: *Repeat of the same story a minute later*

Me: *Feeling of unease*

Me: "Please forgive me, mind, for reacting to you with frustration. It is no way to treat you. I love what you bring into my awareness. I love that you are so aware".

My mind: *Repeat of the same story again*

Me: "Thank you, mind, for showing me this. I didn't realize I shouldn't have been treated like this by this person. Please forgive me for allowing myself to be treated like this. I promise to take better care of us."

My mind: *Repeat of the same story again*

Me: "I forgive all the people involved in this saga."

My mind: *Repeat of the same story again*

Me: "I forgive you (mentioning person by name). I forgive you for…"

My mind: *Silence*. *No more story! Needle lifted from the spinning record.*

Me: "Hooray! Is that peace I hear?"

There is power in forgiveness.

It was as if my mind was telling me a story for a reason. Prompting me to see the story from a new place. A new perspective offered a breath of fresh air. It cleared out the cobwebs. Forgiveness and understanding carried me to peace. It wasn't the road I imagined I would have to travel, but it was a road lined with gold. The repeated voice and negative feelings would disappear when I truly learned how to forgive. My whole being returned to peace. Sometimes it took a few attempts. I learned to really put my heart into it. I would really have to be genuine about forgiving. It wasn't a quick hack to get well, it was life-changing. Forgiveness brings heaven to earth. When the mind story came (often accompanied by anger, frustration, or resentment), I would create some time to list all the things I needed to forgive. Then I would list all the things I needed to forgive myself for. I would say to the imaginary people in the mind story, "I am sorry for…" and say all the things I had done. Even if I didn't feel guilty, I would still apologize. The dramatic stories in my mind were often replays of real-life conversations which hadn't gone well. With this little technique, the mind-movies halted, and I became more of an empty vessel. There was spaciousness within me, spaciousness to hear the singing birds.

Me: Hello?

My mind: *Nothing*

Me: YEAH! I'm free!

Dan puts on a dance song and dances around the room.

MAKING MIND FRIENDS

MAKING FRIENDS WITH my mind was a very important relationship I forged during this time of stillness. Initially, I was angry with my mind for being judgmental, over-analytical, criticizing, and negative. I often used to talk harshly back to my "mind voice". It was "me" versus "my thoughts". The part of me which could witness my thoughts was disappointed in what I was thinking. *Where are these thoughts even coming from?* I would often wonder. Over time I realized judging my thoughts was part of the problem. A judge judging a judge doesn't make less judgment. Gasoline on a fire makes more fire. *I wouldn't treat someone else struggling like this with so little compassion, so why do I talk to myself like this?* I realized if I wanted to heal, I would have to begin to love my mind.

Living with a pessimistic mind is a draining task. My mind chose to see the worst, not the best. It was an effort to see the silver lining. It even annoyed me I was now aware of my negative thinking, and I couldn't go back. When I was unaware, life was unconsciously easy. Now I had peeped into a box I couldn't close again. I knew too much! I had too much awareness. I sometimes longed for a mind who wasn't so complicated, where I couldn't hear the thoughts of my innermost rooms.

It was all part of the cleaning process.

To clean the dirt, we must find the dirt.

To make light which is darkness, we must shine awareness.

It was difficult to understand how nasty this constant companion really was to the people around me, myself included. Perhaps it had a reason to be nasty to me? Perhaps I hadn't been treating it like a good person should? Perhaps I drank too much alcohol, stressed too much, ate the wrong foods, or consumed unhealthy media?

Perhaps my mind wasn't to blame at all?

Is a savage dog born savage, or is it treated to become savage?

I didn't have the answers, but I didn't want to be scared of my thoughts. I wanted to befriend them and transform them. To help them along. Lift them up.

I entered into many conversations with my newfound "mind friend".

Some days I thought I was going plain mad. I would often be standing in the kitchen, cooking, cleaning, pottering around, whilst in deep conversation with myself. I wondered, *does everyone have conversations with their mind? Am I the only one with all these different voices?* Some voices were promoting, and some opposing. Oftentimes everyone in my inner-mind family had an opinion. Sometimes the conversations were internal, and sometimes they were out loud. I wondered if my landlord thought I had constant visitors when I was simply chatting to myself. I had read Mahatma Gandhi's autobiography. He said he used to go walking and talk out loud, it was an important part of his daily routine. This gave me consolation—I wasn't the only one edging toward what society might consider madness.

Conversational awareness with myself allowed me to keep tabs on what was happening in my head. I soon came to know my "mind friend" very well. I learned how he operated, what he liked and didn't like. I learned the food he loved to consume and what made him angry or confused. In a relationship, I was then able to coax him toward a lighter state of being.

I became less critical of his harsh words and more sympathetic to his state. I wasn't so thrown when he was being over-judgmental or cynical. "Thanks for all these negative thoughts," I would say. "I don't believe what you are telling me is really going to happen, but thank you for warning me. I know deep down you care."

I learned to talk to myself with compassion. It wasn't a case of silencing a nasty friend, it was a case of bringing a depressed friend back to happiness. It wasn't a stopping of the mind-voice, it was a transformation of it. It was time to change tones. I had a mind for a reason and I needed it to come along on the journey with me, not be left behind or told to sit in the naughty corner forever.

It was easier said than done.

Living with my mind at this time was like living with Mr. Negative in my personal space 24/7. I got scared when I realized I could not get away from this friend. I couldn't go outside for a walk or end the telephone call. My mind was always there. It was always going to be there. My mind seemed to be my only constant companion. What a roommate to live with! "Yes, and it will be like this forever!" my mind chimed in gleefully. This roommate would have failed an interview to rent with me if it was an actual person.

My "roommate" was constantly berating, proposing black or white solutions, and speaking about forever, always, every time. I couldn't complain about my roommate to other people either. I was afraid I might be judged for having conversations with myself.

When I woke up in the morning, my mind was there. When I went to bed in the evening, my mind was there. Constantly sharing his worldview and passing comments on what I and others did. I had been living with this struggling friend for most of my adult life and was only waking up to it now.

I didn't know at the time I was simply in a 'negative mind state', a state which could be changed.

I didn't know Mr. Mind would eventually become a genuine and loving friend.

With determination and many conversations, my roommate slowly came to the positive party.

I invited my mind to live with me in a better space.

MIND AND EMOTIONS

I NOTICED THAT when my mind generated thoughts, I often had an intense inner emotional response. I didn't necessarily express these in words, but internal vibrations created uncomfortable ripples within me. My mind was the instigator, and my heart the reactor.

Here's an example of my internal dialogue during this time;

Mind: "You might be sick forever."

Heart: "I'm scared and anxious now."

Body: "Tensing up, hands clenching, I'm starting to sweat a little, increasing heart rate".

My reaction: Reach for comfort food, distract myself, grab my cell phone, browse the internet, numbing activity.

It started with this seemingly uncontrollable negativity coming from my mind. The discomfort it caused created a ripple effect on my human ecosystem, resulting in actions that didn't help me.

Numbing myself led to stuckness, not healing.

When I eventually became aware of this loop of negativity or anxiety—I wanted to break the cycle, not run away from it. The trick was becoming aware. Sometimes it took me a while to realize

I was numbing or keeping myself busy by distraction. In the beginning, I forced myself to be still. A good way to help me do this was to sit and do breathing exercises. It was doing something whilst doing nothing at the same time. The extended exhales and sitting position in a quiet place calmed down my mind. I would do this until my anxiety either burst through with a reason for being anxious or the discomfort or negativity would dissolve on its own. *Maybe I simply needed the space? What am I processing in quiet time?*

Other times I would change my physical space—walking or gardening outside, driving, or even cleaning my room. Sometimes I would stretch my body.

I wanted to be 'busy' because it calmed my mind, but now it wasn't much of an option. Eventually, when I couldn't do any of the active things I started responding to this inner voice.

I tried to respond with curiosity and love.

Mind: "You will be sick forever."

Me: "So what?"

Mind: "You will have to quit your job and probably leave Cape Town and all the things you love…"

Me: "That's ok, I understand this. It's not the end of the world."

Mind (threateningly): "But then you will lose your friends and family too." (mind smirks)

Me: "That's ok. My family will always love me wherever I am. Maybe I can be a cobbler in Italy, maybe I'll own an organic farm, maybe I'll be a shoemaker… they can visit me there!"

Heart: That's exciting!

Body: Relaxed

Mind: "No further comments."

Me: I love you. All of you.

My overall Reaction: Happy, no need for numbing, carry on doing what I was doing before 'mind invasion'.

I was killing the voice with kindness and curiosity. I was moving out of the black-and-white thinking of the mind into new territory. When emotions were stirred up within me, I would have an inner dialogue to bring peace.

I would try to flow past anger and judgment with understanding or forgiveness. I would try to move through fear into excitement and adventure.

Instead of ignoring, running, or changing my mind's problems with avoidant activities, I simply started speaking back. The more I spoke back with soothing and loving intentions, the more I could pacify my unruly inner roommates. The more I played out the imaginary scenarios instead of being scared of them, the more I could relax.

I didn't always notice my thoughts. Sometimes, I would first be aware my body was tense or breathing shallow. I knew this was all stemming from my stressed-out, stretched-out central nervous system, so I tried to make adjustments when I became aware of this.

By communing with the negative, it lost its stranglehold on me.

It was a mind game.

TALKING TO THE FEARS

THE NEGATIVE MIND-VOICE didn't go away overnight, it took a lot of loving.

Mind: "All your businesses will fail if you don't get better soon."

Body: "Tensing neck, creating pain in lower back, clenching fists, shortening breath".

Me: "That may be true, and what will that look like for me?

If the business crashes, we would return to nothing, which we started with anyway. The joy movement would be continued by others. We could possibly start again. I would have more time on my hands. My life would be less stressful. I could pick up another job or take a holiday."

Body: "Yay!"

Heart: "Yay!"

Mind: No response.

I didn't let the original threatening voice get the best of me. They were empty threats if I challenged them and stood my ground. Again and again my body would relax and a small smile would return to my face. My central nervous system would ease. By asking, "So what?"

I was turning over the stones that my 'negative mind' was trying to weigh me down with. I didn't realize how many stones I was actually carrying. Flipping over each stone was stepping through the fear my mind was tormenting me with. Each time I peeked under the mossy stone and answered, "So what?", I felt a little lighter.

Baloo the Bear from *The Jungle Book* sang, "When you look under the rocks and plants and take a glance at the fancy ants…" Well, these fancy ants were getting gobbled up bit by bit, day by day, week by week.

Mind: "You are never going to run again".

Me: "So what? Maybe I'll become a horse rider instead".

Mind: *Quiet*

Me: "Victory!"

Central nervous system: "At ease, soldier!"

Each time I talked back to the fear, there became less fear to affect my whole being.

I peeled back the layers of lies coating me within.

SEASON 8

LIVING THE WELLNESS LIFE

LEARNING TO LOVE

I WAS LEARNING to love myself. Before this time I didn't have wellness practices, self-love time, or mindful moments. Life was mostly a rush, and I was the master rusher. Now I considered my food, my habits, and my routine. I learned about rhythm. Being in harmony with my body and mind's inner rhythm and also in harmony with nature's outer rhythms. Looking up at the stars in the evening. Spending time listening to the crashing of waves. I noticed the season's more. I enjoyed winter, listening to what it asked of me: a time to go inside and reflect. I appreciated summer: a time for exploring, expanding, and extroverting myself into the natural world. This was no longer an "always-on" kind of lifestyle. The lessons from nature made their way into my lifestyle. Winding down after the setting of the sun, rising with the first rays, paying attention to the moon's cycles. My awareness of the natural world helped me come into harmony with everything happening around and within me. On days I was stressed, and in the city, I would look out the window and fix my gaze on the nearest tree. No matter what was happening around me, I would try to *feel* the tree, noting its calmness, its centeredness, the way it minded its own business despite the noise, rushing humans, and traffic. I wanted to be more like the tree. Leafy, beautiful, and peaceful.

I was finally paying attention to what my inner needs were. If I needed more sleep, I would rise later. If I was tired during the day, I'd take a nap. I stopped driving myself so hard. If I didn't feel like doing something—I simply wouldn't. I was exercising my inner listening muscle and would disregard things I thought *should* work or what others thought *should* help me. I was discovering what I needed.

Like the tree in the city, deep down, I knew what I needed. To tap into this, I first had to root into my identity and daily needs.

It was a matter of inner listening.

One day I noticed an old destructive mental pattern creep in. I was looking at a wellness to-do list on my wall. I noticed how many things I hadn't done in the past few days. I felt stressed. I thought, *These things will make me better and I'm not doing them.* This voice was Daniel-the-Productive-Perfectionist again. The list was a paper full of goal-oriented activities for me to get well so I could measure my success. Milestones and goals. Pressure. Stress. What I actually needed was much more simple – rest.

I realized what my mind had done and anger rose within me. I sat back in shock and said, "Thank you for wanting me to be well, I can see your intention here with this checklist, but I think I'm going to take today off." And so I did.

As I had the day off, I shifted my inner world from "needing" to do the wellness list, to doing the wellness tasks when I felt I wanted to. This was a lot less stressful. They would be there as a guide, as something to fall back on when I had the energy to commit to healing, not something mandatory. I didn't want my healing to be stressful. My healing would arrive as a by-product of releasing stress. As I relaxed into my day I entered into a flow state. I was *feeling* what I should do next instead of task orienting myself. I asked, "What would I *love* to do today?" which was a lot happier than, "What *should* I be doing today?"

It was a journey into my heart and another step toward wholeness.

I tried a few experiments during this time, I did things I had never done before. Below I've listed a few which worked for me and contributed to my greater wellness;

AVOID THE BLUE LIGHT

I LEARNED THAT blue light—the dim glow emitted by laptops, cell-phones, tablets, and most household lights or appliances—triggers a chemical reaction in our brains which awakens our nervous systems.

This is because blue light is emitted by the sun and sunshine wakes up the body.

So, I thought, *my body thinks it's standing in broad daylight when I'm in my room at night in fluorescent lighting or looking at my laptop? This might explain the difficulty I have falling asleep.*

I recognized blue light would be helpful at sunrise when it was time to get up, not when I was preparing for bed. Instead of electrical lighting in the evening, I opted for a more romantic option—candle-light. It was akin to a date with myself every night. In the romantic glow, I would make dinner and further converse with myself to find out how my day was. Lighting those little candles was love, and it became part of my routine. My inner rhythm adjusted to a more relaxed state when the sun went down because 1) my body was fully aware it was evening time, and 2) the candle ceremony triggered a rest response. Lighting candles was less budget-friendly, but the reward of greater relaxation was wonderful. As I looked around at the beautiful candle-lit glow, the flickering flames brought ease to my entire nervous system. They created a sense of peace that bright, sterile white lights did not. They softened my days and my emotions. After doing this for some time, my day's rhythm aligned with the earth's and environment's natural rhythm. By tuning into earth's day and night, it contributed to healthier sleep returning. My body created its natural "sleepy chemicals" in the evening because I gave it the space and conditions to do so. By sleeping with my curtains open, my brain could create "wakey chemicals" in the morning in a natural way.

I took great pleasure in the last activity of my day—rolling over in bed and blowing out the final candle.

Poof.

Darkness.

Rest.

GOOD NIGHT TECHNOLOGY

I TOOK IT a step further—no technology after 8 pm. Whenever possible I would switch off my Wi-Fi router, laptop, and cellphone during my evening routine. I read that electrical currents, emissions, and cellphone radiation could be harmful, so I didn't want any sneaky, bad vibrations or electrical currents floating in the air other than my own, especially while I was healing. In the sensitive state I was in, I noticed a difference. With all the devices off, the atmosphere was less busy. A peace in the air presided.

During the critical phase of my healing, I would only switch my phone on after 10 am in the morning. This allowed me space to discover what my needs were before I was swept up in everyone else's demands. This window period of no communication from the outside was vital in helping me listen to what was happening inside me. It gave me a sanctuary in my inner world to deal with things that were coming up. It gave me processing time on a daily basis. When I got the hang of digital self-control, I would greatly begin to look forward to my evenings of tuning out, turning off, and showing up for myself. It contributed hugely to the space I needed to heal without taking a month away on a remote island with no signal.

My "goodnight technology" regime allowed me to be out of emotional reach. Before this, technology was the bridge to Stress Land because I allowed it to be. Even though I was in my home on the forest edge, my phone kept me connected. Now I was learning to "cultivate space". To hear my own needs. To spend time with myself. A daily digital detox allowed my central nervous system to relax. In the evening, amidst the sounds of the nightjar birds and chirping crickets, there too was the sound of my own inner music playing to the world.

WAKING THE BODY

BEFORE I CONNECTED to the outside world or to my grumbling stomach, I would ensure I had done some morning stretches. Most of my stretches were very gentle. Sometimes I would lie in one position for minutes at a time. On days I felt particularly tender, I would move through one or two positions and lie down. If it was sunny, I would head outside. If it was rainy, I would place my mat next to my bed, the only available space on the floor in my tiny room. Rain or shine, I would wake my body gently by giving it the love it deserved. I would begin wherever felt right—the aim was to stretch out any areas of tightness and stiffness and create a "relaxed" environment in my body. Even though I wasn't moving around much, I noticed certain areas of my body would tighten up. *How do these areas even get tight?* I asked myself. At the time I thought stiffness and tightness could only be exercise or activity related. Yet, tightness now found its way to various parts of my body without much "doing" at all.

I noticed how my spine felt tight. My spine was like a rusty slinky struggling to extend itself in any forward bending movement. I wondered if the inflammation from the M.E. was fusing together the once supple parts of my spine. Each day I would try to stretch through the inflammation and my more supple spine brought better feelings and a clearer head.

After many more mornings of stretching, I noticed different body parts were stiff depending on my emotional state. It was remarkable to me. If I was noticeably angry or frustrated with someone or something, I would develop pain around my liver area. If I was feeling fear, I'd experience discomfort in my lower intestines and usually have a loss of appetite. If I held back emotions, my hips would be stiff for days. Stretching my hip flexors and my general hip area would often result in a kind of release, either shaking, strained breathing, or sometimes light sobs. I didn't know why. I simply went along with it. I was experiencing the mind-body connection first-hand. Sometimes when I really paid attention to a stiff or locked-up area, stretching it to release, a mini stream of emotions would slide into my awareness. Pictures or people would emerge in my mind. Painful situations. They just arrived out of the blue. And I let myself feel them.

One particular morning I took my mat outside onto the wooden deck. My mind was so foggy I couldn't concentrate, and my body was so broken I could only lie down. Luckily the sun was shining after about four days of bad weather. I decided to take my shirt off and simply lay down. I was too tired to move, so my only stretch was lying on my back, absorbing the life-giving sun.

After 20 minutes I went back inside.

I felt better than before.

My mood had shifted considerably toward the positive.

I was happier.

Twenty or so minutes of sun had improved my mood, enhanced my body's well-being, and overall I felt better.

So I included it in my daily routine as well.

MORNING BREATHING

BEFORE OR AFTER my stretches, I would try my best to do some breathing exercises. I had learned about breathing years earlier—when the panic attacks first came—because the doctors told me that drawing long, deep breaths would be helpful. With this information and my intuition prompting me to try some focused breathing techniques—I included it in my routine.

It was hard.

"Don't you know how to breathe?" my mind asked.

"Are you becoming a baby that you have to teach yourself how to breathe again?"

My mind only wanted one thing—measured productivity. Breathing was not high on its morning agenda.

"You've got better things to do than this," it would chime almost daily.

Yet, I committed myself.

No matter the mental chatter, I would sit beside my bed and attempt to count my breathing. I would count to four in my mind whilst inhaling. Then I would hold for a moment. Then I would count to eight whilst exhaling. This was my "conscious breathing".

I felt decidedly better if I managed to do this for a few minutes.

My brain fog would lift and I would have better clarity through the clouds of M.E. Some days were harder than others to sit down for breathing time. Sometimes my exhales reverberated as if I was gently sobbing. My body would shudder. I released something on the exhales and inhales. I didn't know what was happening but I continued because I felt better after the session.

If I was too distracted, and it was too hard to count, I would change the type of breathing I was doing. Instead I would take short in-and-out breaths through my nose. Kind of like a puppy panting, except through the nostrils. It was easier to do because I didn't have to think about it. After a few minutes of panting through my nose, I would lean forward, draw a deep inhale, sit up, and slowly exhale. Breathing like this was amazing. If I could do a few rounds I felt a positive shift in my mental state. I became more clear-headed and mental chatter slowed. Sometimes emotions pulsed out. This breathing cleared a part of me that I couldn't see or understand. Much later I would learn more about having an "emotional body".

At the time, it was simply a way to let off steam.

Even though it was helpful, my mind didn't want to sit still and make strange breathing noises. I felt ashamed and guilty that this had become my lifestyle. I was nervous the things I was doing were separating me from "normal society" (and the people I loved). I didn't know anyone else doing breathing exercises. I felt alone in a sea of strange new habits. The penny only dropped many months later when I moved in with my aunt. She said, "Daniel, stop fighting it, if it makes you feel well, then do it." She was right. As I balanced my carbon dioxide and oxygen levels, I became more clear-headed, healthy, and energy-rich. As strange as it was, the puppy breathing was helping defeat disease.

Focusing on breathing in the morning also helped me be aware of my breath at other times. I observed alarmingly that I held my breath for long periods, especially whilst checking emails. If I became aware I was sitting tensely in front of my computer (with little or no air moving in and out of my lungs), I would pause and begin my breathing exercises. I would lean back in my chair and begin to draw deep breaths, holding for a few seconds, then extending my exhale. Only when my nervous state and tension in my body relaxed would I carry on working. Often I would have to repeat this process multiple times. Sometimes my mind was so distracted I would be standing in the middle of my room before I realized I was supposed to be doing breathing exercises. I would sit down and start again. Breathing took effort.

Over time, these little techniques and wellness add-ons carried me towards one goal: calming my central nervous system. Moving me from a frantic state to a peaceful state. I tended toward fight-or-flight from years of stress in the advertising industry, and now, I was learning to relax into my life—one breath at a time.

Each time I managed to sit down for breath work, it was a small victory toward healing.

OUTFLOW TIME

"**Outflow" meant giving** myself time and space for things to "flow out" of my mind. For most of my day, I realized I was allowing information only to flow into my mind, not out of it. This left little to no space for my own thinking or processing. My mind was a factory too busy processing everyone else's problems. What about my direction? What about my problems?

I was so engaged in everyone else's problems and emotions I didn't have space to creatively express my own desires and curiosities. My mind was consuming external information day and night. Problems in the world, friend problems, mom problems, business problems. It was a constant stream of information I allowed to pour in.

I remember times I wanted to throw my laptop into the sea. Or smash my phone into a million little pieces. Or walk into the African desert with nothing. I didn't do any of these things, but the desire often arose. This was information overload.

I would be screaming internally, "I can't handle these digital devices anymore!" as I continued to check messages and solve the requests of others.

My "negative mind" was at the end of its tether at these points. I had created this bursting dam of information that my mind could no longer hold.

"These devices are going to make me snap," I would say to anyone who would listen.

In fact, technology wasn't to blame. It was my lack of digital boundaries, friend boundaries, family boundaries, and work boundaries. Technology was simply the means. I didn't know I didn't have to be available to all people at all times. Lack of knowing what I needed was causing me pain. I expressed this pain as frustration.

Where was my ability to communicate my own needs and do what was good for me sometimes?

I developed it after many frustrating moments of pent-up tension. I had to first understand what I needed and wanted, and then I could clearly define my relationship roles. This allowed me to know what was mine to handle and what was not. This would give me space. This would give me protection from taking on too much. My need to rescue everybody and be of service to everything allowed all these problems to reach me. This was the real issue—not the technology.

Outflow time helped me realize this because it gave me time to process and reflect on thoughts, feelings, and emotions. Outflow time allowed a sorting out, a kind of internal audit which happened unconsciously as I did things which didn't fill up my inner dams.

Outflow time for me included activities like gardening, taking walks on the beach (without my phone), slowly drinking tea on the deck, sitting down to watch the setting sun, and coloring-in in the evenings. It was simply a space where I was occupied enough not to be fidgety but not overloaded or mentally overstimulated. Any activity which didn't require high use of my brain or emotional intelligence became outflow time. Outflow time was not spent watching series, reading magazines, or listening to podcasts, as these all carried information that added to my inner pressure. Outflow time was watching the birds without analyzing their species or whether they were endemic to the region. This spaciousness through natural activity allowed me to sort through the old clothes in my inner closet. I took some clothes out, gave some away, and dusted off the shelves. After a while, I had some space on the hangers for new T-shirts, simply because I included gentle outflow activities in my day-to-day.

SOME COLOR RETURNS

It arrived as a birthday present shortly before I got really ill. The book title read: *Anti-stress Art Therapy for Busy People.*

Really, I thought, *who is this book trying to fool?* It was a children's coloring book with a title for my adult ego. Little did I know it would become a valuable asset in my healing journey. It contributed hugely to my evening outflow time. When the candles were lit and the technology was switched off, I softened my anxiety related to the "I-have-nothing-to-do" feeling by reaching for my adult coloring-in book. I would quell the restlessness in me by sharpening my pencils, choosing my colors, and getting down to business. Here I was, this go-getter-jet-setter start-up businessman asking myself, "Should I color the foxes or the honeybees this evening?" It was like traveling back in time to my childhood. It stirred up some old memories. It reminded me of a time when I had time. When I didn't judge myself for "doing nothing". When I wasn't trying to be productive When I had time to build Lego blocks, draw, write, and do whatever I *felt* like doing. Life was certainly different back then, and I longed to be able to do what I wanted to do, instead of being obligated to show up.

As the pages of daisies, ladybirds, and dolphins fell to my newfound coloring-in prowess, a sense of spaciousness seeped into my evenings. I started to look forward to picking up the pages where I left off. Memories emerged from my mind, body, and heart as I tried to stay between the lines. Coloring and coloring, I processed old relationships and negative emotions. Initially, I would play music when I sat down to color, and then I had to stop that too. Using the opportunity to busy itself, my mind would start sorting different songs into future Secret Sunrise playlists and continued to build inner anxiety as I pretended to facilitate dances to large crowds of people. I opted for silence instead or, at best, classical music, so my business-wired brain would not activate. Once my mind got through the "you're better than this" phase, the color returned to my own life.

The empty white canvas filled with the colors of my own desires.

I appreciated the simplicity of it.

A time to relax.

Resting between the lines.

Everything would be okay.

MORNING PAGES

I TOOK UP the discipline of writing in a diary. The idea had come from my homeopath and some friends who had all recommended it as a healthy habit. They called it "morning pages". To me, it sounded suspiciously like something teenage girls did. This was my mind trying to block me from using another incredibly valuable tool.

The tipping point came one day as I stood in the shopping queue to purchase groceries. On the shelf at the checkout counter was an autobiography of a famous businessman.

A rather unusual place for a book, I thought, as I looked at it nestled amongst the chocolates and sweets. Absent-mindedly, I picked it up and read the back cover. It described how this particular businessman wrote in his diary every evening, reflecting on his actions, character, and business so he could continue to improve himself. *Well*, I thought, *if this man did it and became a millionaire mogul, maybe I should try it.*

I bought my first-ever diary and headed home.

The next morning I woke up and opened my shiny, new diary. I stared blankly at the first page, unsure what to do.

Where does one start this process? I thought.

Diary writing was beyond my comfort zone. The last time I used a diary was probably to scribble the names of girls I fancied in primary school. *Melissa has nice hair, but Vanessa is so much more sporty*, came to mind as I stared at the blank page.

Faced with the challenge, I asked myself again: *What does an adult write in a diary?*

I remembered my mother's diaries. They were full of facts, memories, and milestones from her day-to-day life.

It wasn't the sort of writing I wanted to do.

Then I remembered my homeopath's advice. "Don't judge yourself," he had said. "Begin writing whatever comes to your mind. Let it flow freely."

I put my pen to the paper.

Morning diary, I have no idea what to write in you…I don't see the point in this. But I am going to keep writing until something happens. What am I going to say? Oh Lord, please help me.

Writing those sentences helped me get through my own judgment and unlocked the next few sentences.

I'm stuck. I need direction, I need help. Where do you want me to go? What should I do? How do I get out? Why am I doing this? What's the point?

And some more sentences unlocked.

I guess I'm feeling lost. Like I don't know what I'm doing. Maybe I should seek some help from other medical practitioners or people who practice alternative forms of healing.

Bingo. My first gem. The diary uncovered new ground. By noting I was lost, I took a step toward becoming found.

I'm scared to see new healers or alternative doctors, but I think I could find ones that friends have recommended and research them first. I won't just see anybody, I will see people I feel safe with.

The diary helped me on my journey by providing some solutions. As the thoughts whirled, I could sift through them for clarity.

I could observe them.

The words on the paper expressed a clearer path and turned my thoughts and emotions into directions. Sometimes the words were exactly what my heart needed to release. Sometimes the words were whispers of ideas that were to become realities. The helplessness of my greater life became evident in the first few pages. The tip of my pen was my therapist.

I finished writing that first morning. I probably wrote for 10 mins. Where it all came from, I didn't know. I felt lighter.

From then on, I mainly wrote in the mornings, my resistance lessening with each pen stroke. I started writing more easily in a flow that had less judgment. The more I wrote, the more I noticed the patterns. I noticed things were bothering me and which feelings were sticking around—sometimes for days or weeks. It allowed me to identify challenges in my life and deal with them accordingly.

My diary was the cheapest psychologist I ever had, patiently receiving my inner world every morning. My diary was a doctor who constantly listened to my woes or my joys and reflected things back to me with clarity. Turning to my morning pages gave me a non-judgmental space to free-flow the workings of my inner world.

Why is this bothering me? I would write.

Then I would list the reasons and as I witnessed them land on the page, revelations sprang up to meet me.

It was particularly helpful to write in the morning. My brain was more relaxed, and I could tap into a deeper part of my being. Often I had to try to steer myself away from listing goals, achievements, and to-do lists, and as I did, words would simply flow. Things emerged which surprised me.

"I feel like I need to leave this place and discover myself somewhere else, so I can return later with new friends."

Where did that come from? I thought as I watched the pen scribbling on the page as if on its own accord.

My morning pages became a bridge to my heart.

Soon I was able to journal whenever and wherever without criticism, without structure, with only pure flow.

It helped to locate me in the world of busyness and tuned me into my inner world. It was my little sanctuary.

During the free-flow, emotions would sometimes spill onto the empty page: "I AM SO MAD THIS MORNING, THIS STUPID BUSINESS IS KILLING ME. WHY AM I CHOOSING TO SUBJECT MYSELF TO THIS?"

As the words glared back at me from the paper, it was suddenly much more real. My secret world became manifest on the pages. Seeing what I was feeling helped me make changes. I knew it wasn't good for me to get so emotionally charged in situations, no matter what they were. I knew this was making me sick. After some time I also developed an introduction for writing in the morning. These few words would help me get started; "Good morning, Morning Pages, today I'm feeling…" and then I would let the rest flow. No agenda. No point. Just pure writing as it comes. By asking myself what I felt, I would tap quickly into the language of the heart.

The scribbles in the morning pages weren't necessarily about what I was *thinking* or what I should be *doing*. It was a chance to become present with my heart-self. It brought to the surface what was happening deep in the chambers of my heart. It helped me to begin to speak the language of my own heart.

The types of diaries I bought got more expensive as I placed greater value on their practical presence in my life.

This practice connected me to myself. The ability to listen to things happening in me beyond the goings-on of the material world. I heard the secret whispers of the heart, which were sometimes like a fleeting breeze on a summer's night.

This technique helped me later in my healing journey to overcome the final bouts of disease because I could tune below the noise and hear my heart's intelligence on difficult matters. Re-reading my pages from time to time allowed me to see through the feelings of anger, madness, scaredness, overwhelmedness, and hear what messages these emotions were really bringing to me. Other times, re-reading the pages helped me to see the change in direction life was calling me to through incidents or conversations.

My morning pages was a million-dollar therapist who provided a safe mirror into my own world.

THE MOON

As my wellness practices deepened and I lived a healthier life, I gravitated towards including more nature in my day. Sunrises, sunsets, the grass under my feet. My goal was to live harmoniously with nature. In my corporate advertising days I was so wrapped up in concepts, emails, board meetings, deadlines (and the imaginary world of the mind) that I didn't even know what the month was, let alone the changing of the seasons or weather cycles. Now it was a daily mission to observe the natural world around me. To train my consciousness to tune in and befriend the natural elements.

I adopted a new routine of looking up at the night sky before I went to bed. I scanned the sky to locate the moon and tune into its bright, yellow softness.

My mother loved the moon. She passed this gift to me and it resurfaced as I sought a deeper connection with nature.

In our childhood, my mother would often rush inside the house and excitedly pronounce, "Quick, come see the moon!"

She would usher us outdoors and point to the sky, "Look!"

Gathered like a small herd of gazelle under the evening stars, our eyes locked to the yellow orb of attraction. We would stand for a short while, trying to appreciate it or imagine pictures on the moon's surface, then head back inside. One by one. She would often linger for many more moments, finding something we did not.

I never forgot those moments. Even though we would often feign irritation with her, it was a treat to secretly share in her sense of wonder at something so simple and natural. It stirred awe in me.

Years later, at her funeral, a stranger whom I did not know stood up and said, "I remember a day Michelle drove me all the way to town to buy some airtime. On the way back, she stopped the car on the side of the road so we could watch the rising moon." I could also sense his awe and appreciation. Tears formed in my heart. It sounded exactly like something my mother would do.

Watching the moon became a part of my daily wellness routine. I could appreciate nature without leaving the city or being on holiday. It was a stay-at-home vacation. Instead of going to bed with a head full of digital thoughts, I would fall asleep with the contentment of connectedness to all the earth and creation. To do this, I would go outside and gaze for a minute or three at the night sky whilst generating a sense of appreciation for all the stars, the planets, the entire universe, and the fact I made it through another day. It was as if in those moments I could find a sense of my place in creation. Tiny and insignificant in stature, yet big and expansive in awareness of it all. Looking at the stars and the moon gave me a sense of wonder. It carried me to a place of awe. *I am a part of the entirety of creation. I am small, yet I am big. The stars are up there, and they are in me.*

This habit inadvertently brought me to uncover something quite extraordinary to comprehend. After watching many moons, I noticed its direct effect on my emotional biology. I noticed my moods and emotional states were linked to peak moon cycles. New moon and full moon often brought with them my worst or most uncomfortable days in my struggle with illness.

This is so bizarre, I would think to myself. *It is nearly full moon, and I feel at my worst again.*

Do I have a "time of the month"? I thought.

"Can't be," I said, "I'm a man." Yet, reading my morning pages and paying close attention to my highs and lows, I couldn't deny the evidence. A full moon was, more often than not, inner chaos for me. A new moon was also often met with extreme difficulty and discomfort. Whether I was experiencing inner turmoil or outer turmoil, I was almost always highly uncomfortable being alive during those days around the changing of the moon cycle. This usually reached a peak at some point and then dissipated. It was like being squeezed by some invisible force.

Sometimes the inner tension was unbearable. I wanted to run away from myself at these moments. Being extremely sensitive, I started feeling an oncoming new or full moon days before it was due. I didn't have to look at the night sky or my moon phase app to know the moon's cycle. I felt it. Only after I did much healing could I stop associating the moon with pain or discomfort. The cycles of the moon, which pulled the tides of the oceans up and down the beach, also pulled the tides of my inner emotions. Pulling up things I needed to attend.

When I had more joy, the moon enhanced the joy.

When I had more pain, the moon intensified the pain.

The moon helps us face the inner tides of our emotions.

My mother committed suicide on a full moon.

DREAM JOURNALS

WELLNESS TIME ALSO extended into paying closer attention to my dreams. I kept a "dream diary" to record what came to me at night. I had no idea why, but I thought it was time to start paying attention to all parts of me. At the time, I was listening to a song whose lyrics kept playing in my head: "Whose dreams we are dreaming we don't know". I loved that line. It stirred a curiosity in me. *Where were the dreams coming from? Was it from my mind? Wasn't my mind resting? Who is witnessing the dreams?*

Sometimes dreams stirred up emotions and feelings. Sometimes dreams raised questions. Sometimes dreams were about others, and sometimes dreams were incomprehensible. *Why was I even having them?*

Before this time, I didn't pay much attention to my dreams. Later I dreamed of my friend Claudia's death before it happened. That changed things. *How was this even possible?* It was a big enough wake-up call for me to pay a lot more attention to my mind-movies-after-midnight. Dreams were more powerful than I had given them credit for.

One day, before this time, I'd had what I would call a "powerful dream". I didn't know what a powerful dream was, but I knew this dream was special. It deeply impacted me; I somehow knew it was more than a dream. It was so real, yet it wasn't a memory. It was crystal clear, yet I hadn't experienced it. It was simple, yet it nagged me for attention long after waking.

In the dream, I could see a giant granite-looking rock. It looked similar to the stones at Stonehenge. Yet I somehow knew it wasn't Stonehenge, partly because the big stone was on its own. No circle, no structure. The rock was about four times my height and about five times my width. It had a special feature in it too. Down the middle of the rock was a gigantic crack. Not just any crack, it was shaped like a zigzag running straight down the center. It was the Harry Potter of rocks—a lightning-shaped scar.

In the dream, I was staring at the rock. Standing beneath it, looking up. Then the dream ended. I was touched in my heart and in my mind. It made such an impression on me that by lunchtime, I was still pondering this "Lightning Rock". To put my curiosity to bed, I searched the internet to see if I could find more details. *Maybe it was a famous landmark? Maybe it's somewhere I need to go?* I felt a pull toward this rock but didn't know where to start. *What is this dream saying?* I typed in the search bar of my laptop; "giant cracks in rocks." Thousands of images with cracks in slabs, stones, pebbles, and rocks appeared in the results. Fail. As I mused this rocky mystery like Sherlock Holmes, I pondered, *How does one find their Lightning Rock amongst all the stones in the world?*

I tried some other search terms. Frustratingly, Stonehenge kept popping up. Stonehenge appeared to be the most famous rock family, receiving internet fame and attention. None of the other stones had achieved this rock star status. *Maybe I should go to Stonehenge?* I thought. There was no way I could travel with my illness, so I tucked the idea away for future consideration—ready to remember light-ning rock if it ever popped up, or if I ever needed to stand amongst some large fallen stones in a green field.

The rocks gnawed at me all day.

Little did I know, Lightning Rock would change my life.

GOOD MORNING, MIND!

REFLECTING ON MY dreams and doing my morning pages showed me the importance of how I started my day. It brought awareness of how I really was before I revved up my engines for the things I needed to do. It also helped me realize that if I began my day with a worried or anxious mind, the flow of my day would follow suit. I placed more importance on what I was saying to myself first thing in the morning. I created a new platform to build my day by saying out loud, "Good morning! This is going to be a great day." Sometimes I would look in the mirror and say to my reflection, "I'm looking at you in the mirror, and you look great."

As simple and silly as this was, it helped my mood by changing my mind.

My morning practice got revved up a notch when my aunt sent me a five-step process claiming to create a happier life. I wrote out the five steps and stuck them on the ceiling above my bed. The first thing I saw when I opened my eyes was this: "What are you grateful for?"

It would trigger my brain to start the day with gratitude. No matter how sleepy, I would list reasons in my mind to be grateful:

I'm grateful for the sound of the birds right now.
I'm grateful I am warm.
I'm grateful I have all my arms and legs.
I'm grateful for my aunt, who deposited money into my bank account.
And so on.

An internal rewiring. My thoughts had been conditioned for years to start the day with a to-do list – planning the day ahead as I opened my eyes or mock running-through meetings happening later in the day. Morning practices were now changing my brain from a reactive negative-mind to a grateful positive-mind from the moment the day started.

Once I felt grateful, which didn't always come right away, I would move to the next question: "What can I forgive myself for?"

With my eyes sometimes still closed, I would continue voicing in my head:

I forgive myself for being too hard on myself yesterday.
I forgive myself for talking badly to myself in the hammock.
I forgive myself for hurting women in my life that I have loved.
I forgive myself for trying to be too in control of everything.
I forgive myself for not listening.

When I first started the forgiveness practice, I would naively take about a minute to complete it. I didn't think I had much to be forgiven for. As I progressed with this routine, it became the longest and most difficult part of my morning practice. As the scales lifted from my eyes, I could see how much pain I had been causing myself and others. It was powerful. Tears often followed as I humbled myself enough to repent.

Step three of this process was taking five deep breaths. More often than not, I didn't want to. My mind was itching to get out of bed and start the day. The revving mind voice would say, "Okay, you've spent long enough now. Skip the breathing and let's go!" I could literally feel my mind throwing its little invisible arms in the air with exasperation saying, "Come on, *surely* not today?!" I would have to resist the urge to get up and rush out of bed. I couldn't believe trying to take five deep breaths could be so hard. I'd begin. Inhale. Hold. Exhale.

"This will make you better in the long run," I told my fighting mind.

The last two steps were: "Smile for 30 seconds" and "Love yourself". Smiling was almost as hard as the five deep breaths. Looking like a madman, I would lie in bed, grinning for as long as possible. *This isn't doing anything for you*, my mind-friend would say. "Actually," I would reply, "I've discovered it's scientifically proven that smiling for more than 30 seconds boosts the brain's serotonin levels. I will get my feel-good chemicals this morning, thank you very much!" I would then put my hands to my heart and still smiling I would say, "I really love you, Daniel." I would do my best to mean it. I would try to *feel* it. I knew the healing was in the feeling. My morning battle with my mind would then be over. I was then free to go on my way.

My mind didn't want to get better in the morning. It was happy where it was, clinging to its negative state. It was comfortable. It didn't want to change. It liked to be in control and wanted to stay that way. It took a lot of willpower for me to reclaim my position as the parent. After many disciplined mornings, the state of my mind transformed from negative to positive. It was like servicing a car. After years of neglect, it was a difficult service, but eventually it paid off, and the reward was tangible. After sticking to my morning routine for a few months, it eventually became normal for me to wake up positive. My mind now reached for thought particles that infused happiness into my day. My focus was on the good of life. My inner mental health slowly bloomed. My brain began to automatically enter the 5 step process without having to look at the steps on the ceiling. "What are you grateful for today?" it would start. This was "positive mind" auto-pilot. It didn't matter where I was in the world, wherever I was waking, I was in my routine. The steps before I started my day laid the foundation for a happier life. I tuned into myself. I tuned into happiness. I programmed a positive mind long before the influence of the day led me to believe otherwise.

When the rest of the world was snoozing alarms or creating "to-do" lists, I woke up with a grin.

LIVING PRAYERFULLY

I WOULD TOP off my "lying in bed" routine with this prayer:

"Dear God, you are inside of me, within my very breath, within each bird, each mighty mountain. Your sweet touch reaches everything, and I am well protected. Thank you God for this beautiful day before me. May joy, love, peace, and compassion be part of my life and all those around me on this day."

It was simple, yet it was a big deal for me to pray.

I hadn't had a prayer routine since I was a young child.

I discovered this prayer in a book my homeopath lent me. Amongst the "remedies from a 5000-year-old medical system," written by Vasant Lad, the prayer was nestled amongst advice for holistic wellness. The prayer had struck a sweet chord with me. There was something in it that touched me. I figured, "Well, if Indian doctors prescribed this 5,000 years ago and it's still around, I should try it."

Little did I know how prayer would begin to build my life. It would take my consciousness back to its true home. To the place where I could receive not only physical healing but divine healing from the Master Physician.

Little by little, the simple prayer shifted the focus from "me" trying to save myself and encouraged my mind to explore a vastly bigger place to reach for help. This "bigger place" was universal and cared for all the creatures. This "bigger place" ensured harmony. This "bigger place" provided for the ravens and crocodiles who had nowhere to buy food or doctors to call for help. I mostly called this the "Universe" at the time, "God" was too scary a concept for me to entertain. I figured "God" was a word better saved for churches and doctrines, and I didn't have a great relationship with either.

After reading the prayer each morning, the love and peace in my heart grew. I enjoyed praying it. It brought me comfort. It expanded my little heart in awe. At the time, I didn't know it was my spirit feeding off the sweet words on the page. My spirit grinned as I acknowledged God and connected to the divine nature of existence. Little by little, I grew to enjoy God and all of God's creation. Little by little, I let go of thinking God was religion and instead held to the belief God was in me and everything. God was all of creation. I developed a God-is-out-of-the-box-and-in-the-box attitude. It sparked this recurring thought: *If all the birds, bees, dolphins, and seals have their plans and their place in the world, then surely I do too. Surely God didn't skip over me when God designed the atomic molecules which make up the fabric of existence. I certainly did not create myself, so God must have my back too.*

I thought, *if God had a plan for all of this, then surely God had a plan for me and my little illness.* I started trusting. After all, M.E. isn't really difficult to overcome when you have the creator of the whole galaxy supporting you.

It was a big deal, that simple thought. Learning to hand over responsibility. Not in an irresponsible kind of way but in a trusting kind of way.

I mused over this often: *If the whole of the creation, the natural world, is in perfect harmony, and I am a part of this creation, then I will be in perfect harmony if I allow it.*

I needed to allow myself to come into the flow of this harmony.
I needed to stop resisting the flow.
I was learning to trust something which wasn't my own intellect.
But was I ready to truly surrender to the current of life?

CLUMSY PRAYERS

BEGINNING TO PRAY was a clumsy experience for me. It was like learning to ride a bicycle again. I felt like a child. Sometimes I felt silly. My big ego said, "Really, do you think something in the sky will make things happen for you?!"

I didn't have a choice. I was in desperate need of money. I was sick, with no salary, no capacity to work, and no energy to generate income. I couldn't do much else but pray. I had to experiment with prayer. It was the perfect opportunity to see if God had my back.

Before praying, I thought about how I could make money in my current situation. When an idea came to me, I decided to pray for it. "God, please give me someone to rent my panel van so I can have income."

I prayed and prayed and prayed until I felt sufficiently prayed out.

How did I know The Universe heard me? I didn't, but I put my heart into the prayer as best I could.

After my prayers, I uploaded pictures of my vehicle onto a buyers-and-sellers website and hoped someone would see my advert. I decided to pray every day as often as possible until someone reached out.

I had very few other choices.

Three days later, it happened.

I received an email from an interested renter. He wasn't only interested in renting the van for a couple of days which I had planned. Oh no, he was going for gold. He inquired about an ongoing monthly rental so he could use the car continuously for his electrical business.

I couldn't believe it.

Tears filled my eyes.

I would have an income indefinitely simply because I wasn't using my own vehicle. I would be taken care of financially so I could heal.

It was a miracle, the burden of my finances was lifted.

Had God done this for me?

Was The Universe really listening?

I enjoyed the first few months. I could pay rent without sweating about where my food would come from. I was able to focus on my healing instead of worrying about money.

This vehicle rental honeymoon period ended a few months later. The man stopped paying his monthly installments.

He also didn't return my car.

The stress monster returned.

Now I was down on income and minus a vehicle. Worse than when I started.

As I waited at the police station to get someone to help me find my car, I asked, *Why didn't this work out?*

There were lots of earthly reasons, but I looked deeper than this.

Hadn't I prayed? Hadn't I been in the flow? Didn't God run everything?

The answer popped into my head like a bubble of revelation. It was because it was *MY* dream scheme. *I* had thought about a way to make money and had prayed for it. I hadn't asked God to send me money. I had planned it all and expected God's help.

He did help, but I realized he helped my flimsy plan. My plan wasn't the best for me. There was a much bigger plan which I couldn't see. This is because I hadn't surrendered to God's wisdom.

I had tried to save myself again. This time with the addition of prayer.

I got my car back, but I learned a crucial lesson.

Let God provide. Don't try to tell Him what to do.

When I did things from my own strength, I didn't allow infinite potential to step in.

When I prayed for solutions, I could only pray from the limitations of my own mind, wisdom, and circumstance.

When I let God act, the richest person in the whole world had my back. *Why would I limit my income to a panel van when the Creator of the entire universe could resource me with the flick of a finger?*

I revised the prayer in my head. *God, please give me the finances from any place, any means, or any source. Your resources are infinite, and I am open and willing to receive them all.*

I learned that a monthly salary and renting my car were not the source of all income. Once I started praying for Infinite resources and believing it with all my heart, God showed up to support me in God's fashion.

Sometimes, without doing anything, I would look at my bank balance to find it had increased. Money had appeared out of thin air. Sometimes it was a tax rebate, an old loan, a piece of inheritance, money from a friend, or a gift from a family member. I even received cash as a late birthday present. All I did was keep praying. I kept fighting my financial battle from my bedside. I couldn't rely on my own energy to generate money. I had to rely on Infinite energy. Sometimes I would track the source of the income and I'd call and ask, "Why did you deposit money in my account?"

The response: "I felt I really wanted to support you because I know you're in a tough time."

God was working through others to support me. I didn't need to ask them. I needed to ask The One who sent them.

I was letting go and letting God.

I was trusting God to provide.

I was learning miracles happened when prayers came true in a way I could not have planned.

I decided after this big lesson to stop manifesting what I thought I desired and stop trying to be the master of my own destiny. I changed my prayer to: "God, please bring me what is right for me right now. Please bring me what will serve my highest purpose and the highest purposes of all those around me. Please bring me what will serve Your plans for the highest good of the world."

All that was left for me to do was to put out my hands to receive.

I was prepared to give into Eternity's vision for me.

I was prepared to build a relationship with God through prayer.

I was ready to give more space to God for the miraculous.

It was a dangerous thing to do.

My life changed in ways I never imagined.

MEETING GOD

I NEED TO clarify some things about my relationship with God before I continue to share my story with you. In the upcoming pages, I will refer to God a few times, and I'd like to give you my unique understanding.

Firstly, I know God doesn't have a gender.

Well, at least to me, He doesn't.

Or maybe She does?

I don't know.

I've chosen to refer to God as He, and I'll touch on this soon.

I want you to know when you read the word "God", it comes from a place of reverence in my heart for That-Which-Is.

That which cannot really be named.

The Beyond the beyond.

Our Creator whom I met along my journey whilst trying to heal. Whilst trying to ignore my spiritual reality.

Now I know that God is with us and for us.

Now I believe that *God is who God is*.

I cannot really understand or fathom God.

The particles. The atoms. The molecules. The vibration. The cosmos. The quantum field.

In the beginning, was the Big Bang, The Word, the cosmic sound.

Was I there when the atoms were created?

Was I there when the cornerstones of the earth were laid?

I use the word God because it comes from a place of having experienced divine intervention. A place where the miraculous meets the material world.

I've experienced this meeting place a few times. Enough to convince me.

You will read about it in these upcoming pages.

Oftentimes I did not want to believe what I was seeing and experiencing. Sometimes I still find it hard to believe. Whatever the case, impressions in my mind and treasures in my heart have been formed. I have now experienced things beyond the comprehension of my known reality.

God came to meet me in this way.

I call God He because it's natural and comforting to me. Maybe it's because I grew up in a Christian influenced society. Maybe it's because I didn't have a great relationship with my earthly father, so I needed a heavenly one.

Maybe it's because I always loved the words "Big Poppa," and now I have a "Big Dad" I can rely on. Maybe society and pop culture infused patriarchal, religious ideologies into my subconscious. Maybe I'm searching for a masculine figure to look up to?

It doesn't bother me because I've accepted it's my way of relating to the Great Spirit. Not everyone's way, just my way. Over time, the words "My Father" entered my prayers. On the darkest nights and loneliest roads, it felt true in my heart to cry out, "Father, help me".

It felt safe to me.

It felt like home for my spirit.

I speak with God in a way that is true to my heart.

It makes me come alive.

It hurts me how many religions denounce the feminine aspect of Divinity. I am pained to be a part of this wounded culture. I wish it were otherwise.

For me, and my Father in heaven, I trust I arrived to use this language by Divine grace. Maybe one day we'll all acknowledge a Father-Mother in Heaven, and then we can stop fighting. By kneeling at His-Her feet, we can realize we are all children of God who can do little without His-Her protection and provision.

I like how this keeps my ego in check.

As I continue, I invite you into my personal relationship with God.

I won't hold back my words because it is my child-like road to spiritual revelation, which ultimately played a huge role in my healing.

My innermost world of conversations with Big Dad.

Even though I am healed, I still get on my knees and make myself small at the feet of His divine presence.

I try not to over-analyze gender bias anymore. Instead, I focus on my relationship with the Highest Love and pray for more love on this earth. My heart comes alive with the sweetness of prayer.

What is more important to me is a relationship with the God-inside-it-all. If I could rewrite the historical scriptures, I might find an old papyrus sheet of paper, grab an ink pen, sit in a cave, and re-edit the scriptures to include a feminine gospel. The Father-Mother who cannot be named. In this way, I believe we might be a little closer to including the all-encompassing nature of God.

I'm sure half the world shivers at the thought of me penning through any holy scriptures, so I won't go there. I just want to tell you my story.

Now you can read it with a greater understanding of what and who God is to me.

Let me share what's on my heart:

I pray right now that God is with us as we
journey together into this book.
I pray we may see ourselves as what we rightfully
are, children of The Most High.
One family.
I pray we hold each other in love and understanding and forgiveness.
I pray the entire world is healing and healed.
I pray as you turn the pages of the book and look into the open pages
of my heart, you will have acceptance in your heart for who I am.
I pray for less judgment in ourselves and others.
I pray as I share my intimate experiences with you,
which happened within myself and with others, you
come along tenderly and understandingly.
I pray heaven comes down.

I don't know it all.
I don't know why it all happened to me.
I am following my heart.
It is the hardest journey I've ever taken, and the most rewarding.

GOODBYE ANXIETY

UP TO THE SURFACE

THE PRAYER TIME, spiritual expansion, wellness practices, and body and mind purification carried me toward an interesting place.

Complete purification.

All the rooms in my inner hotel were being cleaned out.

It wasn't a seven-day-juice-fast kind of purification. It was more like a life-fast kind of purification.

My entire life.

Without alcohol, sugar, wheat, dairy, distractions, stress, or constant multimedia messages, the purification process created a blank canvas onto which the pus of my life poured out. Poison hiding beneath the top layer for years was now being stirred up to the surface.

Pus was rising, and it was not pretty.

I remember these days of extreme inner discomfort. I didn't know where to turn. It bubbled up for no reason other than being ready to release itself. Like a volcano ready to blow after years of dormancy, it had its own natural timing. I would wake up edgy, anxious, and strung so tight I was sure something invisible was about to snap. My body was jumpy, and my temper short. I wanted to run away, but where? No matter if I went somewhere else, I knew the feeling would travel along with me, putting others in danger of being dumped on. Something was breaking free inside of me. I thought, *I'm eating healthy, sleeping healthy, abstaining from unhealthy habits... Why is it so uncomfortable to be alive?*

I was in withdrawal symptoms, a "cold turkey" from years of self-abuse. The things I had suppressed now had their chance to emerge from the deep.

Some days the mood-of-the-day was extreme discomfort. I wanted to move, cry, scream, shout… something, anything, but not lie still in my little room. These were attacks of multiple bad moods on steroids. I could hardly face living inside myself, let alone try to face the world. My inner world was heaving like a stormy ocean.

"Time to go for a run!" My mind would shout as the inner emotional turmoil was building.

I can't go running, I'd reply, *M.E has taken care of that.*

Flat on my back, I was forced into the rising pus from the volcano of my emotions.

MEETING ANXIETY

BEFORE THIS PERIOD, it hadn't occurred to me that I had been the victim of this mental suffering. It hadn't occurred to me that I had suppressed or hidden anything within myself.

My green hammock was now revealing the truth.

My mind was all over the show, and my body could not be still.

I constantly needed to be doing something.

I was seldomly in a state of peace in body or mind.

I wriggled around a lot.

I thought it was a part of my jack-in-the-box nature which I had grown up with.

I was wrong. It wasn't me. It was anxiety made manifest in my body and mind.

I saw the pattern—Busy mind, busy body.

I realized a "negative mind" was dominating my body. I noticed the tone of voice with which the negative mind used to speak with me. It was not a friend you wanted to have around. Negative mind was the "party pooper" of my life.

I hadn't always been this way. I recalled a time when I could look at the flowers happily, smile at the birds and light, fluffy, joyous thoughts filled the membranes of my mind. I knew in some faraway place, "positive mind" had existed.

At present, Mr. positive mind was in hibernation.

How can I help it arise from its slumber? I thought. *How can I return to a mind which doesn't make my body writhe all over the place? How can I return to a mind which doesn't interrupt me with inappropriate thoughts irrelevant to the situation or context? How can I soften the destructive nature of the voice of my negative inner friend?*

I had tuned into a negative mind radio station, and the DJ was Captain Anxiety.

Because of this, being still was torturous. I was squeezing out the anxiety from the inside. It didn't want to go.

I was in a fight, wrestling for the healing of my mind.

THE ANXIETY MONSTER

I REFLECTED ON my life before the period of the green hammock and noticed a rather alarming, repetitive pattern. I would push myself to the limit with exercise, driving my physical body to its edge, then I'd collapse to the floor and pick up the pieces to recover. It was a never-ending cycle of: intensive activity, collapse, rest, repeat.

It seemed natural at the time.

It was "who I was".

Then I asked myself, "Why do I always have to go to the limit?"

I had justified it was the right thing to do, to seek my edge. I didn't realize this extreme behavior was also directly proportional to feeling good afterward. The harder I went, the more rewarding the appraisal and recovery. During the "collapse" phase, as my body finally came to stillness, so too did my mind. I had discovered a way of creating a feel-good brain chemical all on my own. My strategy was simple: keep moving. The more I moved or played physically, the quieter the thoughts became.

With a fit, healthy body, anxiety was something I could literally run from. As the anxiety monster emerged from its hiding place in bushes, I would put on my running shoes and head for the mountains. I would sometimes damage my body to calm my mind. It was a game I couldn't win. If I wasn't running, I was drinking alcohol. Drinking to the point of mind peace. The more I drank, the more I floated into a peaceful nether world.

The harder I pushed, the more temporary peace I received in the collapse.

The cycle continued.

Push. Work harder. More anxiety. More exercise. Repeat.

It was a catch-22 situation with one result… burnout.

My therapist helped me see I had been dancing with anxiety for years. I exercised not to be physically fit, but to be mentally fit. I exercised because I needed the post-exercise endorphins and feel-good brain chemicals.

I pushed my body to experience peace.

As I lay in the green hammock pondering this cycle, I noticed my foot twitching and wriggling. Tap, tap tap. More often than not it had the jitters. I noticed on some days it constantly tapped—during rest, meetings, at my desk, reading a book, wherever. It was as if my foot wanted to run, dance, and play.

My body had this inbuilt restlessness inside. My hands would rub each other. My fingers would touch my face frequently and automatically. I had a perpetual pent-up frenetic energy within. When I was healthy, I used to blow off this steam on mountain trails and physical activity, now, it had nowhere to go, and the steam was building.

I noticed my thoughts, they were filled with worries, worst-case scenarios, and predictions of disaster. I noticed my breathing in this state. On some days my breathing nearly stopped altogether. It was so shallow and short I was sipping tiny bits of air at a time. My whole body was tense. I was constantly in fight-or-flight, ready for the worst. Except I wasn't facing a bear or angry mammoth at the entrance of my cave. I actually had nothing to really be anxious about.

"I don't think this is how I should be feeling on a day-to-day basis," I said to myself.

"This is not normal; my body shouldn't feel hunted by lions while resting in the garden."

I was in a state of "bad buzz" a lot of the time.

THE MONSTER INTRUDES

To manage this anxiety, I tried to spend more time in nature. I went for slow gentle walks in the forest. I focused specifically on the smell of fresh pine needles in the air and the sensations of the soft earth beneath my feet. I escaped difficult thoughts by focusing on sensations in my body and the beauty of nature. Instead of bumbling along unconsciously, I would focus my awareness on the incredible qualities of nature.

One day, whilst gazing up through the trees, soaking in the last rays of sunshine, an intrusive voice appeared. It was the anxiety monster, coming to steal the peace.

"That's a perfect branch to tie a rope and hang yourself on," it said.

"What?!" I thought, "Where did that come from?!"

I was trying to enjoy myself in nature, and the anxiety monster had followed me.

"I would never do that," I defended myself.

As the sun glistened in the trees, I tried to push the invasive thought aside and keep enjoying the moment.

The monster wasn't easily push-asidable.

The aftershock of the thought had me reeling.

Where do these thoughts come from? What is wrong with me?

This battle stole my awareness from the beauty around me. I was trapped back in my own head.

I didn't invite these thoughts.

They robbed me of my joy.

"Why can't I just have the 'look at the pretty leaves' kind of thoughts? Why does this monster come out of the dark and attack me?"

The invading thought was usually sudden and quickly disappeared.

However, the lasting effect of the intrusion would leave a spillage of anxiety behind. Like a slime trail behind a snail, the anxiety monster left its mark. I was worried for days afterward. The thoughts could appear from nowhere and were dramatic, fearful, overwhelming, intense, and sometimes terrifying.

I started reflecting on other times this had happened. I rewound the clock in time to my advertising days. I remembered a day walking onto the balcony of my office. I was taking a break for a breath of fresh air and I looked over the edge of the ten-story building. As I stared down I thought to myself, *Would I survive if I jumped from this height?*

I surveyed the street pavement below and I played out the scenario: *If I landed on that person, would I die, or would they die, or would we both survive?*

I never questioned these thoughts at the time.

They were normal to me.

Living in this negative state of mind.

The anxiety monster had made itself my friend.

What I didn't realize was that other thoughts could take the place of these disturbing thoughts.

I didn't have to be tortured.

I could have replacement thoughts like: *Look at the design of these beautiful buildings. Doesn't the sky look especially blue today? I love this place!*

The anxious thoughts had a theme to them: destruction, harm, fear, pain, death, disappointment, worry. They could stir the anxiety pot for hours or days.

Another memory surfaced of a time I was hiking.

What would happen if I jumped off this cliff? I looked down to ascertain if I landed among the rocks or hit a specific tree, what were my chances of survival?

The monster was playing games with me.

Gosh, I said to myself as I lay in the green hammock. *Is this really normal? Is this what all minds tell their people? Is it normal to hear a voice saying, "What will happen if you drive off this road?"*

"It's only a joke," my mind would say.

It isn't hilarious, I would say back.

I realized these thoughts had been with me for most of my adult life. I hadn't been aware of them or given them much attention. Now I was taking stock of the inventory of my mind, and I wasn't pleased with what I was discovering. I had pressed on, pushed on, pushed myself to block out these thoughts without assessing 'why' or 'where' they came from.

The thoughts weren't always outrageously alarming, but they weren't welcoming either.

I was about to face the intruder head-on.

A MONSTER PANIC

WITH THE CHANGES happening in my mind and body, the anxiety monster was getting uncomfortable. It didn't want to be swept out. I was bringing out the vacuum cleaner.

By doing "nothing," I was actually doing "everything." I was giving space for the anxiety to flow out from the recesses of my mind. I had stopped running and faced the thoughts the anxiety monster presented. Sometimes my brain felt like a big orange being squeezed in a juice press. The squeezing of the juice sometimes induced panic attacks.

It was not pleasant.

It manifested as a deep discomfort lurking in the recesses of my inner world—a fear coming from the dark unknown.

This fear would interrupt my life like an unwelcome phone call from a stranger.

One day whilst riding in my friend's car, my inner panic started ringing—the stranger calling from the deep. I slowly started slipping into the abyss. I clutched the car seat as I was falling off a cliff in my mind. Panic gripped my entire being. The driver's voice tuned out. A deep fear of dropping into the unknown rolled over me. My breathing momentarily stopped. I heard a distant voice saying, "Are you ok?"

"I don't know what's happening," I said.

"You're having a panic attack," she said.

Meg explained she was a panic sufferer too. I was shocked but also grateful. I had known her for years and never saw her grappling with the monster.

She knew the stranger lurking in the deep.

She gave me some useful tips and dropped me at home.

The thing about the monster is this—its after-effects lurk on. Once you've been gripped, the trauma of *when is the next* continues to haunt the psyche.

Will it get worse?

What have I done to create this?

On the outside, I looked normal, shiny, happy.

On the inside, I was in a war.

How many people does this happen to? If it's me and Meg, there must be a lot more.

What are we carrying in our inner chambers, which are secret from the world?

I wanted to be free from hiding.

I wanted to be free from anxiety and panic.

I knew that sharing my inner world was a step toward freedom.

THE BATTLE

ON DAYS WHEN the monster came in full force, it was chaos. If I managed to stop what I was doing and make it to my bedroom, I would lay down and start tossing, turning, and writhing in torturous discomfort. My inner tension was unbearable. It wasn't a physical agony but a mental and emotional one.

On bad days, it was full, blown panic.

On others, I can only describe it as an inner tension.

A tension within my body, mind, heart, soul.

It was as if something wanted to break free.

I needed to release it, but what?

To let off the steam I figured that lying still was the best medicine.

By resting I could let it break me and shake me. I needed to feel it. All of it. Let it through.

When I gave myself space from people, food, emails, work—the monster surfaced.

The tension became seen.

The ship trying to break free was released into the open ocean.

Sometimes I cried for no reason. When I lay down long enough, the tension turned into sadness. When I felt sadness, I would play sad songs to encourage the sadness out of me. I cried. For whom? For what? I didn't always know. It didn't always matter. I only knew that sadness needed to come through me.

Other times, anger rose up. I would feel it burning. I would see the faces of the people who provoked it. I would let my resentment through. I punched my pillow. Only after the anger, could I ask for forgiveness. First anger, then forgiveness, then peace.

Sometimes new ideas were birthed, then the tension settled. I wrote in the pages of my diary about upcoming trips, business solutions or wellness itineraries. It was as though I was being spoken to, and I needed to hear it so that the inner phone stopped ringing.

Other times it was pain, hopelessness, frustration or fear of the unknown.

It didn't matter.

I simply came to realize that inner tension, without being addressed, became panic.

It was better to head into battle when I became aware, and venture into the dark cave to poke the bear.

In the early days, before I knew my inner music was trying to break free, I would be in so much inner tension that I would walk around in circles, not knowing what to do. I felt like I was spinning. Floating. Ungrounded. Unable to concentrate on anything. This was an emotional process squeezing through the tubes of my consciousness, asking to be felt.

Why is this happening to me? This is not normal.

I needed to be still in this moment if I wanted to be free from it.

If I had the courage to face it, to quiet myself and listen, then I could ride through it.

Then I would reap the reward.

Another layer of healing peeled back.

The 'tension rising feeling' often triggered me to distract myself first. To fly away. To eat sugar. Reach for crunchy chips. Play on my cell phone. *Anything else but here.*

Sometimes I distracted myself unconsciously to avoid confrontation.

After a time I realized if the monster didn't catch me on this day, it would catch me on another.

It was better to face it.

I was dancing with the depths of myself, with things that had been hiding in the dark.

The space had allowed me to shine the spotlight of remembering on all the parts and moments I had previously abandoned.

Now I had the tools, time and space to piece together the bits that needed rebuilding.

DIFFERENT FORMS OF ATTACK

THE MONSTER WASN'T always full on.

Sometimes it was more subtle.

This could be; anxiety bubbling when I saw an email, repulsion when my phone beeped another notification, or dread when I saw a person calling from a stressful situation.

I felt stress for situations that never used to stress me out.

It might also be a thought-out-of-place kind of attack or a moisture-under-the-armpits thinking of tomorrow.

Sometimes it was the I-can't-deal-with-these-work-emails-anymore.

And yes, sometimes it was the full-blown writhing-in-agony-on-the-bed kind of ambush.

The expression depended on the mood of the monster inside.

I also realized the monster's attacks were related to what I was feeding it.

Anxiety loved me when I didn't choose happiness and wellness.

If I ignored my heart and what it was asking of me, the monster used the opportunity to open the door. Also, if I fed the monster alcohol, overwork, unhealthy food, and unhealthy media—the monster made itself at home.

At this time, my sudden shift in lifestyle to a clean, pure, natural state of living, now threatened the monster's survival.

The warfare began.

The anxiety within me was looking for somewhere to go.

I surrendered and got on the roller-coaster with the bear.

I let go.

It was a terrifying ride.

WRESTLING WITH THE BEARS

As the roller coaster tossed and turned, I sometimes thought I would die.

Or lose my mind.

Or have a heart attack.

Nothing like this did happen.

It was hard to face the roller-coaster. It was hard to say "no" to the daily chores, distractions, and to-do lists. It was hard to lie on my bed when I wanted to buzz around. It was hard to have no intention but to let whatever was inside me come up to the surface. It was hard to dance with the devil on my back. It was hard to lie down with nothing but extreme inner discomfort and a prayer for ease and a lighter burden to carry. It was chaotic and cathartic at the same time.

At this stage, I didn't know if what I was doing was actually helpful or healing. It was weird and I hadn't read about it anywhere. I knew I didn't want to live with discomfort following me around. I knew I had to break free. I also knew after each roller-coaster ride, I came out feeling lighter and happier. I came out often with a revelation or insight. I came out knowing which area of my life I needed to change or who I needed to forgive. Including myself.

I was dancing solo through the minefield of my mind. After a while, I decided I needed to talk to someone about this dance. I booked another appointment with my friend, the homeopath.

"How is everything going?" he asked me as I sat in his room. I explained about the roller-coaster. I told him about the panic which rose out of the bushes like a bear and incapacitated me. I told him about writhing in my bed.

I waited for his response. The judgment. The labels. The psychiatric prescriptions or psychological referral. I waited for the "d" word, expecting him to say, "You are depressed. You should take medication like your mother." My worst nightmare.

He leaned forward in his chair, concern and compassion written on his face.

"What are you panicking about?" he asked.

I was caught off-guard.

What am I panicking about? I repeated in my mind. *Isn't he listening to me? I'm panicking, isn't this bad enough? How am I supposed to know what it's about?*

I was silent for a while, then looked to read his face to see if he was maybe joking. His face still showed genuine care.

No one had ever asked me this.

Smiling and gentle, he repeated his question to me, "Dan, describe to me how you feel when you are panicking?"

I searched inside for an answer to his question. I felt resistance. I didn't want to revisit the last place of panic. I thought again of all the coaches, psychiatrists, friends, and therapists. They had never asked me such a thing. They had only wanted to try to prescribe solutions for the panic. Not to understand it.

I paused. Hesitant. I repeated the question out loud, "How do I feel when I am starting to panic?"

I replied slowly, "I think… I feel… I don't know. I guess I just feel so much pressure building up in me. Sometimes a release of emotions comes pouring out. Like I'm crying, and I don't even know why. On a bad day, I just feel so overwhelmed I want to throw my phone into the ocean and stop communicating with the world. Sometimes I'm at breaking point from all the people. Sometimes I feel so helpless. I want to smash my laptop into little pieces. It all feels too much. I don't know what I'm doing, and at the same time, I feel so needed by everyone. I can't handle it anymore. I want to run away to the mountains or become a monk or something, to find peace and quiet and myself."

I breathed in. There it was. I had said it. The theme of my panic. Not any generic panic. *My* panic. My panic at *this time*. I had described my wrestle with the bear. I had revealed to myself and the homeopath what the real problem was.

Overwhelm.

The solution was immediately apparent to me—I needed space.

Space to breathe. Space from being needed by everyone. Space to process everything I had stored deep inside myself without even knowing it. Space to deal with old trauma. Space to deal with old hurt and relationships. Space to dance with the bears so we could dance no more.

His simple question revealed it to me effortlessly.

I only needed encouragement to look a little deeper for the answer.

It was like searching in the bushes for the bear itself.

And now I had it on a leash.

I asked myself what practical solution might help with my inner overwhelm. It was clear—I needed a few more months off. A freedom from responsibility and relational trauma. This would allow me the space to release my baggage.

I needed space to stop hearing everyone else's voices to gain some inner direction. Where was my life going? I wouldn't be able to know if I kept forcing myself to deal with everyone else's problems.

I needed space to listen to myself. To process. To file. To dust off. The anxiety bear had come to tell me this.

Panic attacks weren't an alien, foreign, or incurable disease. They were a signpost; "Slow down, process, release, or I will keep clawing you."

My homeopath had helped me go beyond shallow solutions to start figuring out what was causing the panic. Without trying to stop it, I could now focus on fixing the root cause of the panic. It was a revelation to me.

There was nothing wrong with me. I was panicking for a reason.

The panic was in my body, and my mind was telling me I needed to rest mentally or take a break from nervous system stimulation. Not a quick daily break, but a much longer rest. A system reset. A chance to step out of overwhelm and sort out the old filing system to create space for something new. The break was rest, so something could be born out of rest. Before this, I feared the panic. I thought something was "wrong" with me. I thought I was broken, dysfunctional, insufficient, weak. Now I could see it was a neon signal asking for change. The way I was going was over.

I had to make a turn.

When I investigated my inner world as to the causes of panic, I discovered the secrets, and the anxiety bear never returned.

BENEATH THE LABEL:
SEEING INNER SIGNS

IT'S HARD TO describe how important this finding was—my panic and illness were unique to me. There was nothing wrong with me! I simply had to discover my own, original path to healing.

I grew up watching my mother and her friends experimenting with various remedies to calm their anxiety. Over time I realized the solution didn't lie in a one-size-fits-all. There was not one pill, one capsule, one tincture, or some special exercise which could magically dissolve anxiety. The root cause of anxiety was unique to each mind. To each emotion. Unless the underlying cause of anxiety was rooted out, any short-term remedy was a never-ending bandage on an ever-bleeding wound.

No amount of pills could cure it.

Only a shift in perspective could.

Anxiety is curable, not chronic.

I identified certain mental patterns which caused my anxiety.

Instead of thinking, "I am an anxious person", I rather asked, "What is causing this anxiety?" This is more powerful than believing I had an illness.

No one is destined for lifelong anxiety—if they are willing to investigate and make necessary lifestyle and behavioral changes.

This got me thinking.

If my anxiety was unique, then surely my chronic illness and lack of happiness were unique too.

I dived deeper into the bushes of my mind to discover more bears:

Why am I feeling depressed?

What is beneath the label of my chronic illness?

This time I was willingly investigating, instead of being a victim.

"Well", I said to myself, "I guess I have a lack of joy for good reasons; I don't have direction in life, I can't do anything I used to for fun, I can't do the work I enjoy, I no longer have a community of active friends, and I don't feel like I have a home". I looked at the list of factors. "These seem like good reasons to be unhappy!" I said to myself. I felt more content. I felt more at ease. It was ok to not be ok. I had compassion for myself. Instead of being a victim asking *Why me?* I could instead be a friend to myself, showing love, patience, and kindness. I replied with a comforting voice, *There's nothing wrong with you. This is only a tough part of the race. We'll get through it.*

I shifted from focusing on the negative and instead cultivated compassion for myself by understanding what I was going through. The key for me was not to slip into a pity party. I saw my challenge as a set of factors that could change over time. "I will learn to love new things," I said to myself. "I will grow a community of friends". "I will change my work."

I was now willing to hand things over and become new. Moving from victim to leader was another important step in my healing.

Instead of labeling myself with the idea I had a mental health disease called "depression", I labeled it in my inner world as a *phase* I was moving through. I wasn't "depressed". I was "moving through a depressed phase". This always allowed me to know I was only visiting. And it was a necessary visit. I needed to pay attention to what my heart was telling me. I needed to pay attention to what my heart was feeling. Instead of using the stretchy label of "depression," I preferred to be more specific on my inner experiences. "I am feeling sad today," I would say to myself. I practiced expressing myself more and more. When I woke up in the morning I'd ask myself, "Daniel, how are you *feeling* today?" I would respond, "I'm fine." Then I would say again, "Daniel, how are you *really* feeling, go deeper, go into your heart."

"Ok", I would respond, requiring a bit more effort. I would search around in my heart, trying to distinguish how I really felt. "I'm actually feeling slightly annoyed," or "I am feeling desperate," or "I am feeling sad," or "I am feeling lost." It required more effort, but I realized there was a feeling beneath the layers. Each layer represented something closer to the truth. If I could drop beneath the lazy, shallow labels we've been given to describe ourselves in a fast-paced world, there were clues to my healing waiting for me. By slowing down, resting, I could discern how I truly was in that moment. It was a game of emotional monopoly. Beneath the layers were the clues pointing me toward healing.

I came to recognize that many of these inner emotional textures were not happy or joyous feelings but were important voices. They were whispering directions to guide me toward the light. The voice of depression—led me to joy. The voice of lostness—gave me new found-ness. The voice of confusion—asked to slow down and get clarity. The voice of fear—asking to look at what was scaring me. I gave myself space to hear the whole family of voices and emotions in me. This is not to say I reacted to every whisper, but I certainly considered them, as they are all part of my inner family.

I noticed that each whisper or feeling had its opposite. A "negative" or uncomfortable feeling was only a positive feeling in disguise. As I listened and acted, the negative became positive. If I allowed the sadness to move through me and understand what it was about, it transformed into happiness. Emotions are an invisible kinetic energy. They want to be heard and felt; the more we transform them, the more we increase our energy. The trick is looking through the misty glass and sifting through their meaning. If I figured out the lostness, a feeling of centeredness followed. If I wrote down my stresses and added solutions, peace followed.

If I ignored the difficult emotions, other negative feelings would attach themselves like velcro. Unkempt emotions become a negative chain. They attract each other. If I ignored the *I'm-not-fulfilled-by-my-job* feeling, other emotions joined the chain. These emotions included; emptiness, lack of purpose, lack of joy, doubt, sadness, anxiety, and depression. The longer I ignored the *I'm-not-fulfilled* feeling, the more negative emotional friends gathered at the party. If I did something about the original feeling by communicating it, planning it, asking what it wanted and why it was there—it would inevitably point me in a new direction or a small evolution. It would be transformed, and there was an end to the challenging emotion. Emotions are like rays of light. When you see light, you don't realize there is an entire color spectrum that makes up the visible rays—until you see a rainbow. Once you have looked at each emotional ray making up your own light field, you channel your light, clear the blocks, and discover the gold beneath your very own rainbow. Once difficult emotions are transformed, new emotional friends have space to join the party. These friends include peace, happiness, wellness, contentment, and joy.

The signposts of these emotions pointed down roads I needed to travel.

Each held the promise of a transformation. Each asked the question of change. *How can we change to help unblock this pressing state of emotion?* By allowing emotional states to do their work in me, I was carried to a healthier internal home. Depression transformed into joy. Sadness transformed into happiness. Brokenness became wholeness. Pain to love.

The trick was to move with it and through it, not run from it. If I was reaching for a cell phone to play mindless games, it was most likely because I was running from an emotion. My mind didn't want to give the voices of my heart the space to be heard. To listen closely. To experience. To face it. When I did, my emotions became fuel for positive action.

If I was sad a few days in a row I learned to stop and ask myself, "What are you feeling sad about?". I would answer the question either verbally or in my diary. I would face it. In the past, I would say, "You have nothing to be sad about," but now I gave this sign-post more importance. I would take time to list the factors which were making me sad. I would express them. I would ask, "Is there anything else you want to do about this?" Sometimes I would write a letter, sometimes I would imagine myself apologizing to the person, and sometimes I would put on a song and cry. I take action to help release the tension of the emotion. Each emotion required different release activities, so I became inventive. I don't believe any emotion is more negative or positive than the other, but it illustrates the movement from "uncomfortable" to "comfortable" emotions. Unpleasant sensations to pleasant sensations. This form of expression played a huge role in my healing. I imagined a new definition of M.E.—(M)ore (E)motions—and chuckled. It accurately described how I was healing.

Here is another example from one of my low days:

Daniel: " I am feeling so 'burned out'".

Daniel: "What exactly does 'burned out' mean to you?"

Daniel: *Grabs a piece of paper and begins to list; "I feel tired, energy-less, unmotivated, scared to do work, stuck, confused, anxious, tense".

It was cathartic going into details on how I felt instead of saying "burned out". It comforted me to know exactly how the inner pieces of my world were moving. Once the initial uncomfortable emotions were released, I took myself deeper:

Daniel: "What do you think is causing this burnout for you?"

This question helped break the cycle of burnout. If I expressed myself without taking any action to change my habits, I would be caught in an infinite loop of getting better (by reclusing and recharging) but heading back again to burnout (by repeating unhealthy patterns).

Daniel: *Makes a list of burnout causes; "Stressful relationship with a close friend, not sure where money is coming from, worried about my mother, stressed I can't exercise," etc.

My next question: *What do you think you can do about this right now?*

I would then write solutions or things I could do to make changes. Answers could be; "Apologize for what I said, heal my relationship with so and so, ask my family for financial support for this time period, Take a break from digital technology, release some responsibility to my business partners, learn more about burnout".

Next question: *What is the next step for each of these points?*

I would then answer this, providing meaningful and tangible action points that I could implement—all leading to change. Most times, there were things I could change immediately. It wasn't something I needed to do next month or next week, they were things I could do right away. It would usually take some form of communication, and the stress would ease. Emotions and communication are two sides of the same coin. To free yourself, you have to free your words.

I created steps to hope for myself by following this process: 1. Confessing exactly how I felt (to myself or others) 2. Identify detailed key feelings 3. Identify causes of these feelings 4. Identify next steps to resolve feelings

I've shared this example of my approach to inner emotional

clarity because it illustrates the simplicity of how we can dive into our inner worlds with pen and paper (at any moment).

Burnout is a hopeless place, but the details unique to you will help you rise from your own ashes.

COMMUNICATING ME

My **adventure started** when my next step was to "learn more about burnout". My action point was obvious—read up about it. I didn't want to spend too much time on my computer, so I got a book called *The Joy of Burnout* by Dina Glouberman. I read it slowly when I had the energy. It helped me tremendously. It gave me hope. It gave me insight into the foreign world I was living in. It was an example of how I took a difficult emotion—"stuck in burnout"— and transformed it into "learning about burnout". It showed me others had been through the same thing. The more specific I was in identifying and expressing my problems, the more specific the answers came to me. When I was clear on what I needed, help materialized very quickly. The trick was taking the time to know what I needed each day. Each 'inner clarity' session was a step to a brighter future.

The same applied to communicating my inner world. When I was first diagnosed with chronic fatigue syndrome I would tell people I was "extremely tired," or "feeling sick," or "not feeling well". This didn't create much velcro for the universe to stick its solutions onto. "I'm feeling sick" is about as broad a statement as the ocean saying, "I'm feeling wet". People's responses to my feelings were,

"Ah shame Dan, rest up" or "get better soon". This was remarkably different to when people knew I had M.E.

The more specific details I could give, the more specific help I could receive.

My healing was also up to me.

The same was said about the depression I was experiencing. If I told people I was 'depressed', no one would know what to do. Depression is a vague word used to describe a broad spectrum of symptoms. In my opinion, depression is a lack of joy. Everyone's joy is unique. So how can everyone's depression not be unique too? The lack of feel-good chemicals in the brain is the same for all depressed people, but the pathway in and out of depression is unique for everyone. I needed to be more specific by describing my phase of depression if I was going to receive the help I was looking for.

What are you really feeling, Daniel? What is beneath the unhappiness?

I needed to do some searching. If my lack of joy was because I was lost or worried, these details were more helpful. "Lost" is not the same as "overwhelmed" or "stressed out", which could all be causes of depression. If I expressed my "lostness" instead of my "depressedness", then people would ask, "Why are you feeling lost?" This was a lot more helpful because we could begin to search for solutions. People would help me go beyond the feeling instead of being stuck in it. This is the power of speaking about what you are feeling. This is the power of not hiding your inner world. A tree can only thrive in a forest of other trees—each knowing what is happening inside the network and supporting it to higher heights.

Sometimes I was lost in my own forest, and it took the simple expression of how I felt to get back on the path to wellness.

Essentially, by breaking down the discomfort like this and going into the bushes looking for bears, I could work through various feelings to guide me back to safety and comfort.

I moved on to find what was beneath the M.E.

I decided to start by researching chronic illnesses in general. I asked myself, "What does *chronic* really mean?" I looked up the definition online – "persisting for a long time". I pondered this. To me, it meant the M.E. could be around for a while, but this didn't mean forever. I sensed it wouldn't be a passive going away but there was hope. I would make it my daily mission to get to the bottom of it and not quit until I was fully healed. A full-time focus. I wouldn't pity myself but rather participate in my own active healing process, not waiting for it to come from somewhere or someone else. It would have to come from me. A long time was not till the end of time. I would do it. I thought about the book on cancer and HIV/ Aids my doctor had given me to illustrate chronic illness recovery. According to science, these diseases appeared to lurk around and had to be managed effectively, never really going away. This wasn't good enough for me. I wanted a future life where I had totally forgotten about M.E.

My mission was to return to joy.

I was angry at the doctors. Furious they had suggested this was the life God had destined for me. I thought doctors were supposed to inspire hope. These ones didn't. And I didn't believe them either.

I believe God has set aside a Kingdom of Heaven for each of us.

I refused to accept I could live anything less.

I rejected the doctor's diagnosis that I was chosen to live with a dim light. I decided I wasn't going to victimize myself by believing a 'managed life' was the best I could hope for. It was time to start my own research. My own journey. To stop putting my life in the hands of others. By digging into the uniqueness of the disease in me, I created hope where there was none, and with God's help, I found it.

I also asked myself an important question based on what I had learned about labels. I asked; *How is this chronic illness **unique** to me?*

"Well", I replied, "this specific form of chronic illness ***slows me down,*** and it ***fogs my brain,*** so I can't think straight."

These were my two most prominent symptoms and biggest clues. I looked beyond hundreds of suggestions about diet, movement, meditation, chemicals, supplements, treatments, and asked myself with child-like innocence: *Well, how do I get better then?*

With the 'slow down' and 'brain fog' clues in mind, I replied, "Well, I should probably **slow down** and **use my brain less**!"

"It's that easy!" a little inner voice shouted out.

So what exactly does that mean for me?

I sat with the question.

I had reached an important point of discovery.

It was a new direction for my healing.

I knew my return to joy lay in the simplicity of this, but I didn't have the details on how.

I was uncovering the longest road of my life… The journey from head to heart.

I just didn't know where to start.

"Do not worry about tomorrow,
for tomorrow will worry about itself…
Each day has enough trouble of its own."

[MATTHEW 6:34]

HEARING MY HEART

I NEEDED ANSWERS on "how to use my mind less."

From somewhere, anywhere.

Sitting in my chair, staring at the blank wall in front of my desk, I closed my eyes.

I summoned up a level of determination and intensity as I fixated on the question, *How do I use my brain less?* I repeated this to myself again and again. I directed all my inner focus to the question. Searching the very depths of information in my brain, I reached a dead end. Nothing. I experienced a level of emptiness. I paused in the stillness.

With no thoughts, there was space for something new to emerge.

What I heard in the stillness was the voice of my heart.

As I let go of thoughts and constantly figuring things out, a level of receptiveness pervaded, asking for answers rather than creating them. The ears of my heart were on full alert. I had no idea what I was doing but I had put the training wheels of my heart on, and I was going for the first ride.

Suddenly, a pebble of information dropped into the pond of my heart.

In the spaciousness, a new sensation emerged.

A wave of knowing washed over me. *I must start following my heart on a daily basis.*

I could feel what that life was like. Peace, joy, contentment, happiness.

Guided by Heart Intelligence I would end up fulfilled, content, and healthy.

My heart would enable me to become present with everything as it is. Not living in the future or worrying about the past. Living life in each moment and asking for guidance in each moment. A heart-led life would never be lonely. I would have love and direction. I knew I had to build a relationship with my heart and God, which would require trust, faith, and timing. It was more than a "follow your heart" commercial or "live your dream" philosophy. It was a solution to give my mind a break, to trust, to hand over the steering wheel to my heart, and enjoy the ride. It was a new attitude, a new positioning with life. I was cultivating a new compass for living, a daily heart compass.

I had no idea how to start following my heart each day.

I remained paused in the silence of receiving Divine guidance.

Heart Intelligence.

I waited for more answers.

Suddenly I had an urge to phone my friend Sebastian.

I tentatively reached for my phone.

I had no idea what I was going to say. I was simply trusting my newfound heart impulse.

I dialed his number. It started ringing.

He answered almost immediately.

"Dan bru! How you doing?!" his jovial manner uplifted me.

"Howzit Basil!" I greeted.

"Ya man, how you doing my bru?!" he asked.

"Ya, I'm sitting in my room and I've had this realization. I think for me to get better, I need to heal my body, mind, and **heart**."

I paused.

He was listening intently, I could feel it.

I continued, "I know about the body and about the mind thing, but I don't get this whole 'heart thing'. I don't know how to listen to it or improve it. I know I've used my heart for some major decisions in my life, but I don't really know how to live daily listening to it."

There was only a short pause on the other end of the line.

"Dan", he said, "you've been following your head for the last ten years, so if you could follow your heart for the next ten I would just love that my bru."

Energy pulsed through me as he said the words.

I transformed from unsure and confused to totally uplifted.

His words of encouragement connected with something my heart knew to be true.

He said it so confidently I felt he was right alongside my journey to the heart.

God had brought me someone who understood what I needed for my path.

Although probably a non-event in Sebastian's life, this incident totally changed me. Something in my heart made me reach out, and the result was that I was supported.

I suddenly had direction and knew what I needed to do—Heal my heart and listen to its sweet whispers. This would help take pressure off my mind.

It felt right.

With his agreement, this heart-led life went from a crazy idea to my natural next step of healing. Sebastian helped set the wheels in motion. I was encouraged that the secret to my total well-being lay within the treasures of my heart. I sensed God had sent Sebastian to me as a friend to teach me more about this 'heart-led' existence. We had done it when we had started passion projects together and lived outside the corporate normality, but here was an invitation for the heart to be heard and followed every day.

I reflected on Sebastian's heart-led life.

When everyone went to university, he didn't. When he wanted to pursue things others didn't approve, he did it anyway. He had very few things figured out, yet he was tremendously alive and happy-go-lucky. This was a side effect of following one's heart... happiness and fulfillment.

He was walking proof.

My short and sweet conversation with this 'heart-led man' was a turning point in my own journey.

Thinking less, feeling more.

LANGUAGE OF THE HEART

FOLLOWING THE HEART is madness to the mind. The mind cannot understand it.

My early experiments were filled with doubt and fear.

I was losing my mind to find my heart.

M.E. shifted me from mind-based living (what I thought was right) to heart-based living (what I felt was right). I did not follow every emotion, but I paid close attention to what impulses I had and what my intuition was calling me to do. I had to learn to carefully discern the voices inside and dissect which ones had the potential to lead me to health. When I sought the place deep in the center of my heart and made time to hear the whispers, a direction became clear.

Listening to my heart also meant expressing myself more, standing up for things I believed in, saying "no", and heading into the unknown.

It meant following a 'pull', a simple feeling to do something.

I often didn't want to do what my heart was asking, so I would test myself by rather asking, "Does it feel right **not** to do this?"

This question circumnavigated the mind's responses.

The mind wanted to say, "but, but, but, but," instead I allowed my intuition to respond, "no, it feels like we need to do this for some unknown reason right now. It doesn't feel right to skip it."

Later the things I did made sense.

A life lived with heart only makes sense when you look back.

In this way, I could stop planning, stop thinking ahead, and I gave much more opportunity for my intuition to speak.

I let the voice of my heart back in.

I learned it was better to keep moving, even in the wrong direction, than to get stuck in the mud of my mind's comfort zone.

I didn't want "managing a disease" to become a manageable zone of contentment.

My heart was a light in the dark where millions of options and opinions were confusing and overwhelming.

My heart led me to new pastures.

I created an idiom for myself: "Heart-led, Mind fed".

To me, this meant following my heart, whilst using my mind to keep me safe. My mind was still very important but wasn't leading the charge. I tried not to blame it for being controlling, it simply needed to rediscover its rightful place. My Mind-Heart balance was the key. For example, if I felt my heart calling me to do something, I wouldn't shut down the idea. I would ask, "Hello mind, how can we safely make this happen?" The mind's voice and heart's voice were equally important.

To begin to feel a direction was scary and risky. *Where will I end up?* My mind cared for my safety and wanted to know the details which my heart could not give. Often my mind and I walked one foot in front of the other, one day at a time, one week at a time, while my heart called me to some unseen paradise. The picture begins to complete itself in hindsight, not in foresight. The God of my heart takes care of the details.

Reasons I was scared to follow my heart included; I didn't want to always be on the move, I didn't want a gypsy lifestyle, I didn't want to be poor, a drifter, going nowhere. I wanted to contribute to the working economy, earn a living, to be "normal" in an economic sense.

My heart had its own way of creating stability.

The game is still as real today as it was then. Often my heart trusts completely whilst my mind is doubtful and afraid. My heart welcomes while my mind judges. My heart desperately tries to love while my mind encourages separation. I listen to both of them. I try to love both of them. I remind myself they each have their place and correct positioning in my life. They are the captain and the wind, helping me sail the ocean of my life. My heart is the wind, blowing me in a direction. My mind is the captain, making sure we get there in one piece. Without the wind, we would have nothing to ride.

It's good to feel the wind before flying the kite.

To position my mind to 'help and not hinder,' I would ask myself this question; "Mind, what do you need to come along in this direction?" I would then list the fears and judgments my mind would present. After consoling and considering my mind, I would feel peace, and we could then move forward as a team. I might also ask this; "Mind, what are you afraid of?" I write all of it down, either on paper or type it on my laptop. Sometimes the lists of fears are long. When I complete the list and go back to re-read the points, they are often silly fears. Yet, to the mind, it is not silly. Although it is the future, it feels real now to the mind. I try not to judge my mind's fears and choose rather to respond with kindness, solutions, or considerations. An example of a fear I had before leaving my home was this; "I am afraid if I pack up my room and go traveling, I will lose contact with all the people I love". This fear kept me from heading out on an enriching journey for months. Looking at it now, it seems silly, and irrational. We all have digital devices to maintain relationships if we lie. Yet, this fear was real to me and caused much discomfort. I was scared to lose the few connections I had in my community. *Who would I meet? Would I be alone? Would I be lost?* were the kind of thoughts plaguing my inner world. After I wrote it down I could look at it much more clearly. Seeing it in writing I wrote next to it a column of solutions; "set up digital dinners and regular connect sessions online with the people that you love". My mind calmed down. Peace returned. I could carry on working on my campervan without this concern in me. I could start getting excited.

The danger is that unconsciously the fear had been floating there for months, holding me back and keeping me in one spot. An unidentified fear is like having a wheel lock on your wheel. You can't see it, but you spend your life waiting in the parking lot. Checking the wheels for wheel locks gives a little nudge to help the mind go, "ok, that's not so bad. We can remove it and get going slowly". It can also be the difference between doing something with fear and anxiety or joy and excitement. If I don't remove the locks, the tension between my mind and my heart grows. When I neglect the growing calling of my heart, I become sad, unfulfilled, and depressed. This signals that it is time to rest and listen—to stop and identify my inner roadblocks. Once clear of these inner checkpoints, happiness returns, and the momentum of my heart fills my inner world with love. The things my heart desires fall into place and are supported by my mind. I can then step onto the field of fulfillment.

This is the power and beauty of a heart-led life.

I also speak to my heart.

Instead of asking, "What do you think I should do?" I speak to my heart in my own language.

*What would I **love** to do right now?*

How do I FEEL?

*What would I **love** to do this month?*

*What would I **love** to do for someone else this week?*

*What is the most **loving** thing to do here?*

These questions carry me toward love, joy, and peace, and this is what I consider to be a successful life.

Life is built on the right questions, so when we begin to uncover the language of the heart, we can ask our hearts the right questions. I have questions for my mind, heart, body, and spirit. They each get their say. In this way, love can be our guide.

My life has become an adventure. Things beyond my wildest dreams come to meet me because after all, my mind couldn't dream of things only my heart knows.

For me, this is a life lived with God.

"Man looks on the outside while God looks on the heart"

[1 SAMUEL 16:7]

LOSING ANXIETY

Leaving my mind also meant leaving my anxiety.

Using my brain less (as M.E. was ordering me to do) actually helped me to enter this state; *Less mind, less anxiety.*

If you don't put petrol on the fire, it can't burn.

To be more specific… When I didn't put too much pressure on my mind to have all the answers or perfect solutions, it enabled me to live more freely.

My new voice was;

I am not in control.

I make mistakes.

I am not perfect.

I don't have it all figured out.

I don't always have the answer.

This was helping my mind to follow my heart and realize again its right place—to be supportive and not the "star of the show".

It also helped take the pressure of constantly performing out of my mind.

I started asking others for their opinions instead of "knowing the way".

I sought advice.

I changed from having "excuses for not performing" to "I am sorry" or "I am scared".

The anxiety dissolved more.

A friend told me, "Why waste an opportunity for a *good apology* on a poor excuse".

The more I sought forgiveness, the calmer I became.

This was a healing balm for my anxiety.

The lessons were daily. When I needed my home to be perfect, the dinner to be perfect, the email to be perfect, life to be perfect… it created a condition of low-lying anxiety for me. When I had to always be a good, friendly, or nice person, it created a kind of silent "always-on" anxiety. I noticed it in myself and how I was creating it for myself. I didn't 'think' I was anxious because I couldn't see I was the master creator of my stresses.

When I lived with heart and showed up to things I wasn't prepared for or didn't know a lot about, I was more humble. To stand in the unknown and simply say, "I don't know". In this trickle of humbleness, I discovered my feelings.

I learned bottling up my feelings created tension and anxiety.

The healing was in the feeling.

The wellness was in the expression.

Expression led me to my purpose.

FEELING MY WAY

I BEGAN TO sense the difference in texture between my emotions and feelings. Whilst emotions were reactions to situations, thoughts, or experiences, *feelings* were a little different. They could arrive on their own. They were a mood, an intuition, a "gut pull"—they were true sign posts for a particular direction that was sometimes inexplainable.

Whether emotions or 'feelings'—all these inner voices were telling me something important about my life.

Instead of blocking them out, I paid more attention.

For example, if I felt stressed checking emails, I would pause and interrogate my reaction before mindlessly replying or pushing through it.

"Dan, what is really stressing you right now?" I would ask.

I would ponder and answer my own inner question before taking action in my outer world.

I might ask myself, "Why is this stressing you all of a sudden? What has changed? This never used to stress you."

Sometimes I would do a job for months or years, and then one day, a feeling of tension simply appeared. The tension lingered. Where there was peace, now there was stress. This time, I didn't blame myself or try to push on. I went to my inner world to find a solution.

Why?

I learned that if I ignored an ongoing feeling like 'emptiness', eventually, it would be joined by 'hopelessness' and/or 'depression'. Instead of blocking the discomfort, overriding them, or calling them 'silly', I became friends with these feelings. I listened and discerned. *Are these loving signals worth following, or are they unloving signals based on fear?*

Do I need to make changes in my life?

After investigation, some feelings required inner change (mental patterns, overcoming fears, judgments) and some demanded outer change (job, location, friends etc.) so I could head toward fresh new pastures.

As a man, I have more feelings than I'd like to admit—scanning my inner world taught me this. The difference between men's and women's emotional landscapes (generally speaking)—women express, men suppress—but both sexes have rich inner emotional landscapes. This might be the result of societal conditioning or other various factors, and it is changing, but I know we both have an inner dialogue of the heart, and it is in both our interests to make known in a loving way what is happening inside.

Our world depends on it.

I experimented with expressing myself more.

I tried to speak the inner textures of my heart when I was aware of what was happening within. I stood up for myself more (beliefs, needs, wants) and trusted what I was feeling.

I shared my heart.

To become more sure of myself and my feelings, I confided in people I trusted, sharing my heart's whispers with them until I got to the bottom of what was happening inside.

This helped me to trust myself more and gave me clarity on what I needed to do.

This process gave me peace.

Eventually, as I became better at expressing myself, the habit became effortless. At any moment I could access what I was feeling. The trick was learning to express myself without hurting others. As I learned this a lightness of life returned. I didn't carry so much emotional stress or inner anxiety. I put a voice to it and what was weighing me down dissolved. I could now lay down a lot of the emotional baggage I had been carrying.

I admit it was rocky at first because my first expressions of trapped feelings were difficult and painful. I was slowly reclaiming my truth and needs which I had long forgotten. I no doubt hurt many people in the early days of learning the art of expression. I am sorry for this. My strong friends stuck around and are still around because they knew I was changing for the better and healing.

The light in my eyes returned too.

Like rain from the clouds, I released past emotional traumas.

The fog lifted.

My foot stopped anxiously tapping.

My hands stopped anxiously wringing.

I allowed things to flow through my heart and like a running river, it gave me energy, power, peace, and direction.

Me being able to express me.

Whether it is easy or not, broken or whole—feelings are true for all of us.

Each time we express, we move higher.

Another thank you to those who endured my discovery of expression—you brought me to a light I could not see.

THE ART OF DYING:
HANDING OVER

GOODBYE MICHELLE, MY LITTLE ONE

LITTLE DID I know, anxiety wouldn't be the only thing leaving. There were a few more goodbyes to happen, which I had no control over.

The first goodbye came on an idle Monday afternoon after a full moon.

An old work colleague had pleaded for me to drop off a digital wrist GPS with him. He was completing a volunteer fire rescue course and needed it for navigation. I really didn't want to do it. I was feeling low and didn't want to see anyone. Also, I was dealing with an unusual situation. Nearly all of my clothes had been stolen from my laundry basket. I'd left my dirty washing on the front seat of my friend's car as I intended to take it to the laundry. I didn't have the energy to do my own washing and I didn't have a car.

Before I could drive to the laundry, a thief broke the passenger door and stole everything. This was about the sum total of all the clothes I owned. Instead of heading to the laundry, I went to the police station to file a report of theft. The policeman was not hopeful I would see my clothes again.

What does this mean, God?

I guess I will have to start again then.

My old work colleague then called again.

He was desperate for the GPS.

I was tired from the day's events but I decided to go.

It was not easy.

A short time after I arrived, he began sharing his emotional and mental struggles.

I guessed this meet-up was not only about the GPS.

He told me he would have committed suicide if it were not for his little daughter.

Why do people do this to me? I remember thinking.

They don't do it to my other friends, why me?

I really didn't have the capacity to be of support. I was struggling enough on my own.

I left his house feeling heavy. Wondering if I was destined to be a drama-magnet.

Pondering my sticky situation, I was driving the short stretch of road home when my phone rang.

It was my stepfather calling.

He was straight to the point.

"Dan, I have some bad news…"

A pause.

"Your mother has killed herself."

I broke.

The moment my ears caught the vibration of the words, my heart exploded into pieces. I saw a flash of white light, and something in my chest shattered into a million tiny fragments. Shards of my heart were flung to the peripheral edges of my being.

Like a star exploding in a galaxy, pieces flew into outer space.

A firework of trauma.

I pulled over the car. My vision blurred.

My stepfather asked, "Are you okay?"

I was speechless. I was completely unprepared for this moment. Even after the struggles and threats from my mother about suicide, I was not prepared for the actual experience of losing her.

I was experiencing worse-case scenario.

I didn't have the words to reply to my stepfather.

"No, yes, I don't know," I said.

"I've already called Grant," my stepfather replied, "He's coming over to be with you. Can you get home?"

I looked through tears at the road ahead, "yes, I think so".

That was it, the total conversation. Short and sweet. As I was pulling back onto the road, the voice in my head boomed like thunder to the Heavens… "Why, why, why, WHY? WHY? WHY ME? GOD. This cannot be happening. WHY?"

I thought I was starting to climb out of my dark pit of disease and burnout. I thought I was figuring things out. I thought things were getting better.

A bomb had exploded in the plans of my life.

Grant arrived at my house a few minutes later.

I don't think I had ever heard him cry until that moment.

"I'm so sorry, Dan, I'm so sorry, Dan, I'm so sorry, Dan." We hugged. We cried. He too had been there for the long journey with my mother. He knew all the ins and outs and how I had tried to help her.

The walk with Michelle was finally over.

Grant suggested I come over to his house. He still lived in my old stomping ground in the beach house of Camps Bay. I was clueless and in shock and agreed to accompany him.

Someone cooked dinner. I wasn't really tasting the food. I sat at the table with my friends whom I hadn't seen since recovering from my illness. We made small talk, no one broaching the topic of my present reality. How could we?

I realized we are quite unprepared for circumstances like this in the Western world. There is very little equipping for the inevitability of death. I had never spoken much about death or experienced its aftermath, so when it appeared that night, it was a gray area for all of us. Especially the kind I was facing.

Amid the trauma of sudden death, I realized the impact of my mother's depression was finally lifted off all of us. No more threats, no more hospital visits, no more worries, no more stressing. My friends had been as much a part of the journey as I had. With her leaving, so too did a kind of baggage, the stress of not knowing if your loved one will be ok. In its place arrived a mountain of pain, regret, anger, loss, confusion, and frustration. It was a new emotional territory. The old story was over. The new wardrobe of emotions had arrived.

Dinner at the house was gray. I was split between two worlds. One world falling apart and the other carrying on as normal.

When the evening came to a close, Grant drove me home. I stepped back into my room alone. It was surreal. Everything was the same, and nothing was the same.

Climbing into bed, I faced the fact I no longer had a mother.

LITTLE DUCKY

I thought I would never get to sleep. I was angry with God. *How could I deal with this on top of everything else? What was I to do now? How was this all happening?*

I thought I would lie awake all night reminiscing about my mother. In fact, the opposite happened. I had one of my best night's sleep in a long time. So much so I was guilty when I woke up. *Aren't you supposed to be grieving and lying awake all night?* I said to myself. I didn't know what to do. My phone was off. I was happy to be alone. I didn't want to see anyone. I decided to give myself an hour or two before allowing the incoming family requests and condolences. *How is my sister doing?* I thought. *Oh God, I hope this doesn't completely shatter her. Why is she mixed up in all this mess? She doesn't deserve this.*

I went over to my induction stove to start preparing some breakfast. I was shattered. I was standing mindlessly over the stove like a robot on autopilot. I pressed the button and heard it beep as the plate heated up. I was trying my best to focus on making porridge. It was hard to focus on anything.

As I stared blankly through the kitchen window, I heard an unusual sound.

"Beep beep beep", it went.

I looked down at the stove.

"Beep beep beep", it went again.

I strained my ears, trying to figure out if the stove was malfunctioning. Then I realized the sound was coming from outside. I also realized it wasn't a "beep" but more of a "cheep".

"Cheep. Cheep. Cheep," came the sound again. It was rhythmic in evenly spaced intervals.

I looked out the window, trying to see what was making the sound.

The sound came closer.

I stared into the foliage above my window sill.

Its little head popped out of the succulents.

Making its way towards me through the garden was a baby duckling.

"Cheep, cheep, cheep," it constantly called as it approached me. I was stunned. The little duckling was heading right for me with no fear.

Something special was happening.

My kitchen window was ground-level because my cottage was dug into an embankment. I was eye to eye with the little duckling as it clumsily scrambled over the last bits of foliage. My mind started to react in fear and awe; *Is this a message from my mother? Is this God? What is happening right now?* Feelings rushed up inside of me.

My oats in the pot started boiling over.

As I moved the pot, I witnessed the baby duckling hopping and struggling up the window sill. Ducky was insistent on surmounting this obstacle to get inside. Instead of helping it, I took my phone out and videoed the moment. *No one will believe this.*

As I was videoing, the duckling successfully mounted the ledge and dropped rather hazardously onto the kitchen counter.

The stove had cooled sufficiently and Little Ducky raced across and pressed up against me.

My mind: *There is a duckling pressed against my stomach.*

My emotions: **rollercoaster*

The moment was overwhelming.

Tears flowed from my eyes.

Why me? I can't handle this anymore, God. It's all too much. I sobbed and sobbed and sobbed.

I looked down at the little brownish, yellow duckling.

"Cheep, cheep, cheep," it said, nuzzling my belly.

I didn't know what to do. I was frozen. Eventually, I reached out my hand, picked Little Ducky up and put it in my jacket pocket.

A softer little "cheep, cheep" sound reached my ears momentarily and then quietened down.

I gave my pocket a soft prod to make sure Little Ducky was still ok.

"Cheep, cheep, cheep" came the response..

Little Ducky had found its happy place. It was home.

I switched my stove back on and continued making breakfast like this was normal.

I didn't know what else to do.

My heart was touched.

My mind surrendered to the moment.

I carried on like it was just another day.

For me, it was.

A DAY WITH DUCKY

I HUNG OUT with that duckling for most of the day. I lay sunning with it on the deck. I have a wonderful photograph of Little Ducky sitting on my chest. I told my stepfather about it. It was consoling and comforting for me to have this encounter. A small distraction and moment of lightness from the tragedy. I was chatting with Little Ducky and Little Ducky was chatting with me. "Cheep, cheep, cheep," Little Ducky would say. Sometimes I felt like I was talking to my mother, saying all the things we couldn't say whilst we were both alive.

Later I went to my landlady to talk about my newfound feathered friend. I knew I couldn't look after Little Ducky forever. *What if it dies while I am looking after it?* There was no way I could handle any more death or loss.

My landlady suggested I take it to an animal rescue shelter. She also pointed out Little Ducky was, in fact, a Little Goosey. She surmised it came from a family of geese who were nesting nearby. I agreed the animal shelter would be the best home.

Don't try to rescue everything, Daniel, came the voice in my head. *Look what happened when you tried to rescue your mother. Give this little bird to people who really know how to care for chicks.*

It was a hard pill to swallow. I realized no matter how hard I tried, I couldn't save everything. No matter what I did, I was not a goose or the best person for saving it.

I handed over Little Goosey to the lady at the bird sanctuary. Pain and sadness caressed my heart. It was as if I was handing over the responsibility for my mother to someone else's care. I was letting go of my need to save things, to constantly be the rescuer.

"It will have a good home here," the lady said. "We've got an incubator with a bunch of other goslings, it will fit right in."

I thought of my mom not being able to "fit in" anywhere while she tried to find her new life and community. More heartbreak. I was on the verge of a real sobbing explosion. I imagined the lady behind the counter staring at this grown man having a mini breakdown at handing over a little goose. Little Goosey was only a part of a much bigger parcel of pain.

"Goodbye Little Ducky," I said (forgetting again Little Ducky was actually Little Goosey). "You have come to the right place now," I said as I comforted the little chick and myself.

"You will fit in and be loved by your new ducky friends".

The lady allowed me to walk inside, all the way to the incubator. I peeped in to witness a whole array of little chicks hopping around in their see-through home. I was comforted as I watched these buoyant, little, yellow fluff balls tumbling into the beginning of their new lives.

I said goodbye to them and the staff. When I got to my car in the parking lot, I could no longer hold the tears back. The dam was too full. Grief seeped out of my already saturated being into the hands I held to my face.

When I returned home feeling sobbed out, the hollowness returned. A palpable inner emptiness. Now that Little Ducky was gone, I was forced to turn from the distraction back to the sad reality of my own life. Alone. Sick. Mom-less.

Despair returned.

I searched my mind for an anchor. Something to do or look forward to.

There wasn't much. I was living on the low end of life.

What can I do right now? I asked myself.

I still didn't know what I should be doing.

Then I remembered a weekly meditation session happening a few houses up the street. It was scheduled for the following morning.

Is that okay to do? I thought. *Should I not be doing something else? Should I not be grieving? What does one do in this situation? How does 'normal life' carry on?*

I didn't know what was right or wrong, so I figured I would see how I felt when I woke up in the morning.

MY AFRICAN LADY APPEARS

I WOKE UP in a haze and mild state of shock.

Losing someone so important to me was like losing my footing on the earth. I had no idea what to do. My compass for life had been cast into the open ocean. I was floating in an unreal dream state amongst the stormy sea.

I decided to go to the meditation session.

I needed some form of human company to help carry the inner load, even in silence.

I got dressed and slowly walked up the road toward the meditation gathering. As I was halfway up the narrow road, a lady opened the door of her red car right in front of me.

"Hi," she said with a big smile. She bristled with confidence, friendliness, and power.

"How are you?" she asked, radiance still beaming off her.

"Not good," I replied.

I hesitated whether to give her my actual circumstance or opt for a polite societal reply. This would be the first time I was verbalizing my trauma to someone outside my trusted circle. I fumbled in my mind for the words. I didn't really know how to say it. It felt too heavy.

"My mother killed herself two days ago," I replied.

I was shocked by the truth.

I waited for some kind of surprise, an uncomfortable consolation, or an awkward reaction. Instead, her eyes changed to deep compassion.

She looked at me with firm tenderness, "This must be why I have come here this morning. I have never attended this meditation before."

I was taken aback. *Where were the condolences? The niceties? She was expecting this?*

Was this another God moment?

Another God-incidence?

Am I being supported Divinely?

My inner world rattled whilst my spirit soared.

She spoke more.

Her words calmed me. Affirmed me. Strengthened me.

I was stunned by her authority.

She knew exactly what to do.

As we walked toward the home of the meditation gathering, she gave me her business card and told me she'd dealt with situations like this before. She helped people on their journeys through life. She knew some traditional African rituals which could help me deal with grief.

I took her card.

I was bewildered.

Where did this all come from?

My life felt like a movie. Not in a good way.

I knew I would desperately need support and couldn't do it alone, but I was unsure if this was the support I sought. *African rituals? Grieving processes? What even is this?*

"Send me an email if you need support," she said as we headed into the meditation session.

Needless to say, the entire meditation gathering was a strange experience for me. Gathered with a group of people on a wooden deck alongside a trickling mountain stream, everyone sat cross-legged and serene whilst a nuclear bomb exploded in me. I became distinctly aware of the precious space inside each of us. No one could tell the warfare happening in the chambers of my inner mansions. I sat carrying my own secret existence, which few had access to. I realized we don't really know what is happening within those around us. What demons are people really wrestling with a forced smile on their face?

I picked at some food after the meditation.

I made short small talk with strangers.

Enough, a feeling arose inside of me.

I said goodbyes to the strangers and hugged the woman who gave me her business card. I slowly headed back to my room, dreading to face myself and my life situation again.

I placed the business card next to my computer. I lay in bed and let more grief and confusion cloud my mind. I mindlessly fumbled through my daily routine and probably chatted with some family members during the day. I thought about the duckling. I re-watched the video of it climbing through the window and sent it to some family members.

Time passed in a haze.

Nearer to evening time, I noticed the business card again. The word *Phakalane* stood out in bold. I searched the retreat center online. The website showed a large, beautifully built center nestled on the slopes of Hout Bay. I was still unsure of the idea of these "African rituals," but her homestead's chic modern pictures and landscape looked safe and inviting. Also, considering the circumstances, my need for help outweighed my fear and doubt. Her name was Claudia, and I decided to email and enquire about what help she might be able to offer and what these "African ceremonies" might be.

She responded quickly.

Her email was to the point, and two days later, we were having tea in front of a warm fireplace in her home. Her home was magnificent. She had built it herself, with her own hands. She told me "phakalane" meant "hawk" in an African language.

Of course. Obviously this is the place of the hawk, the exact animal sent from beyond to guide me through all of this. I am the sick hawk, and I have found a place of refuge.

Phakalane felt like a new home to me.

Claudia felt like a new mother to me.

The words she spoke offered me much comfort. She had a way that made me feel entirely safe. I could sense she had no other agenda than to be of service to my grieving process as an amazing listener. She knew what to do and say, and everything she offered me seemed like perfect advice.

She explained the African ceremonial process to me.

It would mean for 21 days, I would have to abstain from distractions so I could really be with my grief. I would abstain from eating strange food, eating out, going to social places, no movies, no TV, no hugging strangers, no pleasuring myself, and limiting as much office work as possible. It was designed for me to be present with everything I was feeling.

It was exactly what I needed. No one in Western society had offered me this or suggested it. I realized how ill-equipped in the West we are to deal with death. I was lost and confused. Claudia was my guide through the tidal wave of grief. I would only come to know years later how other cultures have beautifully structured processes for the death and grieving of lost loved ones. At this moment, all I had was the advice of some family members and friends; "Bury yourself in work" , "You'll get through it", "It'll be ok". Nothing was going to be ok. Nothing was the same. Everything was different. I no longer had a mother and I needed help. I wouldn't find solace in a 1-hour memorial service. Although the road with Claudia would be harder and unknown, I knew I needed a unique approach. Death changes things. It was another important layer of my healing and being in the world.

I started with something Claudia called the "ashing process". First, we built a fire together and stared quietly into the flames. Out of the silence, the questions emerged. *Are you angry with your mother? How do you feel now?* We spoke. It was a sharing-of-the-heart process with no agenda. It was freeing. It was a heart-to-heart turned to the volume of level deep. She encouraged me to speak about my feelings and cry if I needed to cry. Until now, I had not yet been guided into my real pain. No one had asked me to describe it. Claudia did. She was helping clean the wound. Until now I had received a lot of "I'm sorry man, you'll get over it" or "Your mother was a great person, just remember the good times". This kind of comfort has its place, but sitting here with Claudia, I was supported to explore a grief I had subconsciously buried in the secret chambers of my heart. This grief was the unattractive kind that distorts faces and convulses bodies. Claudia thought grief was beautiful. I could sense it. She strengthened and lit up as the conversation became more real and raw. There was no space for shallowness beside the fire. Beyond the sobs, I experienced a great peace. It felt right to be sharing this way. For my body to be aching with a kind of betrayal that broke me inside. An ancient memory searched my brain for other times I may have needed this kind of support, and I wondered how others would deal with moments like these without their Claudia. How many people had never experienced this kind of release or even understood what it was to take a deep dive into their grieving chambers? I didn't even know this level of honesty was possible.

To honor my mother in this way felt like the perfect way for me to be held through death. I would come out more alive and strengthened than ever.

I distinctly remember Claudia's own vulnerability at our first session. I remember her sharing her own experiences concerning suicide and depression and family members dealing with grief and mental illness. I cried openly in her presence. Her safe atmosphere provided the container where I could experimentally express these new parts of myself. I felt liberated. I could say it like it was. She guided me through the valley of the shadow of death. I am forever grateful for this.

I checked in with her a few times during the 21 days. She encouraged me to give myself time and space to deal with the trauma. She encouraged me to be as free as possible from distractions and let the trauma move through me. Rather than bottle anything that could get stuck in some dark part within me and cause trouble later on. I am again forever grateful for this. She helped me to get closure on the initial part of the grieving process.

The ending of the ceremony was in an enclosure she had built. She heated some rocks in a fire and then put them into cold water in a tub. Steam was created in the enclosure. We sat together and sang a goodbye song to my mother. It was incredible. It was so releasing. So freeing. I had experienced nothing like it in my culture. Where were the rituals for death for western people? Ceremonies designed to help deal with real life. The best I could look forward to was a one-hour memorial service with pats on the back.

We exited the enclosure and sat by the fire. I was basking in the tenderness of a goodbye. Awe and reverence for this African culture filled me, ancient traditions had helped me so much.

She looked at me and asked, "Daniel, what do you want from your new life?"

I had not even begun to consider this.

Claudia had given me perspective on the whole ordeal and helped me to realize I was now free. Free to become a man, not a boy desperately trying to save his mother.

I began to imagine a new life.
One without the responsibilities of a suicidal parent.
"Joy," I replied.
We looked up.
A rainbow appeared in the valley suddenly beneath us.
"That is for you," she said confidently.
Tears filled my eyes.

IT'S YOU OR ME, PERSONALITY

I MAY HAVE gotten out of the frying pan but I certainly was not out of the fire. There was much letting go and 'burning' happening in my inner world. It felt at times like I was witnessing a personal suicide each week. A death inside me. My inner world. My personality.

Unhealthy patterning in my personality was holding me back from getting better. Who I thought I needed to be was not actually who I was inside. This divide caused illness. My personality did not really want to change to accommodate, it didn't want to become someone else. It liked who it was. It did not want to see life in a new way. My personality didn't want to be experiencing all that was happening to us.

These things happen to someone else, my mind would say. This was not life according to a personality which my mind had created.

I realized my personality was entirely constructed.

It helped me to fit into my Cape Town lifestyle, get what I needed in the workplace, build a friend circle, and grow my organizations. It helped me survive, thrive, gain popularity, attract clients, attract a mate, and get heaps of attention from most around me.

Is my personality really me? I wondered.

Is it not changeable and malleable?

I thought of myself before I arrived in Cape Town. I reflected on who I was then.

I was different. I asked myself, *Where is the Daniel who loves to write poetry? Where is the Daniel who loves to lie in bed reading books? Where is the Daniel who loves creating things or playing in nature?* I wondered what happened to the introverted part of myself who didn't care for attention or social gatherings. *Where is he?*

My new personality was not honoring parts of myself that were integral to my wellbeing. My personality wasn't fake, it was simply biased. It had forgotten other important parts which needed expressing.

I realized parts of me had been put in a box and stored deep in a closet with a "maybe later" label.

My new "Cape Town personality" prevented my true maturing self from emerging. I was trapped in a self-built cage that needed some sides to fall down so I could start unfolding other aspects of my life.

There was a self in me who was being drawn out from beneath the layers.

The musical self.

The mystical self.

The spiritual self.

The compassionate self.

The writer.

There was a self who wanted to dance with his hands in the air in front of thousands of people.

There was a self who wanted to recluse, to write and reflect and sit in quietude for days without judgment.

There was a self who was dying to know God.

The problem was my personality had built a box of all the things I did and didn't do. What I liked and didn't like.

For example:

I didn't like spiritual things which I couldn't explain rationally.

I didn't like dreadlocked hippies.

I didn't like scatter cushions.

I didn't like cats.

I didn't like people taking party drugs.

I didn't like general societal norms and standards.

I didn't like Saturday markets.

I asked myself, *Whose dislikes are these? Where did all this judgment come from? Why do I have lists of do's and don'ts and likes or dislikes?*

Is this really me?

I was a construct of my circumstances.

I created a Self to fulfill my need to be loved and accepted. I was built by me for me. The things running me were things I could change at any time. I knew I could learn to like anything my personality deemed off-limits. I also knew I probably had to start doing this to grow or move in a different direction. It occurred to me my wonderful persona was being enjoyed by everyone around me—at a cost to myself. The persona of 'the helper', 'the fun guy' , 'the intellectual' ,'the Mr Can-Do-It-All', were built to cover my inner needs.

Having an unbalanced Daniel was not leading to the deep fulfillment my soul was searching for. This persona created a "soul in a box" kind of life.

I knew my personality had to change. It had to become flexible, and soften.

I had to be open to things I didn't like before.

I decided I would no longer have Life desperately knocking on my door with signs and synchronicities pointing me in a new direction while my personality had its "thanks, but no thanks" attitude.

It was time to reinvent the pleasure my personality was seeking and replace it with the purpose for which my soul was calling.

MY EGO'S ON FIRE

I was letting go of who I thought I was. It was very painful. The dream of the house, the car, the life, the wife, and the expectations. They were all crumbling. As they crumbled, my personality rumbled. It did not like the changes. It let me know. My mind was the voice of my personality. "You are going to lose all of your friends, Daniel. People will think you are weird and will reject you. You will end up living in a hut in the forest with an animal skull on your head. You are going to disappear from all the conventional reality you love."

None of this came true. But it was my fear at the time. This was a daily voice I had to live with as I was coming into my purpose. Wanting to do one thing but being told by my mind the reasons I shouldn't. My ego didn't want to let go, and it was putting up a fight. Its future was threatened, so it tried to stir up fear to hinder me. It didn't want to hear the music which was wanting to pour out from my deeper parts. My ego knew it meant the death of certain parts of itself. It was now creating enough fear to slow the dance of my soul. It was holding on for dear life.

Then one day, we faced off.

A glorious battle fought in the mind.

Me against me.

Sitting rather peacefully on the wooden deck one afternoon, enjoying the beauty of the small riverine forest at my feet, the voice came in like a missile from the unknown.

"That looks like a perfect branch on which to hang yourself."

What? I thought. *Where did that come from?* The voice did not fit the scenario I was enjoying. It was the torment of my mind again. Playing some trick to bend me into doing something distracting or harming. Me running from me.

I was done with this.

I was done running.

I was done with that voice keeping me from the fullness and promise of an abundant life.

"You are going to end up like your mother. It's in your genes, and you can't escape. You were born like this. There is something wrong with you. Your whole family is like this." My mind was in full-blown attack, throwing petrol on its own greatest fears. It was going right for my Achilles heel—inducing a fear I would end up like the rest of my family. Drugs. Death. Distracted. Or disturbed.

Panic panged inside of me. I thought I had been through the worst of it, but this was something different to my chronic anxiety. This was facing my deepest darkest fear. This voice was savage. My mind was using my current life situation of having recently lost my mother to fuel its own darkness. It was hitting me while I was at my lowest. It genuinely scared me. Would I lose control and end up like my mother?

I had doubt and fear.

Sitting on that deck, I knew it had to end.

I had to tame these suicidal thoughts.

TAMING SUICIDE

ANGER ATTACKED MY inner world.

"Why do I have to face this torment?" I was screaming inside, "Why can't I have peace?"

I didn't want to run anymore. I didn't want to be scared anymore. I knew my thoughts were only thoughts, no matter how scary, but I didn't want to deal with those kinds of thoughts anymore. It had to stop. For me to completely heal, I needed to move beyond this right now.

I paused in my inner dialogue. In a brief moment, I prepared myself for battle. I would face this fear head-on. I made a conscious decision to go into it. It was like going into a deep scary cave within me, but I would go.

A voice rose up inside my heart, "I will not let this fear be a part of my life. I choose a better life."

The massive internal battle was about to begin. It was petrifying. I was going to go to the place I feared most.

I brought the intrusive thought back up to the surface of my mind… "That is a perfect branch on which to hang yourself."

To go into it, I knew I would have to imagine it. I would have to see it through. Fear welled inside me like a tidal wave as I ventured on in my imagination.

If I pictured it, would I end up doing it? My mind threw another spear into the battle of thoughts. It was creating more doubt and fear to stop the journey.

I pressed on.

I pictured myself hanging from one of the trees in front of the wooden deck. I saw my feet swinging. I wondered if the landlords would see me first or someone from the road?

I allowed my mind to completely play out the scenario.

"Come on, mind, what have you got? What's your worst? I will face you," I said with all my heart. Terrified, but standing like David before Goliath.

I continued.

I allowed myself to imagine going to the hardware store. Which one? I imagined buying the rope… which one? A thick white coarse sailors' rope or something more modern? Would the police be able to trace my purchase back to the store and ask them questions about me? Would the police have access to my bank account? I chose the sailors' rope. I imagined the feeling of it around my neck. So much fear welled up.

A memory flooded back. I remembered a friend in university who had met the same fate. He lived in my residence and hung himself next to the dining hall while we ate lunch. I was traumatized. I didn't tell anyone, but the death of that amazing, kind, and lovely man touched me so deeply. How could he have done this to himself whilst the rest of us were having the time of our lives? I allowed more to surface.

I remember, as a child, hearing a gunshot from next door. My next-door neighbor shot himself in front of his kids and fell down the stairs. The neighbor was shocked. My stepfather asked me if I had heard the shot. "Yes," I replied. I was too young to really understand the gravity.

The suicide monster had been lurking near already then.

My mother was the final home run.

Now it was attacking me.

I switched back to my own tree in front of me. I went all the way through with it in my mind. Every detail. When I finished going through it, I thought with terror in my heart, "What does this mean now? Am I going to want to do it? Is the feeling stronger? Is the next step the hardware store?"

I waited. I still felt the same. I was tuning into the voice of my heart. What was there? I felt peace. I felt the same. I felt ok. It was only a silly, controlling thought. Had I done it? What now?

The anxiety and panic were gone, and the fear lifted. I entered the darkest, scariest cave of my life and expected to find a bear, but I only found bat guano. No monster. No grizzly bear.

I peeped in the terror box and found nothing. Only now, with the box lid open, it was lighter. The darkness had turned to light. The fear was gone because my heart had spoken. All I was dealing with were dark thoughts. Dark thoughts hiding in the recesses of my mind, secretly controlling and tormenting me. Claiming me as a victim whenever I wandered too close to the cave. I had brought awareness now they had fled.

I wanted to banish these thoughts forever and destroy this fear completely. I wanted it to be the last time I would be tormented.

I sat waiting. Listening to my inner world. Tuning into my heart again. "What is the next step to destroy this?" I asked.

A question arose…

"Daniel, do you really want to kill yourself?"

More fear emerged instantly.

I did not want to answer this question.

I did not know the answer.

Instinctively, I knew I needed to go into it again. The battle was won, but the war was not over. It was another box with another big monster. The only way to defeat it… open the box. I took a deep breath. I allowed my mind to run the details.

"Firstly," I thought, "I don't feel like I have a life right now anyway." I asked myself, "What am I even living for? I thought of my life; "I am a walking zombie. No mom. No health. Everything I know is no longer. I don't know where I am going or what to do. Nothing is the same. I am useless, and days are passing in a haze. Why am I even alive?"

My mind's point of view was rather bleak. It wasn't a "yes", but it wasn't a "no" either.

"Undecided," was the final verdict of the mind.

Then, for one of the first times in my conscious life, I asked my heart the same question. It was direct communication with my heart. A heart-to-heart with myself.

"Daniel, do you really want to kill yourself?"

I searched my heart for the answer.

It was warm and confident.

I slightly rephrased the question, "Daniel, do you really *feel* like killing yourself?" I had learnt *feeling* was the language of the heart.

I listened.

I sensed comfort.

I sensed contentment, happiness, and peace were present within me.

My heart knew this was exactly where I needed to be.

It knew everything was going to be ok.

As I 'felt around' in my heart for an answer, a sense of excitement emerged for my future. My heart told me this was all part of a wild adventure through life and we would overcome it. Eventually, we would step into a new life which my mind could never have imagined. It simply didn't have enough information to know where we were going.

More excitement welled up in my heart.

I was listening deeply.

"A new life!" my heart shouted with glee.

My heart confirmed I still had much life to live. Sure, it wasn't happening now, and the situation wasn't rosy, but this was a passing moment in a much longer scale of my life. Something was built into my heart's intelligence, knowing we would get out of this mess eventually. My heart didn't want to quit or cheat its way out of life.

"This demon of suicide ends here with me," it said.

"This whole scenario is a small blip on the radar of your entire life."

"No," was the verdict of my heart in matters of cutting my precious life short. It was a big "NO".

My final answer depended on who I was listening to.

An "Undecided" from the mind and a big, definite "No" from the heart.

That was it.

Something inside me snapped.

I was suddenly freed. I had certainty. Direction. Conviction. The fear vanished. The cards landed in their place. I reached some kind of definite conclusion by way of the majority feeling that no matter what happened, I would not take my life by my own hand. I had too much life to live. My heart revealed this to me. Something new came over me, or something old left me. Or both. I couldn't tell but I knew I had jumped over a massive hurdle. I had, by grace, conquered something monstrous in my life. A mental pattern, a sick spirit, a curse, generational baggage plaguing my family for centuries—we were free. The gorilla on my back, who had been hanging around my neck for years, had now been faced. With the power of my heart, the fear of dying like my mother was burned away.

I said it out loud to be sure; "By my hand, I will never take my life."

I let the statement sit with me.

It was true.

I had committed to living a full life. Free of torment. In total peace.

I felt solid, confident, grounded and sure. The matter had been dealt with and put to bed. I could now move on.

Life force surged within me. I repeatedly committed to the promise, "By my hand, I will never take my life." It was easy and hard because now I would have to find a new way. I could begin a new life where the torment of suicide was no longer welcome or present. I had regained the power over those unwelcome thoughts and could now start looking for solutions instead of being trapped in a fear dungeon. Now I could focus on healing because I didn't have another option. Now I could create a different life because I ruled out the 'quick exit' strategy. I said to myself, "If I need to become homeless, insane, live in the wilderness, or become a shoemaker on the coast of Italy, I will do that rather than take my life." It was revelatory. I was willing to change. To be malleable. To be refreshed. The black-and-white thoughts which plagued me for years were lifted. They were handed back to the place of darkness from whence they had come. By the sheer grace of God and His presence in my heart, I had faced my demons and busted one of my biggest fears.

COMPLETE HANDOVER

IF THOSE WILD, unhealthy thoughts ever tried to resurface, I was prepared for battle. Like a warrior in full armor drawing his sword, I would immediately and confidently say, "Sorry, I've decided I'm not going to kill myself."

It was liberating. They were chopped down mid-attack. *Did my family line run from these thoughts? Did people all over the world deal with these out-of-place interruptions? Did these thoughts bend us to their will before we realized the life we were living was not ours but one based on fear?* They were sometimes subtle and dangerous as well as loud and terrifying. *Perhaps,* I pondered, *that's why there is a family line of addiction to drugs and alcohol in my lineage.* I had made a stand against it. I would not be passing this curse to any of my blood. There was no longer a contract for the thoughts to hold onto. I was a new creation, willing to forgive and forget. I prayed God would dissolve and forgive anything someone might have done in my family for us to deserve it. I was covering all the bases. Not only with my own but with God's healing power, it was over.

Those thoughts died forever.

The demon of suicide left.

There was no more space for it.

Paralyzing fear was replaced with prayer.

The extra 'head space' I received became filled with gratitude and life.

I decided I would no longer live my life in "black and white." The journey of the heart was a more "in-between" existence than a "pick this or pick that". The Heart knew the way but my mind didn't know the detail. I would trust this process. *How can I know the plan God has for me? To realize it, I have to let go.* Surrendering to my heart I was happy to be whatever God wanted me to be. Whatever Life was calling me to be.

Not knowing.

Trusting.

Forging of a new personality which would serve my highest good and those around me.

A personality that supported my purpose and found pleasure in becoming who I was set aside to be.

With some major fears wrestled, more peace returned to my heart and mind—but the surrender wasn't completely over. A final phase still loomed. The journey to real wellness had one more major battle.

The tipping point between my old life and my newer version arrived on an idle weekday.

I woke up feeling highly uncomfortable in my emotional body. As usual, there was nothing I could really pin it to. My inner world moved restlessly, while my outer world was mundane as laundry. From deep in the dungeons, a feeling of despair and hopelessness crept up.

"Oh God, why me? Why am I still in this? When is this going to end?"

I was lying in bed pleading with our Creator. The slowness of my life and recovery weighed on me more than usual. My heart was breaking for a taste of my old life. Grief and frustration bubbled in my inner soup of turmoil.

I got out of bed, desperate to change my space and create some freshness. I opened my bedroom door and went to my deck. Waves of grief overcame me, for my life, my mother's life, for the things I had and hadn't done, and for the difficulty of real life. I walked onto the patch of grass where I had seen 'little ducky' only days before. I had nothing left to give. I was nothing.

I paused on that patch of grass.

I lifted my head to look up at the sky.

I watched the clouds, the deep blue, then I fixed my gaze beyond, into the infinite.

I gazed into the Beyond with the eyes of my heart.

I lifted up my arms open wide, open to the sky, in a posture of total receptiveness and surrender.

From the depths of my heart, a prayer pleaded itself up to the heavens;

God, if You're out there, I give up.

My heart was cracking open as I continued.

I thought I was at rock bottom and now I realize I don't even know what rock bottom is.

I sobbed at the pieces of my life.

Only You know God. Only You know what is to come. I know nothing. I can't handle any more of this. I give up. I give myself over to You. Take my life. Use it. It's Yours.

Silence.

I dropped to my knees.

My arms still open to the sky.

Then I crumbled into a little ball.

Humble before the mighty infinite.

Small.

I handed my entire heart over to God.

I felt it.

I gave it all up.

I needed someone else to take the steering wheel.

I wouldn't fight anymore.

I didn't know what to fight for.

I surrendered.

I surrendered my heart to God.

I gave it to Him.

To have and to hold.

To make my life a success or a mess.

To mold me into who I needed to become.

I opened the gates of my heart so Heaven could pour in.

I didn't think about surrendering. I felt it.

It was God's turn to save me.

Not by my strength, but by His.

I gave up on who I thought I needed to be.

I gave up on thinking I was able to handle anything.

I gave in totally to God.

I committed my heart into God's infinite hands.

Tears flowed from my face as I remained in a little ball on the ground.

Humbling myself before the King of the Universe.

I remained there for some time, gently sobbing, knowing I had truly given up.

I knew in my heart from that moment on, I was ready to completely trust in Him. I would listen to His voice in my heart and follow it relentlessly and obediently. I would trust He knew where I needed to go. I would give it my best shot until I 'arrived' somewhere. I would put my own agendas aside and see if I could follow God's agendas instead. I would no longer do what I wanted to.

In one sense, it was like dying whilst I was still alive.

I was becoming less so He could become more.

I was scared, but I had nowhere left to turn.

I had given everything I had.

Little did I know this death would make me more alive than I had ever been in my entire life.

It wasn't a 'giving up' as much as it was a 'giving back'. Giving back my life to the God who sent me. A submission to an Infinite authority who knew better than I. A recommitment to the intelligence of the heart, which draws its wisdom from heavenly places.

This moment would carry me to True Life. Eternal life and eternal aliveness.

It would give my soul its purpose and fulfillment.

I died so the dance of my heavenly self could flow forth.

I died so I could hear the music again.

I surrendered to the song of my soul, seated up high.

SURRENDER EXPERIMENTS

AFTER THE GREAT handover, my life didn't change radically overnight, but a deeper peace arrived, knowing I was no longer in control. I was now a servant of Love. The change in my heart brought smaller changes in my life. One of these changes was in my prayer life. I shifted from asking for things like 'money' or 'health' to; "God, please guide me as to what *You* need me to do" or "God, please bring me what *You* know I need".

It wasn't about me anymore.

I was slowly losing the "me first" attitude.

I slowly opened up to receive His wisdom.

I prayed to be protected and walk in step with His will.

I prayed I could trust in God to help me through this.

Then one day… something did happen.

It was to take my surrender to a new level and shift forever my question if God was really with me.

It was a day when the cold, gray weather perfectly matched my inner landscape.

I was lying in bed and thinking, *Why is everything so gray? Haven't I handed myself over?*

Why is nothing happening?

Why aren't my prayers being answered?

Despair turned to anger within me.

"God, are You even out there? Why aren't you helping me? I've given you what You want."

I channeled my anger up toward the heavens.

"God, why are You doing this to me? Why am I stuck, not able to do anything? WHAT DO YOU WANT ME TO DO?"

I demanded help fiercely in my heart.

Where was this supernatural intelligence of the world now? Why had I not had another miracle or even some direction since the 'Great Handover'?

I cried out from my heart, "You need to come right now and guide me to something that will help me. I don't know what to do anymore. Are you hearing me?"

This anger gave me energy.

Sheer frustration motivated my ejection from bed.

I put on my shoes and marched out of my room.

If God wasn't bringing me a sign, I would go out and get one.

I decided to walk out of my front gate and just go. I would "let go and let God" and see what happened.

No plan. No destination.

Will he lead me?

Will he be there for me?

I had asked Him to, and now it was time.

My intention was to leave the house and see where I was guided. I would simply listen and watch for a sign. Not by my will, but by His.

I decided in my heart that God was going to guide me because I was going to let Him.

I couldn't spend another hour in my tiny room.

"Ludicrous," my mind said as I started walking away from my house.

I exited the garden gate and walked about 20 meters until I reached the stop sign at the beginning of the cul-de-sac.

What now? Where are you, God?

I listened. I looked around.

Nothing.

I turned my attention upwards towards the heavens again. Fixing my heart on the direction of the Infinite.

"Which way do You want me to go, Lord?"

I stood in the street waiting for a sign, a feeling, anything.

"Seriously, God, show me. Left, straight, or right?"

I stood still.

What am I even waiting for? I didn't know, but I would not move until something guided me.

"Left or right? Left or right?" I repeated.

Nothing.

I paused.

I shifted all my attention and focus to my inner world. If I couldn't see anything outside, I would listen on the inside.

Suddenly I had an impulse to use my awareness to scan over my body. I was reminded of a book where the indigenous tribes of Southern Africa spoke about asking for guidance from the Great Spirit so they could *feel* where the animals were to hunt.

If God guided them, why wouldn't He guide me?

I wasn't exactly tracking animals but maybe God would direct my body too.

I scanned my physical body with my awareness up and down.

"This is crazy," my mind chimed in.

I stood there. I felt my entire body waiting for something.

My entire awareness was focused on the inside now. I wasn't looking for birds or cars or signs. "Come on, God, if you can do all the other stuff with me, You can guide me like this. I am Yours".

I kept praying in my heart; *I'm completely submitted, I'm completely submitted.*

Use me.

Dance me.

Puppeteer me.

It was the subtlest, tiny sensation on the left side of my body. Like a little tingle. A little pull. It was so easily overlooked I was doubtful. *Should I go left? Is this real? Is this really something? Did I imagine it?*

I did another internal check, waiting for the Master Puppeteer.

"Left?" I asked myself. I felt a small *yes.*

I could feel something subtle and invisible there.

"Right?" I asked. I felt absolutely nothing. A hollow abyss.

"Left?" I asked again.

The softest, tiniest, smallest voice somehow gave the gentlest feeling and sensation toward the left.

"Right?" Nothing.

Fine, I'm going left!

It was madness to my mind, yet here I was, in this great surrender experiment.

So off I went to the left.

Down the road.

I arrived at another stop street 50 meters later.

"Ok, same thing… left, right, or straight, God?" I stood there. Determined I would wait for a signal again. I would not move on my own accord or according to my own thoughts.

I pleaded again. "Please, God, show me the way. Use my body. Talk to me through my body. If you created this and I am a part of this great whole, I know you can use it to speak to me. Guide me. Lead me." Again, I brought awareness to my body to feel if I should go left, right, or straight.

"Left?" Nothing.

"Right?" Not sure.

"Straight?" Bingo! A definite sensation to go straight rather than right. *Why does straight feel better?* I had no idea. It just did, I couldn't deny it. It was the subtlest of intuitive guidance, but it was there.

I was feeling my way through this journey of surrender.

I crossed the street and went down the steps onto a grassy path by a river bank. "Oh God, where am I going to end up? Is this complete madness? Please look after me." Again, the same thing, another junction. Left alongside the stream or straight through the parking lot?

I waited. Not moving until I was sure. Scanning. Asking. Feeling. Praying. Then it came. Definitely a small sensation on the right-hand side with the tiniest pull to go to the right. Off I went along the bank to the right of the nursery.

I had nothing to prove. Nowhere to be. No destination.

I was walking with God.

I noticed some people on the street below where I was standing. I thought about what they were doing in their worlds and what I was doing in mine. "Has anyone ever played this game?" I thought. *When people see me on the outside, do they realize what I am going through?*

I kept walking down the main road. I didn't care where I ended up, I had nothing to lose. At every turn, I followed the sensations in my body or the gut feeling I had. There was always the subtlest of pulls if I listened closely enough.

Eventually, I walked down roads I had never been before.

This style of adventure was taking me off my normal track.

I worried I might run out of energy to get home.

Then I said, "This is on You, God. It is You leading me. It is Your responsibility".

I was committed to seeing the experiment all the way through.

I continued walking.

I was headed towards a rather dangerous part of the town now. *Will I get killed?* I could see the headlines already: 'Hout Bay man stabbed near township'.

"Well," my mind said, "at least it's an easier road out of your current life situation."

Suddenly, my body called to veer off the main road and take a right turn up a side street. I had never been up this road before, but I was happy I was no longer heading toward potential danger.

"Thank you, God," I said quietly to myself.

After a few steps, I noticed a single tennis court on the right-hand side, nestled amongst some suburban houses. I felt a strong pull to sit on some concrete steps alongside the court. In my heart, body, and intuition, it was clear I needed to sit and watch the two old men playing tennis. It was certainly not my desire to intrude on this tennis match. I felt like a strange, creepy person staring at men enjoying their private tennis game. But I couldn't deny it—this was where the Puppet Master wanted me to be. He was pulling the strings, He was resting me here. I was practicing obedience. I had arrived simply from listening. It was not my will.

I remember thinking clearly, "Well, look at your amazing life, Dan. Here you are watching two old men playing tennis on some random day of the week whilst losing your mind."

I could hear the judgment of my mind's voice loud and clear, but it didn't matter. I was going to stay there until I felt like I had to move. I reflected upon my small bedroom where I was earlier, "Anything is better than lying in bed all day," I said to comfort myself. "If this is where surrender has brought me, I will not leave until I feel like something significant has happened."

Lost in the tension of my mind's accusing and critical thoughts, I didn't notice a change of sides in the tennis match. As I looked up, one of the old men was at the fence in front of me, reaching for his water bottle.

I suddenly had the strongest urge to make conversation with him.

This was surprising for me. I seldomly ignited small talk with anybody.

As the man unscrewed the lid of his water bottle he suddenly said to me, "Great day for a game, hey. Perfect weather. How are you?"

He looked happy and content.

The chains on my mouth suddenly broke. Before I could calculate a reply, I blurted out, "Ya perfect weather. As for me, I'm not so okay, actually. I've got family stuff going on and I'm really struggling with a disease called M.E. You've probably never heard of it. It's a virus taking all my energy, so ya."

The words automatically came tumbling out of me.

I was embarrassed by the sudden outpouring of feelings.

Here was a complete stranger onto whom I spilled my dramatic life and medical woes. I waited for his apprehensive looks or judgment. He appeared completely unphased. He bent down to put his water bottle back into his tennis bag and casually replied, "Well, look at me, after having M.E. for 15 years, I can play tennis again."

He walked to the other side of the tennis court to continue his match.

My mind exploded.

Three simple sentences. That's all it took. I was speechless. I was stunned. Shocked. Of all the people in the whole world, my walk with Surrender had led me to a fellow chronic fatigue and M.E. sufferer. A person who likewise would have been bed-ridden, energyless, and in complete despair at some point in his life. A friend with chronic illness. Yet here he was, playing a game of tennis with his friend and running around the court.

His few words flipped my world upside down.

Did this experiment actually work? Had the sensations in my body really led me here? Was this a coincidence? Was God guiding me? What on earth just happened?

Tears welled in my eyes as uncertainty bubbled in my heart.

I felt connected to something much bigger than my own little life.

I wanted to cry and hug him and hear his whole life story.

I finally had hope.

Meeting this man was a living example; I could return to health and joy.

It was exactly what I needed.

It was possible.

My heart burst with reverence and humility.

I decided I would recommit all my energy to this mission of conquering my chronic illness. With God's help.

If I surrendered, I could get there.

God had brought me the miracle, a shining a light at the end of a dark tunnel.

There was no more doubt left—I could win—with God.

THE DANCE OF THE
SCATTER CUSHIONS

WITH ALL THE death and dying, shifting of perspectives, truth bombs, surrender, and supernatural encounters, I tried my best to keep up and give myself extra love. I started to treat myself in ways I never had before. This sometimes meant buying myself comforting things from the shops, visiting Saturday organic markets to purchase the healthiest food, going for massages, haircuts, or other things I thought would nourish my body, mind, and soul during this challenging time. By exploring this new frontier of self-love, I broke more of the boundaries of my personality. Stretching myself to include new things, "hippie" things, alternate things, and strange things, which often turned out not to be alternate or strange at all. They were simply new experiences I had previously judged. They were useful and necessary for creating a healthy, holy, balanced life.

A real revelation of how far I had come arrived one day when I went to a local shopping center.

I went with the intention of buying two scatter cushions for my little room. Two simple scatter cushions might seem normal to most, yet, I could hardly believe what I was doing. It went against every-thing I thought I would do in my life. Until now, I had always been wary of extra household items, especially scatter cushions. When I was a young boy living at home with my mother, I would ask, "What is the point of these things on the couch? Why do I have to have these on my bed? What do they even do?!"

In my mind, they were the epitome of materialistic commercial-ism—a waste of material objects destined to somehow pollute the world. Sebastian and I had previously discussed the futility of these tiny cushions, which we deemed could not be used for anything practical. What was the point? They hogged the space on couches, beds, and sofas around the world. For what? Yet here I was now, in my new life, following the subtle calling in my heart which spoke—*two scatter cushions will look nice in this room*. I had to overcome myself to follow this. As simple as it seems, it was the first in a long line of "breaking self." I was stepping through judgments my old self had created to forge into a new territory of personality. It wasn't the task of purchasing the cushion, it was a test of obedience.

My dance of the scatter cushions wasn't easy. It was time for me to be a normal consumer and enjoy it. I was growing up. When I arrived at the local store, embarrassment accompanied me as my shopping partner. I strode sheepishly across the floor to the shop attendant.

Oh gosh, I thought, *he is going to judge me so much.*

"Do you have any scatter cushions?" I asked, the words coming out like thick porridge.

He didn't flinch and walked me straight to the shelves.

It was my own judgments judging me, not anyone else's. Buying scatter cushions was normal to most of society, but not to me and my mind.

I had no idea what I was doing or looking for. What made a good scatter cushion? I was deeply out of my comfort zone. He showed me the shelf and left me there. I reached out my hand and felt the texture and patterns of some. *What does one look for in the ideal scatter cushion? Where was a teammate to help me choose? Shouldn't I call a female friend for help? Is that a sexist thought? I'm lost!*

I reached out to them on the shelf. Small, big, hard, soft. All kinds of fabric covering them, all kinds of colors. Immediately I discarded the ones with a rough outer cover—the kind which imprints a pattern on your arm or face once you've fallen asleep. I didn't want to doze off in my chair to wake up with indented pictures of embroidered flowers on my cheeks.

Aha! I thought as I moved to the bottom shelf. There they are.

Sitting on the shelf were two beautiful, light green, medium-sized scatter cushions. I knew immediately these were the ones.

Exactly what I'm looking for!

I was chuffed with myself.

I wonder if this color will work with the new picnic blanket I recently bought?

Oh God! I thought. *Who have I become?*

A new person. Thank you, God.

MEETING THE MIRACULOUS

SUPERNATURAL HEART ENERGY

LET'S REWIND THE clock to when I had to participate in two major events which frightened my energy reserves. The first—host my mother's memorial service on our country's east coast. The second—fly to her last place of residence and pack up her belongings. I had ample support at both these gatherings, but these were two things that were very far from my M.E. radar: 1. flights and 2. crowds of people. I would have to do a lot of both. This was not my plan. God had his own design. I was scared. Worried I would slide backward into disease. Worried it might set me back months.

I had no choice.

Life was calling the shots.

After stressing about my wellbeing and packing all the nutritional supplements I could fit into my bag, I headed for the first commitment—the memorial service on the east coast of the country (nearest to most of our family).

I slept on the floor of my sister's apartment.

I was at my wit's end.

I recited a poem for my mother on the day of her memorial.

One I had written. I called it the "Bush Baby". My mother loved the bush.

It was heartfelt.

It was surreal.

Standing up to speak about the most important person in my life with whom I would no longer have an earthly relationship with. No calls. No messages. No feeling of a sense of home in her presence. No love being poured out on me.

The weekend passed in a haze of family members, memories, tears, and pat-on-the-back condolences.

This is real life, I thought. *All the other stuff I've been worrying about is trivial compared to this.*

I did have one moment I thought I wouldn't make it through the weekend. I was at breaking point. I didn't know where to turn. What to do. I walked outside my sister's apartment and put my yoga mat on the ground. I did some stretches and tried to calm my mind. Waves of feeling crashed into me; anger, depression, fear, sadness, tragedy.

My emotional body was overwhelmed and sick.

It is difficult to fall apart gracefully.

The weekend was a blur, but I made it through. I arrived back in Cape Town stunned and hollow.

Surprisingly, I wasn't any sicker than when I left.

I wasn't better, but I was still ok considering all the driving, traveling, emotions, eating poorly, and lack of routine. The trip proved—what I thought I needed didn't always matter. I was ok. It was mind-boggling. Usually one-tenth of that activity level could bed-bound me for a week. Yet, after all the random people, sleepless nights, endless handshakes, and hours of talking—I was standing. It didn't make sense; I had energy.

God won't take me to it if I can't get through it.

It seemed when there was no other way. I was supported by a Life force that didn't come from me, it came through me, to do what I needed to do.

When the Grand Puppet Master orchestrated the dance, I could boogie all day.

With His energy on His terms, I could ride the storm.

The trip to the north east interior of the country would further cement this belief.

A SORTING TRIP TO THE BUSH

MY MOTHER'S LAST abode was on the opposite side of the country from where I lived. I needed to fly for longer and be gone for a longer period of time than my trip to the east coast. More exertion would be required—the energy expense of sorting through her things, packing cars, moving boxes, driving long distances to get to various places. Not to mention another memorial service we were hosting in the nearby town. This meant another speech for me, another stream of tears, and more pats on the back. On top of this, I contracted a rather intense case of the flu before the trip.

Double sick and stressed to the max was no good start to this adventure. Any M.E. sufferer will tell you that getting out of bed for a few hours is a good day. This trip would be a few days.

I flew in on a small plane to the local airport—it was the closest town to where my far-flung family lived. As they put our luggage on an open trailer on the runway, I watched various tourists gearing up for the African experience of a lifetime. Meanwhile, I was gearing up for a different kind of African experience of a lifetime.

My family was waiting for me, and as we reunited, I'm sure the same thought floated in all our minds, *lovely to see you but a pity about the circumstances.* Why do we need death to bring us together?

We spent the evening catching up and immediately started sorting through my mother's belongings.

Tears flowed from the eyes of various family members. My aunt broke down sobbing as she picked up some artifacts that reminded her of their shared youth.

The next day we went off to my mother's last place of residence. The scene of the crime. It was off the beaten path along dirt roads as she resided and managed a lodge in the heart of the African bush. I had really wanted to visit my mom a few months before but couldn't at the time with my health crisis. She had encouraged me a few times, and my response in a voice note was, "I don't have the energy, mom." Yet, lo and behold, here I was.

As we arrived and got out of the car, the staff greeted us warmly. They were obviously expecting us. They took us to the lodge and I could see touches of my mother's presence immediately. In the paintings on the walls (which used to hang in our family home), her office desk, the way the staff members' eyes lit up when they found out we were the children of Michelle. I could feel she had been much loved there.

I remember being guided toward her room by the staff. With each step, resistance and fear pushed against me. Unspoken anxiety, contemplation—deep soul-stirring music filled the invisible orchestra of unspoken conversations amongst us. *What will we find? Will it scar us for life? Am I ready to face these facts that I won't be able to forget?* These were some of my life's longest and scariest steps, trodding across the dusty African ground toward her cottage.

We arrived at the door. I looked around outside. It was the perfect environment for her. Nature, bush, wild animals, quietude. Everything she loved.

Someone opened the door and we walked in. It was small and

tidy. I imagined her busying herself around her room, cleaning, as she loved to do. Her room was neat. I wondered if she tidied it purposefully moments before the end. I walked up to the side of her bed.

There on the bedside table was her diary. It was open on a page. The last page she ever wrote. I paused nervously. *Should I read it? Will this haunt me for life?* The other family members were busy in their own thought bubbles, so I nervously glanced down. *Do I really want to know her last thoughts?* I steeled myself.

At the top of the page was written, *THINGS I AM GRATEFUL FOR*. It was heart-wrenching. It was the closest I had been to my mother's final moments.

There was a list underneath the heading;

1) The sound of birds.

2) My children.

3)…

Number 3) was blank.

There were no more items on the list.

My heart sank.

Nothing more to be grateful for.

Only an empty number three on a page with lots of white space. The number three kept staring up at me. It appeared my mother had been trying to practice gratitude, and yet she couldn't gather three things to be grateful for. Had she given up? Could I ever know how hard that must have been? To live like that.

I tried to compose myself as my heart tore a little more, and my eyes glistened with grief.

I then saw my sister walking towards the bathroom. I knew the bathroom was the scene of the incident, I followed.

As I entered, I looked around.

Time slowed down. It was a normal bathroom, yet nothing was normal about it. I glanced down and noticed my sister standing in a small, dried pool of blood. It must have been my mothers'. This was where my mother had taken her own life.

It felt like a nightmare and yet peacefully surreal at the same time. Normal time suspended as I stared into the space of disbelief and the unimaginable imagined. Here we were. Sister and brother standing in the bathroom of dreams we didn't dream. The final place. Exit through the bathroom.

Behind my sister was the bullet hole in the wall where it had lodged in the tiles after passing through our mother's heart. What does one say in a moment like this? I felt like a puppet in someone else's life.

Doesn't this happen to other people?

How has this happened to our family?

What are we doing here?

Thoughts buzzed around my mind like a tragic movie.

Other family members joined us at the scene of the crime. The little bathroom filled up. My aunt said when she found my mother on the floor, she looked very peaceful. I couldn't imagine having to face the scene, although hearing it was peaceful was slightly comforting.

We stood like chess pieces before a strategic move on the board. All taking in the moment. Then someone moved, and it was time for business.

We had much sorting to do.

My mother had stuff everywhere with everyone.

We had to clean and clear and clean and clear.

It was like sorting through an entire home that she had somehow carried across the country. *Why had she not sold this stuff or given it away after her divorce or the closure of our family home years before? What was she holding on to?* As we went through box after box, it appeared my mother was hanging onto much—as if she couldn't let go of all of the stuff that reminded her of her former life. I wondered if she was holding onto all this stuff outside of her. How much was she holding onto inside of her? Why did she shoot herself in the heart? Was there stuff in her heart that needed to be released?

So many questions the dead leave to the living, possibly never to be solved.

Standing amid that tornado in our lives, we were processing a lot.

The trip floated by in a haze.

Days of weeping, sharing stories, looking at old memories, and deciding who-keeps-what. I didn't have time to think about my illness. I was mainly on autopilot. As I boarded the plane back to Cape Town, it suddenly dawned on me, "God, where on earth am I getting the energy for this? How am I even moving around still?"

I thought about the doctors I had seen weeks before—they would never believe it. I was a walking M.E. miracle. I realized I had been functioning at normal human capacity. My joy peaked for a moment. I hadn't been able to do anything like it for months. *How had I handled the tornado? Was it adrenaline?* I even had the flu when I left, but somehow I was getting better in the chaos.

It didn't make any sense to me. I had defied what the doctors said was possible for myself. I had gone beyond the rationality of the mind and been supported internally and externally by some unknown life force. I didn't want to accept this, but I couldn't help it. I was living, breathing proof that energy arrived when it had to.

INVISIBLE FUEL

I **BECAME FASCINATED** by this phenomenon. Where had this strength suddenly come from? It was a supernatural strength. I couldn't comprehend that I often lay in bed for days, unable to get up, yet I had accomplished these two major trips and was still on track for healing.

I pondered this deeply: If I looked down at my body, I could still see two pairs of strong quad muscles, a fading six-pack, chiseled sinewy calf muscles from long-distance running, and yet, with all this physical fitness, some days I could still hardly move from bed. Recent tests had shown I was still borderline triathlete-level fit, yet, I could hardly move. The question that tinkered in my brain was this: *If my muscles don't move me, then what does?*

I began to consider what the Chinese had known for centuries or millennia, that some kind of life force must fuel those muscles. I pondered this: *Had the life force carried me through the events of my mother? Why? And why couldn't I have it now?*

It was as if something gave me energy when it wanted and took energy when it wanted. Right now, as I looked at my body, it was as if something was robbing me of some invisible energy that used to feed my muscles but no longer did. *How is this even possible?*

No matter how many chocolates, energy bars, or superfood breakfasts I ate, it didn't generate the energy for me to get up on a bad day. My body was missing some kind of supernatural fuel. A fuel I couldn't see, a fuel I couldn't eat, and a fuel I didn't know how to get. Normally I wouldn't have believed it but the sorting trip to the bush had proved it. I used to believe the harder I trained and the stronger my muscles got, the faster or further I could run. I used to believe the more energy I needed, the more food I must consume. That belief stopped holding weight because here I was with a body of strong muscles but nothing to make it move forward.

Is it possible the virus is eating up this energy? I thought. *What energy is it even eating?* It certainly wasn't eating my flesh, yet M.E. munched on just enough life force to keep itself happy and keep me alive, so it could repeat the process gleefully again and again. The virus never allowed me to be completely empty, but also never allowed me the freedom to be out of survival mode.

I didn't want to think about this invisible force I couldn't see. This was the job of Shaolin monks, maybe a few ninjas or saintly people on a quest for divine knowledge. Eventually I had no choice, I had to learn about energy management because a kinesiologist said it best, "You are in an energy crisis, and you need to learn how to manage it yourself."

THE GREAT ENERGY EXPERIMENT

With this advice and tired of the up-and-down energy cycles, I started my research. It was simple—I would keep a record of things that fueled me and things that drained me. I would rank my energy level each day with a score out of ten on how actions and activities affected me. My plan? Ditch the things that drained me, keep the things that fueled me.

After each interaction, I would discern how I felt. If I were uplifted and joyous, I would note it. If I was drained, I would note it. Watching my calendar and all my actions and interactions, some interesting things emerged.

I found that any stress, particularly emotional stress, reduced my energy drastically. One "bad conversation" or "difficult personal relationship" could have me bedridden for hours. If I was emotionally ill, my brain fog rolled in and incapacitated me. It could take ages to regain normal functioning. I would be slumped in bed.

My emotional body had something to do with my overall health.

I didn't know exactly how, but I could see and feel the results.

Secondly, I noticed I had energy for some events but not others. This was not in my control, it was a fact I had to accept. Whether the event was a business gathering, a personal growth workshop, a trip to the mall or a weekend away, some things I was given stamina for, and others I was not. It was only months later I discovered why.

When you have nothing in your cup, it is easy to discover what pours life in, and what doesn't.

When you have a lot, it is easy to be wasteful with your precious life.

DANCING ON THE MOUNTAIN

One day, a Secret Sunrise dance event appeared in my calendar. This was during my great energy experiment, so it was on my "energy watch list". I was wary because it was certain to entail high physical exertion levels. Even so, my heart was for it. It was a milestone in my life. Secret Sunrise had been permitted to host a dance on Cape Town's iconic Table Mountain.

At this point, after the funerals, the 21-day grieving process, the surrender, and everything in between, I was still facing the reality that doctors had told me "not to overdo it". They'd encouraged me not to use more than 50 percent of my available energy. They called it the 50/50 rule. If I wanted to walk to the beach on a particular day, I would need to walk halfway and then turn around and head home. Seemingly, 50 percent of my energy was for living, and the other 50 percent was for healing. Or so the theory went. Yet, here I was faced again with the decision: do I proceed with this journey to the city, head up a mountain, dance for at least an hour, connect with friends and work colleagues and then return home? It was going to shatter the 50/50 rule.

The motivating factor was that it was a once-in-a-lifetime event. My previous personal ambitions were now a reality. I had dreamt of this day, hundreds of people dancing on the mountain, joy being shared. I simply couldn't miss it. I decided I would rather die dancing than miss the moment of a lifetime. To help myself I would be very prepared—smoothies, breathing exercises, snacks, and energy supplements.

I arrived at the base of Table mountain. At the entrance, I greeted my fellow employees and interns, careful not to expend too much energy on small talk. A cable car lifted us to the top of the mountain, and we walked around a restaurant to the dance floor. High above the city and ocean, we were nestled amongst a colorful group of people and a mishmash of strewn boulders. It was beautiful and surreal. A couple hundred people gathered on top of one of the natural wonders of the world, ready to experience joy. As the live piano played, soft wisps of clouds floated up and over the mountain at sunset.

I climbed onto a big rock and danced on my own. People were on boulders around me, each in their own headspace and heartspace—lost in the wonderful facilitation of the musical guidance that a Secret Sunrise brings. My mind was placed to the side as I moved to the rhythm of my heartstrings. I forgot I was ill. My heart came alive. Joy arrived. Fun flowed. I played, smiled, laughed, and connected in a way I hadn't done in weeks. Wild, free, and expressive. This was Secret Sunrise's promise—Music, Movement, Connection, and I was literally and physically on top of the world. I danced the entire event. At one point I lifted my arms to the skies, tears rolling down my cheeks. This was being alive.

I went beyond the edge of strenuous. It wasn't the 50/50 the doctors had recommended. It was more like 300/50. The dance ended. I posed for some pictures. I was elated. Electric. I was on top of the world. As the buzz slowly faded, I looked in my bag for water and noticed the various smoothies. I gazed at them as I faintly remembered I was supposed to be ill. They were strangers in my suitcase. They didn't seem to matter in that moment. I ignored them. I had more than enough energy to go out for dinner and socialize late into the night. I was still electric when I went to bed. For someone who had no energy most of the time, it was miraculous.

I was overflowing.

I woke up the next morning completely refreshed. My body was slightly stiff from the exercise but I could move around. I got on with my day easily and no brain fog tormented me. Somehow this dance activity was invisible fuel. I'd discovered a secret medicine. It was as if my being knew this was my purpose, and when I practiced it, I was rewarded. I made notes on my energy schedule next to Secret Sunrise dancing—"Uplift," it read. I began to do it again and again.

I couldn't do much else, but I could definitely dance. Secret Sunrise helped the inner sun to rise within me. It was joy fuel. It was healing. It wasn't only me who attended for this reason, many others received the same medicine, but for me, as an M.E. sufferer, it was life-giving. It was like sipping from the cup of life itself. I struggled with this thought, *Why on earth was Life leading me to be a dancer?* I never wanted to be a dancer. I wanted to be a strategist and an advertising man.

I didn't have a choice. My mind needed to come along—my experience of receiving energy was all the proof I needed. When I picked up the microphone to facilitate a dance, it was like coming home. The world dissolved. It still does. The words come automatically. I forget everything and become one with the dance.

Little did I know I was returning to the river of my life. My calling. My purpose. I had spent too many years trying to do what I thought I should do. Too many years on the riverbank, watching the river go by. Now I was being guided back to the main current.

An infinite well of energy was opening up to me.

I wanted to follow it. I had to follow it. It was the difference between going with the river or fighting it.

I chose to dance.

PERSONAL VS. INFINITE

This experiment taught me the importance of "personal energy" compared to "infinite energy". Whenever I thought I *had to* do something and tried to do it, I was running on personal energy. When I *felt* like doing something, I was running on infinite energy. Let's say I had built up a good energy reserve for over two weeks. If my mind told me I had to go into the office to check up on people (out of fear that things were going astray), this action might cost me a day lying in bed. If I did things out of guilt, fear, worry, concern, or stress, I was clearly using personal energy. If I was forcing myself, I was running on borrowed time.

Fear does not support life.

Personal energy was finite.

It runs out quickly.

The opposite was true if I was operating from what I called "infinite energy". These were things I had to do not because my mind called me but because my heart was willing me. These were things I did from a place of love or because there was an unexplainable curiosity or invisible draw to do them. These things were things

I simply had to do. Not by my choice but because Life positioned me in such a way I could not deny them.

When I did things Life was guiding me to (by showing me a few signs or chance encounters or conversations or prayers), I was divinely supported. My energy was constant and sustaining. Doors of opportunity flung open. In these moments I was able to reach beyond my chronic illness limitations. When I truly listened to my heart and did things not from fear but from love, I wasn't running on my own gasoline, I was running on divine petrol.

This concept also applied to the mundane. Every task in my life is measured. Cooking, sweeping, gardening. They are all supported by the same invisible force. That force chooses when to supply. I might receive a supply for a certain task in one week, and not another. In one year, and not another. This is divine timing, receiving the resources from God for the work He has laid out for me. I could be looking at the same laptop, the same emails—the only difference is that some email content on some days would ignite me, whilst on other days, it would deflate me. Sometimes the content felt like life, and sometimes it felt like death. I knew I had no option but to spend time in places that gave me "uplift". If the circle came around again, I would be able to re-handle emails which I could not a few months before. But divinity was calling me to something else in the interim. It is important to listen to this because you never know when God has an important assignment for you.

When we learn to trust in life and how we are being resourced, we learn to spend our energy according to divine plans.

After a period of time with my great energy experiment, a theme emerged for me on what topped me up during this time (which is different now and will be different next year). I was called to do more of these activities: dancing freely, praying, sitting in the mountains, listening to natural running water, meditating on rocks at sunset, engaging in meaningful conversations with new friends, and taking time for emotional releases. I had to make space for these activities. Time didn't appear. I had to include them in my "life-giving" engagements. These activities were 'top ups', but when I was placed perfectly in my purpose, I was fully alive and buzzing with energy. I was electric. I didn't know my purpose at this stage, but I knew when I was *ALIVE*. I figured the two went together.

So, what made me feel most alive, I did more of. Eventually my life became a buzz.

Nowadays, I can "work" 7 days a week, but I'm not really working because I'm not striving for anything. I'm only doing what I am receiving the resources for.

If I feel like I am forcing myself, I stop. I cannot live separate from God.

The only force I like to live on is Life Force. Not from my hand but from the Creator.

Doing "uplift" activities slowly created a life full of purpose for me. By engaging in more real-world examples of aliveness, my purpose unfolds. I try to follow the invisible law of Life's current.

The great energy experiment taught me two valuable lessons;

Stop resisting the current of life.

Be the lightbulb.

THE BIRD AND THE DIVER

TO SOME, THESE energy experiments are common knowledge. To me, this inner discovery was miraculous. During the season of miracles, I wasn't only met with invisible miracles, but I was a part of some undeniably plain-to-see miracles too.

One evening, lying on my "I-don't-know-what-to-do-with-my-life" boulder on the mountainside, I was pleading with God. My heart was heavy and I was praying for a sign. Internally I was crying out for something to happen which would bring a positive change in my life.

I needed His help.

Sitting on the boulder with my eyes closed, flowing between meditation and deep prayers, my eyes suddenly popped open. As they did, they locked on a little bird perched on a stick below me. It was close to the ground. It cocked its head as it peered at me. Hop hop it went, on its springy little legs as it dropped to the ground. It peered at me curiously again. It was rather interested in what I was up to on my rock. I looked at it. It cocked its head again to the side as if wonderfully curious. I kept staring at it. Then, in a single motion, it hopped from its branch to the ground and looked back at me again. I looked at it. It hopped away a little. It looked back at me, then hopped a little way again.

I felt a strange 'pull' to follow the bird. Was it curiosity? Was it something more? A whisper in me said, "Climb down from the rock and follow the little bird—see where it goes". Only moments ago, I had been praying for "anything", and "anything" appeared to have arrived, so I hopped down from the rock.

I thought the little bird would fly away.

It didn't.

He hopped.

I followed.

He hopped.

I followed.

Together down the mountain.

This is madness, said my mind.

"Hey," I said back to myself, "the worst that can happen is nothing can happen! Let's see!"

The bird kept hopping. So off we went down the mountain. Me and little birdy. Hop, hop, hop. Follow, follow, follow. This went on for a good few minutes as we descended together.

After a while, doubt crept in. *Is this really happening? Am I really following a bird? Is it leading me somewhere? God, are you here right now?*

Hop, hop, hop. Follow, follow, follow.

The further down the mountain we went, the closer to the road and the ocean I got.

There was a stone building in front of us now. Little birdy climbed up. I climbed up too.

I kept making my way closer to it. Perched on the edge of the building.

Abruptly, with one last hop, it jumped from the building and flew off. The game of follow-the-bird was done.

I felt alone and abandoned. *Am I losing my mind?* I thought. *Did the bird really guide me? What now?*

I climbed down from the stone house and crossed the road beneath. I walked over to a viewpoint to contemplate the experience. I gazed toward the horizon and interrogated myself.

Game over.

I felt ashamed and silly. *Am I fooling myself?* I asked in my inner world. *Am I creating games in my own imagination?*

The divine game of chase-the-bird having ended, I was doubtful and empty.

I stood, surveying the ocean in front of me. Back to loneliness.

And then I heard it.

A soft but audible sound. It was a long, low-pitched shout accompanied by a series of high-pitched whistles.

I listened more intently, craning my eardrums for more morsels of sound.

It came again.

It sounded like someone far away shouting.

A hiker appeared on the path before me, walking up the mountain toward the viewpoint.

"Did you hear that?" I asked.

The hiker looked at me quizzically and replied, "Hear what?"

"That shouting and whistling sound?"

"No," said the hiker with a shake of the head.

We paused for a brief moment together, listening for any sounds. Nothing.

Am I now hearing things too? my mind chimed in, as if the bird incident wasn't enough.

I stood there, still listening, still tail between my legs, doubting as I stared at the view.

The sound came again. There was no denying it this time. It was someone shouting, followed by a repeated sequence of whistles.

I ran down the mountain.

The other hiker had already left.

I scrambled down the scree slope and through the shrubs to get to the edge of the cliffs.

I paused.

Completely still. Straining for the direction of the sound.

"Pheeeeeew. Pheeeeeew. Pheeeeeewwwwww." The trill of a person whistling coming from the left.

I squinted my eyes toward the ocean. I was hundreds of meters above the sea at this point and it was getting late. It was hard to see. I started scanning the big, black, milky ocean back and forth.

Then I saw him.

It was a man on his back, floating in the ocean in scuba diving gear. He was bobbing about in a remote bay off Chapmans Peak Drive. He was miles from the road or nearest possible exit of the ocean. He was simply lying there, bobbing like a tiny champagne cork in the sea of life.

It was a puzzling discovery. There was no boat in sight, and neither was there any way for him to get to the beach because of the sheer cliffs and rocks. In fact, there was no beach. The waves crashed into the cliffs and rocks below. As I stood there staring at him, I realized this was a significant problem. Night was coming and the Atlantic Ocean was freezing.

I scanned the skies and estimated we were about twenty-five minutes away from total darkness.

What is a scuba diver doing here? I thought.

I heard him whistle again. Pheeeeeew. Pheeeeeew. Pheeeeeew. It sounded desperate. It sounded like a clear, methodical call for help.

This time I whistled back.

There was no way he could see me amongst the boulders of the cliff, I was too high and too far above him, but I began whistling his tune. His whistles grew in intensity. I whistled again, this time a different tune. This time he copied my tune. We were communicating!

I immediately reached for my phone. I very seldom took my phone on my guided prayer hikes. Today was somehow different. I called a national rescue number and got through to the operator. I explained my situation. He said he would get through to the national coast guard, and they would have to dispatch someone.

"How will they find him in the dark?" I thought. "This will never work. By the time they get here, it will be night time". I had to do something.

I stayed on the telephone waiting for the confirmation of the sea rescue or for the operator to put me through to the coast guard. The line started ringing again. In an impulsive moment I ended the call. He could call me back. I had to do something right away. I couldn't stand around waiting on telephone lines while this diver got swept into the black abyss. Standing there, something inside me said, "Walk away from the man and climb to the top of the peak on your right-hand side". I felt a pull to start moving to the right.

I obeyed.

As I reached the top, I looked down to my right, and movement caught my eye. A rubber dinghy boat with three men onboard was frantically zooming up and down. I could suddenly make sense of what was happening. On the other side of the point was the scuba diver bobbing in the ocean, and on this side was the boat. They couldn't see or hear each other. I could see the men on the boat scanning the cliffs and the water. I could hear the engine as it revved, then waited, then revved, then waited. Searching. Listening. Scanning.

Standing where I was from this vantage point, I figured out what may have happened. The diver had gone down under the water, and a strong underwater current had swept him away from the boat.

He had now ended up in the bay on my left whilst the dive boat searched and waited for him on the right-hand side. There was a huge cliff between the two. I was on the point, and they were in two separate bays and not in the line of sight or earshot of one another.

"Pheeeeeew. Pheeeeeew. Pheeeeeew." The whistles for help reached me again from the left. The diver had been quiet for a while. It was so dark now it was getting hard for me to see the gray speck of a human in the great expanse of the undulating ocean.

Still no call back from sea rescue or desire for me to try to get through to them on the phone. I knew what I had to do. I moved along the cliff slightly closer to the rubber dingy. They had cut the motor and were sitting silently on the ocean. If I was ever going to make the loudest scream in my entire life, this was the moment. Joy flicked in me for a split second at the thought of being given permission to unleash my voice fully. What an adventure. I was going to give it everything I had.

I drew in a deep breath.

"HEEEEEEEEEEEEEEEEY!" I screamed with all my might.

"HAAAAAAAAAAAAAAAAAAY!"

I took a breath.

"HEEEEEEEEEEEEY!"

I let loose as much as I had in me.

Even before I started shouting, I'd said a little prayer, "Lord, supernatural voice, please. They need to hear me!"

I looked at the boat.

No movement at all.

I can do better.

No one had ever asked me to scream for a person's life before, so I thought I could give it a better go a second time.

"HEEEEEEEEEEY AAAAAAAAAH!" I screamed. I gave it the loudest shout I could.

I felt scared for the diver and his life. It seemed like this situation now rested on me.

Then it happened.

The people on the boat heard something.

The engine fired up and they raced towards the cliffs near me.

I screamed again.

They moved closer.

The boat was near, but they couldn't see me.

I decided to walk a little closer to the pinnacle. Closer to the diver. I moved to a point, still high up on the cliffs, at the section where the two bays met in the open ocean. I whistled the same tune I had heard from the diver. I watched.

The boat's driver heard it, and the rubber dinghy raced around to the top of the peninsula. I whistled some more. As I did, the diver, who had been quiet for some time, started whistling again.

I watched the miracle unfold—As the boat rounded the peninsula and came to the bay's entrance on the left, they stopped the engine. As the motor cut, in the quiet, the diver whistled one last time.

The men on the boat saw him.

With some final streams of late dusk light lingering, I saw a boat of three men pulling a gray shape out of the water. I heard the engine fire up, and full throttle sent them zooming toward the harbor on the opposite side of the bay. Dusk faded to dark as they melted into the safety of harbor on the other side.

I stood in awe.

The scuba diver was rescued!

I wondered how he was feeling.

I remembered the little bird.

I had followed the bird. I had crossed the road. I had heard the sound.

The bird, the diver, the rescue.

Did the bird save his life?

Did my obedience to follow the bird result in a miracle?

My heart opened wide as I gazed over the cliff.

Did God guide me?

I asked for a sign only moments before, now, I was standing on the cliff at the edge of a last-minute rescue of a life. All because I had followed the bird.

My friends told me later they thought the men were marine poachers stealing abalone from a protected area.

I guessed God loves all His children.

FOWL FRIENDS WARNING

Not long after I had another precious encounter with birds.

I had left my house for a casual Saturday afternoon walk. As I walked to the end of the street leading directly away from my house, I turned right at the stop street. It was the infamous place where I had first asked the question, "Do You want me to go left or right?" It was a place of surrender and trust.

On this particular day, searching for a feeling, still experimenting with tuning in, I felt a little pull to the right. I decided to walk up the road towards the mountain. I had hardly taken a few strides when a flock of about four or five guinea fowl started making a loud noise. A real racket and squabble emerged from the gang. A guinea fowl (which is an African bird) is prone to making a noise but usually flies away with a warning call if you approach. This time was different. They came running towards me.

Before I could react they had surrounded me in a circle. They were running around me, squawking their high-pitched salutations. I paused. I looked around. What on earth was happening? As I stood there watching them running around me, I asked myself, "What are you trying to tell me, little birds?"

I tuned into their energy. I watched them squawking and running and making a fuss. As I tuned into their group guinea fowl chatter, I felt like they were warning me.

I stood. My attention on the inside again. Scanning myself for guidance I checked again. "Yip," I said to myself, "of the hundreds of feelings I could feel, I get the sense of something warning me to be careful". I spoke to the Guinea fowl from my heart; *if this a warning you are giving me, then let me know.* I transmitted the words to them with my will. As if in acknowledgment of their work being completed, they flew off.

As quickly as they arrived they were gone.

What a coincidence! I said to myself. *I don't speak guinea fowl.*

I continued walking, but the mass gathering had left an impression.

What if it wasn't a coincidence, Daniel? I continued to muse.

What if God could talk to you through birds or insects or anything?

"Maybe a car will run you over?" my mind said.

Well, there's nothing I can do about that, I replied.

I pondered deeper.

Maybe it wasn't an obvious warning.

Maybe it was a warning about something in my life.

I reminisced about my thought patterns, living practices, the disease… *should there be something I need to be aware of? Am I doing something wrong?*

What is this warning about?

"Well", I eventually said, "I can't do anything now, so I guess I'll see."

I continued up the road, took my first left, and walked to the end of the street. I turned left again, walked down, and headed home. I didn't have much energy to be walking around this particular evening, but I was in the routine of changing my space at sunset.

I was already walking back to the stop street where the guinea fowl had accosted me when two men came into view.

They were headed toward me.

I stared at them from a distance, discerning if they were friend or foe. In South Africa, one must have their wits about them, for muggings are common.

The guinea fowl suddenly popped into my mind.

"A warning," the voice said.

My hair stood on end.

Could this be it? Could this be the moment they were telling me about?

The battle of my mind commenced.

"Don't be silly," said my mind. "These are normal people".

Get out of the road, my intuition fired back.

"Not necessary," said my mind, "don't be scared because they are locals."

Get to safety right now, my intuition said.

I was standing in the road like a deer in the headlights.

The men were coming toward me.

My mind went for the final blow, "You can't go listening to weird guinea fowl messages, this is nuts."

I looked to my left. There was a high retaining wall.

Climb it, my intuition said.

The inner battle continued.

Hearing both the voices, I was deeply conflicted. I played out the scenario: Pass the men, potentially get robbed. Climb up the wall, potentially look like a racist.

I disliked both options.

I chose the latter.

The previous time I didn't listen to my intuition, I was mugged at knife point, so it was time to do life differently. The worst that could happen is my pride could be hurt.

I turned abruptly to the left. I climbed straight up the retaining wall and onto the concrete fence surrounding a stranger's house.

I sat there.

I stared at the men.

"Gosh, these men are going to judge you so much", said my mind. "As if segregation isn't already a problem in your country, here you are acting like a fearful idiot".

I felt really uncomfortable.

My inner judge was out in full force.

"Do you know the racial damage you are doing right now?"

Everything in my logical mind wanted to pretend I was fixing the wall or looking at the sunset. But I couldn't.

I stared at them. They stared at me.

The men approached quickly and with purpose. They appeared to be on a mission in their own suburban quest.

As they drew parallel to me, one of them looked up— "Do you have a smoke?" he asked.

It was the exact question I was asked on Table Mountain during my previous mugging, shortly before a knife appeared.

My hair stood on end.

The Guinea fowl.

I was on full alert.

I didn't doubt anymore.

I trusted the guinea fowl and my intuition.

This is trouble.

I was extremely glad to be sitting on the wall.

I looked down from my perch and shook my head, giving the answer about the cigarette.

They kept walking.

As they neared the end of the road, I felt comfortable I could make it home safely.

I jumped down.

It was only the beginning of this journey.

I started running.

Sprinting back to my landlord's house I realized it was time to sound the alarm. These men were trouble for the neighborhood.

Sickness momentarily forgotten, I reached the front door.

"Uwe!" I shouted (the name of my German landlord). "Uwe, come quickly! There is trouble on the road."

I heard a shuffle and scurry of feet upstairs. To my surprise, he didn't ask any questions.

He simply grabbed his local security radio and car keys.

"Which way?" he asked.

"To the stop street," I said.

Truthfully, I had no idea where to go. I didn't know where the men were.

"Turn right here," I said. I had tuned to my inner world and felt the pull. I was completely trusting. Straining to hear any signal in my inner world, I was asking God with all my heart—"Show us where".

Uwe turned right into the road to head up the mountain. We passed the place where the guinea fowl had appeared. I was scared. I had no idea if these men were robbers. I had no evidence. They did nothing wrong. I was scared because I was trusting the guinea fowl. I was scared because I was trusting my intuition. I was scared we might not find the robbers, I was scared we might find the robbers.

All I had were the guinea fowl.

It was all based on the intuitive, the miraculous, the invisible.

Doubt pressed in on me. *How will I tell my German compadre about the guinea fowl if we don't find them?* My body tensed.

We were both scanning the road for any out-of-place persons.

And then they appeared.

The two men came into view at the end of the road.

It was a dead end, so I motioned to Uwe, "Pull over. That's them."

He steered the car quietly to the side of the road. We tucked in behind another vehicle.

We were on full alert.

The men walked slowly as they headed upward. Like me, they had walked a small loop of the residential area.

Then came the dreaded question from Uwe, "How do you know they are robbers, Dan?"

I was caught. I didn't know what to say. How could I speak about the guinea fowl? I mused at the answer as I ran it through in my head; *some birds told me*. I definitely wasn't going to say that.

"I just have a bad feeling," I replied.

We watched. Nothing happened. The men looked like they were Sunday strolling now. As I was losing hope and doubting myself, it happened. Right in front of our eyes.

One of the men pulled out a knife.

An unsuspecting girl of about 15 years of age was standing outside her home. She was focused intensely on her cell phone whilst holding a small dog on a leash in the other. The men approached her. I don't think she even saw the knife. Before she realized anything was happening, the man snatched her phone.

They started sprinting immediately.

The dog yapped.

The men bolted.

The girl froze.

A mugging in front of our very eyes! It happened! In an instant my sixth senses were confirmed. Robbers! The dog hardly squeaked out a bark, and the men were gone. Up the street and out of sight.

Uwe was on his radio like lightning; "Bravo one, come in,

robbery in Skaife Street, Scott Estate. Two males, one wearing a red jacket."

The community radio crackled back almost instantly with affirmatives.

The community came alive.

In under two minutes, men were coming out of their houses in Saturday trousers, and car engines were beginning to rev.

I was excited. Not for the girl who had been mugged, but because I had trusted my intuition and the signs, and it had come true. Divine messages from the birds and from God had not let me down. This was communication on a new level for me.

The chase was on.

We zoomed to the top of the road but reached the dead end where the robbers had headed into the bushes. They crossed a small stream and were making a beeline to an adjacent residential area.

Uwe was on his radio again.

Neighbors were emerging already onto their driveways on the other side of the stream. Oozing out of their homes to protect their colonies.

We decided to zoom back to the bottom of the road and see if we could intersect the robbers below the other estate. As we went, I witnessed even more neighbors joining the hunt.

Reports started coming in on the radio.

"I see him. He just jumped under a bridge by the main road."

"I saw him again. He crossed the road. It looks like a getaway car parked by the bridge trying to pick him up."

"I see him. He's messaging on his phone."

As we got to the bridge, the neighborhood cars were already zooming toward the getaway vehicles location. The fugitives had now been separated.

We chased the robbers for over an hour.

Despite all the odds stacked against them, they got away. One jumped off a bridge in front of a police car into a heavily reeded wetland. The other, well, we don't even know. We stood for ages shining spotlights into the reeds, hoping to catch the robber. Others were looking for the white getaway vehicle.

At the end, there was not much to show.

As the dust settled and dusk sank, I thought about the incidents which led us here.

If only everyone on this search knew.

If only the robbers knew who had betrayed them.

A confusion of guinea fowl.

A desire to trust.

A missed mugging.

A drop of inner guidance.

That's what it took to create a circus of people circulating for thieves.

My inner world was humming: *Did the birds speak to me? Was God using His creation to commune with me? Was it all an accident? A miss? A coincidence?*

My life was becoming a mountain of 'coincidences', one joined to the other in a long chain which touched my heart and soul.

DRIVING TO DANIEL

DIVINE INCIDENTS BEGAN stacking in my life.

One evening I headed out to connect with my best friend, Sarah. I had enough energy and agreed on sushi together in a bustling, social part of town. I needed someone to talk to, so I was willing to risk an outing. I was sad. We could no longer connect about skateboarding, mountaineering, ocean adventures, or party hopping. We still had a lot of love and time for each other, but there was now a clear divide. A chasm had opened up—the valley of my own spiritual journey. I couldn't really describe the extent of the incidents happening to me, but we shared what we were up to, had a lovely meal, and I began my journey home.

Little did I know this short drive would have a long-lasting impact.

As I was driving, deep in my meandering thoughts, I rounded a last curve onto the coastal road.

The final stretch home.

As if something turned the car to the left on its own, my body automatically made the movements to slow the vehicle down and pull over.

At the same instant, I saw him.

A man came out of the bushes toward me.

He was wearing a hat and coat and walked straight toward my car. I wanted to drive. In South Africa, you don't pick up hitchhikers from behind bushes in the middle of the night—it is a dangerous game.

I willed my body to go.

It wouldn't.

I was stuck.

I knew this man was coming to get in the car.

I did not want this, but I couldn't move.

My mind was screaming, "Drive!" whilst another part of me seemed totally at ease.

It happened so fast, and then he was already opening the car door.

I was frozen.

He climbed slowly onto the passenger seat.

I inhaled a rich, full scent of an older African man. He still had his hat on his head, a tweed jacket, and a walking stick.

My head reorientated itself to focus back on the road in front of us. I wanted to look at him but I couldn't. My head wouldn't permit it.

I started driving.

As I pulled off, I went to the only place I could, back to my inner world. I was searching desperately for what I was feeling.

Is this dangerous? Am I safe? Does he have a knife? What is going to happen?

My mind wanted to conjure some kind of dramatic story about to unfold.

Yet, I couldn't deny it, there was an atmosphere of peace in the car.

Spaciousness.

He didn't talk.

I couldn't talk.

We were simply journeying together as long lost companions.

I tried using my awareness to scan him. Even after years of traveling and street-smart engagements, I couldn't sense or place his intentions.

Something felt different in the air.

This man's presence was bewildering to me.

Why is he not speaking? Why am I not speaking?

I kept expecting him to say something. My own mouth was glued shut.

Where on earth are we going?

"My name is Daniel," he eventually said.

My being was riveted.

He has the same name.

Oh God, what is happening?

I didn't feel like I was on earth anymore.

Fear and expectation churned in my heart.

"I'm from Amanzimtoti," he said.

Born in the same town!

Bombs exploded in my inner being.

"I'm a Zulu man," he said.

I loved Zulus. I loved the Zulu nation. I had a fascination with their culture.

What are the chances?

Two Daniels. Both from the small town of Amanzimtoti, driving down a narrow coastal road on the opposite side of the country in the middle of the night.

What is he going to tell me next?

"I've been given a good job at the airport," he said.

I was in a trance-like state as he tried to tell me about his job at the airport. He was sort of fumbling through the details like he didn't know himself what he was doing. It didn't make sense to me, but he appeared grateful for the situation. I couldn't imagine how he might be an airport manager in his late eighties, let alone how he made the journey or even gained knowledge of the job, but he seemed happy. The details were vague and odd, but I was happy for him too. He also added his wife came along to support him. I wondered how they both made the journey across the country and where they would be living. Who had helped them? How could they relocate to Cape Town after spending their whole lives in the province of KwaZulu-Natal?

My mind came back to reality. *It's all well and good that he has a job at the airport, but what is he doing on this coastal road? He's miles from the airport and nowhere near the place he says he lives.*

"Where are you going?" I asked out loud, finally able to get my words out. He mumbled something inaudible. I asked another question.

"Daniel, what can I do for you?"

It was strange, like I was asking myself the same question.

"Make a turn here and take me back. You can drop me by the police station. I will catch a taxi from there."

The police station was at the beginning of the coastal road, closer to where I had picked him up. It was in the opposite direction to where we were traveling.

There are no taxis from the police station at this time of the night, I thought. *The hope of transport to where he is going is very slim.*

I was genuinely concerned for him. Here was this frail old man, walking in the dark, heading in one direction and turning back the other way. How could I leave him alone in the dark at this hour, without energy reserves to carry him to his destination? He also seemed very poor. I could tell he was salt of the rural African earth.

Where will he get the money if a taxi picks him up?

I didn't know what to do, so I simply obeyed him.

I turned the vehicle around.

I headed back in the same direction we had come from.

Again we drove in silence.

I was in deep contemplation, and he sat quietly with his hat on his lap.

Despite the confusion, I still felt a sense of peace. I knew I had to do whatever he told me to do. I would have to obey his commands. I was at his service. I was humbled. I was concerned. There was nothing normal about this hitchhiker or this car ride. I felt the presence of "something else". I stopped at the police station. As expected, there was no one there. I instinctively reached for my wallet. The least I could do was give him something. In my wallet was a R200 note. Nothing else. I looked again. *Why can't there be a R10 or a R20?* I was so poor myself. I handed him R200. There was no other choice, he clearly needed it more than me. He received it with the beautiful gesture many Zulu people use when receiving money: one hand on their wrist and the other open to receive. He appeared deeply grateful.

He got out of the van slowly and put his hat back on. He walked across the dimly lit parking lot with a slightly hunched back and his walking stick. Across from him was the ocean, on the left a steep bank, and on the right some strewn boulders on a grassy area. He disappeared into the night.

I sat in the car, dumbfounded. *What was happening? Where did he go? Where had he come from?* I turned the car around again and resumed the journey home.

I wanted to tell someone about what had happened.

How can I?

I was scared of being laughed at.

I decided I would probably keep this story to myself forever.

I would avoid ridicule and I write it off as sheer coincidence—two

Daniels, hailing from the same town, seeking out a life in Cape Town. Lost.

As time went by this story would expand, God was coming for me.

WALKING WITH DANIEL

A WEEK OR two later, I was walking in the mountains to escape the impending doom feeling erupting in my heart again. I sat amongst my favorite prayer rocks high up on the mountainside: "God, take my impending doom away, please. Take my life, God. Help me. Guide me. Send me a sign. Any sign." It was another heartfelt prayer. I was still hopeless, even though I was getting better. I felt hopeless simply at the fact of being alive. I was still breaking apart, even though there was no known reason for it. I was extremely grateful to be on that mountain and considered it my saving grace, but I also knew I would desperately need some divine help when I got down from the mountain.

"Please, God, what do I need to do? Please send me a great big neon sign with flashing fairy lights which I can easily follow."

After finishing my prayers, meditations, and silences, I ambled down the rocky slope back to the road. I started on my normal route home along the tar, sad I hadn't seen any birds or natural signs of wonder. Nothing had happened. I wondered if it would. *Would I get a billboard I couldn't miss?* I crossed the road to get a better view of the ocean.

Suddenly, I stopped dead in my tracks.

"Daniel," I said out loud.

Standing in front of me was the old African man in his coat and hat. His name came tumbling out of my mouth before I was sure it was even him. *Puppet mouth.*

What on earth is he doing here?

Shock melted into humility. I felt like lying and weeping at his feet for some unknown reason. He mumbled something under his breath I couldn't understand. It was definitely him. I felt The Presence again.

Is he the sign I was praying for?

Standing right in front of me was the billboard with flashing fairy lights.

I felt a strong pull to kneel down before him, curl into a ball and touch his feet. To be of service. I resisted the pull. It took energy to remain standing before him. "What are you doing here?" I said with timidness in my voice.

I half expected him to hold out his stick so I could take hold and transcend off the planet.

Instead, he mumbled something about visiting friends.

It didn't make sense—walking along the long stretch of Chapman's Peak Drive alone was not the way to visit friends—especially when you are over 80 years old and live on the other side of the city.

"Where are you going?" I repeated again.

"I'm looking for some Zulu friends," he said.

"Where?" I said. He repeated a story about some people nearby he was looking for.

He said he was alone, missed the Zulu culture, and needed some company. He'd heard some Zulu men lived in a nearby seaside town.

I was transfixed by his story, trying to figure it all out. It still didn't make much sense. If he was going to the next town, he could've caught a taxi there. In fact, he wouldn't have used this particular route at all. As I contemplated his story, we both started to turn and walk back down the hill. Even more strange. Now we were heading in the opposite direction he said he needed to go. It was another U-turn, like when I picked him up with my car on that first night. He was going in one direction, met me, then reversed the direction.

I was perplexed.

Two Daniels.

Both from the same town.

Walking side by side—on autopilot. I was ready to serve no matter his request. My spirit entered a willing submission for this man I did not know.

Here we go again, my mind voiced. Silence. Walking. Looking at the ocean in the bay. Contemplating. I still had not been able to fully see his face. It was as if I couldn't look into his eyes. I couldn't bring myself to face him fully. Hence, I did not truly know what he looked like. I recognized him mainly by how I felt in his presence. By the eyes of my heart.

Would someone see me with him? Would someone offer us a lift? Was he simply a normal man who was lost and I had coincidentally bumped into again? Was this something more?

I didn't know what was going on, but something was going on. Same hat. Same jacket.

Is this all he wears?

We walked back down into the little town of Hout Bay. We headed straight to the nearest cash ATM. We didn't even speak about it, we both instinctively knew what to do. I put my card in to draw money. I looked at my bank balance—so low. It was hard to give away the little I had. I drew R200 again. I placed it in his hands. He thanked me profusely and told me he would pay me back.

How? I thought. He had no internet banking or a way of reaching me.

I didn't bother to ask further questions.

We walked to the nearby taxi rank. My thoughts were still churning like rapids on a raging river. I was in a trance-like state of elevation around him.

We arrived at the small taxi rank outside the shopping center.

He mumbled a goodbye and continued walking towards the waiting taxis. I watched him intently to see which taxi he would take so I could figure out which suburb he was headed to. *Will his stories line up?*

As Daniel merged with the crowd, I lost sight of him. I kept watching the opening doors of taxis to see if he was ducking into one. *He's sure to pop up now,* I thought.

He never did.

I stood there watching intently but never saw him leave.

Maybe he went to the shop or somehow slipped into a taxi.

He was suddenly gone again, mysteriously into the dark, just like the first night I met him.

I was alone again.

I walked slowly back to my room. Crisscrossing roads and heading up the familiar side streets between buildings. I felt different. The hollowness and despair in my heart on the mountain were now replaced by something else. "God, was this the neon sign I was praying for?" It wasn't exactly the neon, flashing billboard I had imagined or expected, but it certainly was some kind of can't-ignore-it sign. It was the sign God had chosen for me for His purpose. I was awakening to something bigger, and I was struggling against it. Any doubt about the existence of God was beginning to dissolve. I didn't want it to, but it was happening, through sheer experience. It was like living in a movie I couldn't tell anyone about.

My prayers were getting answers.

All my conditioning and resistance to things of the supernatural were painfully and uncomfortably breaking down. I was fighting against it, but I couldn't stop it. I didn't want it. It wanted me.

I was still worried I would lose everything I knew.

My friends, family, everything.

Can anyone understand this?

I felt alone.

I never wanted to meet angels, spirits, shamans, healers, anyone, or anything of such nature. I had no reference to even describe what was happening. I simply experienced encounters with birds, animals, insects, and people in ways like never before. My eyes were opening.

I had once tried to read a book about God. It frightened me so much that I put it away.

Now, God was coming for me, writing Himself into my life.

God was listening.

For many people this would be a comforting thought. For me, it was terrifying. It made me realize things were happening behind this world's curtain. Things behind the veil I couldn't see, know or explain. My mind reared up again, "Maybe this is another coincidence. It could be. I mean, maybe Daniel took the day off work from the airport? Maybe he did have a friend he was going see and then turned around and walked back to catch a taxi?"

Maybe.

I didn't know the answers, but I stopped trying to figure it out. I had the revelation I knew less than I thought I did, so I rested in that thought and felt deeply touched and humbled.

I went home and sat on my deck in silence. *Again*, I thought, *I will never share this with anyone.*

It was a year before this story was drawn out of me.

Tears rolled from my eyes as I explained to my aunt what had happened to me.

"An angel," she said, "God loves you".

TO GO OR NOT TO GO

AFTER MY MOTHER'S death, the question of what we would do with her motor vehicle was something my sister and I had to decide on. It was parked in a garage on the other side of the country, and I figured keeping it would be more beneficial than selling it. I would be the one who would have to get it. I didn't know if this was a wise decision considering my health and wellbeing, but I decided I would try a different approach—pray to see what God wanted me to do.

One day soon after, driving with Grant over the mountain towards Camps Bay, I was discussing whether I should go to Durban to fetch the car. My eyes suddenly locked onto a man on the corner of the road. It was Daniel. He looked as if he was hitchhiking again. *The worst possible place to try and catch a lift*, I thought. *Daniel needs a car to get around.*

An awareness was triggered in me. "Daniel needs a car". I thought about the car dilemma I was in. *Is God talking to me?* I thought. I was mid-sentence about it when I saw Daniel. The neon sign seemed to be saying, "Go to Durban".

"Grant. Did you see that man?" I said.

"Um, ya, I think so. Do you want me to go back?" He was hesitant as we were on a rather dangerous corner.

I had that usual feeling around Daniel—a deep stirring.

I paused for a second. "No, it's okay, I thought I'd seen him before."

I was touched again by Daniel's presence, even if he was not in the car with us.

I thought about Daniel's situation on the side of the road— *Daniel needs a car.*

It was an answer to my prayer.

I would go to Durban.

LOOKING FOR LOVE

DISEASE IS A desolate place.

I knew I was heading to Durban soon (to pick up the car), but I was now wrestling with loneliness.

I didn't think I could endure another week or two without some kind of meaningful human connection. An out-of-the-box thought entered my mind:

Why don't you go onto a dating app and connect with someone in the area? Surely there's someone out there up for some hanging out and light friendship?

"No way", my ego replied. "Me, Fantastic Mr. Fox, relegated and reduced to dating sites?!" *No way.*

My mind, trying to be the usual party pooper, didn't get its way. I put my pride aside and set up my profile. *What now?!* I was excited. A chance to connect with someone.

The first picture of a woman appeared on my screen. She looked happy, young, and traveling Cape Town.

What am I even looking for? What is my ideal woman now?

What I was looking for in a partner had changed.

I thought this was a good thing.

I was no longer attracted to the wild party-type who was living recklessly with alcohol in hand. There were plenty of those in Cape Town. I continued to scroll through the pictures. "No, no, no, Not this one. No. Old life, no." I had definitely changed. The type of partner I wanted needed to reflect my new qualities and inner values.

Okay, I said to myself, *what is my real desire here? I can't go flicking through endless images of people, I need to know in my heart what I am looking for.* I leaned back in bed and thought about which qualities would complement a healthy relationship. *Fun, friendly, playful, happy-go-lucky, and very natural. Someone who can communicate well and isn't scared to be forward about their feelings.* My brain wandered through my travels around the globe, searching for cultures that represented this. I remembered Spain. It occurred to me that the men and women of Spain ticked many of these boxes. *Maybe I'll meet a Spanish woman?* I mused. On the other hand, I didn't want to get sucked into the unhealthy party scene either. I knew that fun and free-spirited could also be accompanied by out-of-control and unreliable. So, I turned my ideals to healthier qualities; *Grounded, committed, supportive,* and maybe, I thought with a smile, *someone who loves to cook?!*

"Maybe that's an Afrikaans woman?!" the voice in my mind blurted out on its own.

I chuckled. Traditional Afrikaners are a very pure and conservative culture, and I didn't picture myself at all "good enough" to fit the mold. "Well", I said to myself, "I will see what comes to me. I have the qualities in my mind and it's time to keep scrolling!"

As I scrolled, I said a prayer: You bring me someone. You know what's best.

Within the space of ten minutes, I matched with a profile.

That was fast! Excitement bubbled in me for the first time in a long time. Being sick for so long can be boring. With my first matching partner I sparked up like a twinkling star. I wasn't sure if I knew how to use the app properly, yet I was instantly connected to someone potentially looking for the same thing. I checked her profile. She looked Afrikaans. I chuckled again. She also looked natural, fun, and down to earth. *This time it will be different,* I thought. I wasted no time. I replied to her with a straight-to-the-point message; "Hey! I'm keen to meet up. Why don't you come over for tea sometime soon? I live in Hout Bay." She was also clearly a mover and shaker.

We set a date for the following week.

JUST A TEA

I COULDN'T BELIEVE how quickly my life had changed. I went from feeling dead a month ago to suddenly having a date! It was surreal. Was I even ready? I was unsure but my heart felt good about it. I was craving human connection. As the date got closer I was super nervous—I ran through everything I thought I needed. It had been a while since I ventured out into the wild territory of dating, and I was trying my best to be as calm and cool as possible.

Her car arrived outside my house. My heart was bouncing around like a kitten on a wool ball. *What if she was nothing like I imagined?* I tried to stabilize my emotions as the wool ball unraveled further. My green hammock practice and mind stilling were failing miserably. *What if all the pictures of her had been a lie?*

"Just a tea," I said to comfort myself.

She got out of the car.

Her energy was electric.

My face smiled immediately.

So did hers.

Instant connection.

She looks even better in real life!

It was true. She was lovely. We hugged. I liked her immediately.

We walked over to the little wooden deck. The deck where I had spent so much time lying, dying, and crying. Now there were candles and a spread to celebrate love. We settled down on my scatter cushion to have our first tea and chat. *Scatter cushion, so useful*, I thought. We chatted deep into the evening. I looked around at the surrealness of the moment. All this time alone and now having a romantic little picnic, herbal teas, snacks, picnic blanket… all complete with my scatter cushions.

Life had changed for me.

It turned out she was a born and bred Afrikaaner. Not only that, she could also speak near-fluent Spanish. My internal world somersaulted. *God, are you joking with me?* It was as if, since I couldn't decide between Afrikaans and Spanish, I got a mixture of both. *Anything is possible*, I thought, as my mind jumped to conclusions about wedding bells and horse-drawn carriages.

Our first date went well, and we decided to see each other soon. In fact, that very weekend, she was having a gathering at her house and suggested I attend.

UNHEALTHY LETTING GO

I WAS NERVOUS. I hadn't been out for a long time and I wasn't sure if I could handle all the social interaction. I could feel I was coming to the end of the worst of it, but I still had doubts. Any day I wasn't feeling 100% sparked fear the M.E. monster was sliding in. Instead of letting fear get the best of me, I checked in with my heart. "Heart, what do you feel? Should I go through with this?" Feeling into it rather than weighing up the pros and cons, my heart jumped excitedly. It was clear my heart was game for an adventure.

The weekend arrived and I headed out in my car. The drive was a fair distance from the city and far from where I lived. I had never been to this little suburb before. I remember pulling up outside her house. A multitude of cars were already parked. I pulled over and stopped the car, pausing momentarily before exiting. My nerves twisted inside me like dangling vines off a tree. It had been a long time since I had been on "the scene". I walked inside, trying to look cool and relaxed. There she was. The sight of her lit me up. She was different from anyone I had been with before. She was so natural. So pure. Salt of the earth.

I watched how she gracefully and lovingly interacted with the guests. I watched her play with the kids. She was a born nurturer.

"Marriage material," I whispered to the part of me who desperately wanted commitment.

I didn't want to mess it up, so I switched from cool to "extra cool". I would bring out the best of Daniel in the hopes she would like me. Playing the cool guy around the boys, being charming to the ladies, striking a few good nonchalant poses, and giving her enough space—these were some of my strategies. I was pulling out all tricks of the trade, and my ego was out in full force. This was what Old Daniel had been waiting for, for months. I had opened the door for him. I let him in.

It was a disaster in the making.

The trouble started when a lady offered me an alcoholic drink. I said yes. I hadn't drunk much for over a year. I thought it would be a good idea to fit in. *I could also use something to calm my nerves,* I thought to myself as I received the beverage. It worked. But no sooner had I finished one drink, another appeared in the empty glass beside me. The Afrikaans people were excellent hosts. More drinks arrived. At this point, I was sitting on the grass in the back garden watching live music. I didn't move much as the drinks kept refreshing themselves. The next moment I was inside chatting with the "boss man" who ran the company hosting the event. A beautiful Afrikaans lady with a tray of alcoholic shooters appeared out of thin air.

It was one of the last things I remember clearly.

"Why the hell not?" were the words that entered my mind.

I need to let off some steam. I've been cooped up for months.

I don't remember much after that.

There was a major portion of the day left, let alone the night. I can't tell you what happened. I know a Jacuzzi was involved. I remember some people being upset with me, and I don't remember why. Amongst the fragments, there is only one crystal clear memory. I remember sitting in the Jacuzzi next to a much older man. We were chatting about suicide. He shared with me his father had committed suicide. I remember asking him questions and was impressed that he could talk about it with humility and peace. It gave me hope. He had clearly dealt with the suicide monster. I hoped I could do the same one day. Able to talk about everything sensitive and help others.

Back to fuzzy memories. I may have tried to kiss my date in the Jacuzzi in front of strangers and her work colleagues. I don't think she was impressed.

I woke up in the morning next to my date. I had not planned to stay over. She definitely had not planned for me to stay over, either. She was much too pure to have a drunken reprobate in her house, let alone her bed. I suppose she took me in from pity since I couldn't have gotten myself home. I had the aftertaste of vomit in my mouth. At that stage of the morning, the entire previous day was a complete blank to me. My date did not look happy. I could feel the elephant in the room. I had done some bad things. I had caused irreparable damage to a sparkling new relationship. I was a rogue outlier who had upset the party. Was this my blowout? Did the grief for my mother, my pent-up frustration, and my desperation for a loving relationship give Old Dan what he needed to create a disaster? Yes. Did I mix alcohol and tragedy to the detriment of everyone? Yes. Was I a party pooper? Yes.

My date gave me a vague summary of my actions of the previous 24 hours. I don't think she told me everything because it was probably too embarrassing and uncomfortable for her to say out loud.

I was shattered. I couldn't believe it. The months of healing. The months of tender kindness. The months of commitment to helping myself get better. All of it turned upside down by one night of drinking alcohol. I decided then and there that alcohol was the devil's water. It had no place in my life. My father abused alcohol, my grandmother abused it, my uncles abused it, my ex-girlfriends abused it, and I abused it. It was the cause of great pain in my life. I was no better than anybody else partaking in the poison.

Alcohol spoiled my life and other lives I knew of, and here it was, ruining more lives. The life of my wonderful innocent date. I could see in her eyes how much pain and confusion I had caused her. Everything I'd said before did not match the person I was in front of her. My Spanish-Afrikaans dreams and the trust she had given me were broken. It also turned out she wasn't much of a drinker, and this party scene wasn't her typical night out. I had tried to fit into a place that wasn't even her home in the first place.

I was looking to attract something on the outside of my life but hadn't become what I wanted on the inside.

I hung my head low as I exited the house.

I was too embarrassed to say much to the friends who were still around. We got to my car.

She looked at me through kind and tender eyes.

"You can still give me one more kiss," she said softly and shyly.

It broke my heart.

Her purity was amazing.

It was the last time I connected with her.

She married someone better.

LAST DANCE WITH DANIEL

I DROVE AWAY.

My first big social outing was a total disaster.

A voice inside was pounding away at me, "Daniel, this has to stop. This way of life has to stop." I drove until I got to a petrol station. Once I had filled up the tank, I got out of the car and walked to a children's playground near the back of the food court. I called my best friend Marina and told her what happened. She laughed and said, "Shame, Danny, that is not like you at all. If she's the right one, she will give you another chance." She was right. If it was going to work out, it would. She was also wrong about something. This kind of behavior was actually like me. The culture I was in had made it seem normal. Flashbacks of all the times I had abused alcohol, women, and myself came flashing into my mind's eye.

I cried.

I was standing atop a children's jungle gym trying to hide my tears and contorted cry face. I was totally ashamed. I needed so much healing and forgiveness for the things I had done in Cape Town. I didn't even know what I was doing in the past was wrong. I had lost my moral compass. I slowly realized the man I had become.

It wasn't this perfect, loving, joy-sharing image I had of myself. The true man was much unhealthier than this. Where was the innocent boy with the pure heart who had arrived in this city? Where was the fun-loving, natural, kind-hearted child I used to be? I lay down on dry, prickly grass next to the jungle gym while the sunshine warmed my battered body.

I slipped into a prayerful space.

"Oh God, what do I need to do? Please forgive me," I sobbed. "Please forgive me. Please help me to break free. This has to end."

I lay there for a long time, not really knowing what to do. I thought I was making big strides in my healing and growth but this moment was ground zero again.

Self-sabotage the order of the day.

Eventually I was motivated to get up. I was tired from the poor sleep and my nerves were totally frayed from the evening's alcohol abuse. I had suffered post-binge anxiety many times and the accompanying sinking feeling in my heart was nearly unbearable in my current condition. This was not a day I needed to be having. I decided to head home and get straight into bed.

I walked to my car. I wondered why I had climbed on top of the jungle gym. It felt significant but I couldn't really place it. I remember once leaving a stranger behind on top of a jungle gym. A group of us had promised him a lift back from a festival and we were so drunk we left him behind. We knew what we were doing and we didn't care. These jungle gyms and that scenario represented the worst of me. It brought up memories from days I wanted to forget. From a version of myself I wanted to disregard. I wanted to get as far away from this place as possible. As far away from those days as possible. The location and state I was in conjured up my past.

I started the car engine and slowly exited the gas station.

I made some wrong turns and ended up in some farm lands.

I pulled over next to a barbed wire fence.

Where am I?

My anxiety rippled.

I turned back, trying to find the highway.

Eventually I crossed a bridge and made a loop to rejoin the road in the right direction.

Then I saw him.

The stance. The hat. The jacket.

It was happening all over again.

Daniel.

I pulled over slowly on the onramp.

Daniel opened the door and got in.

The familiar smell. The familiar silence. The familiar presence of something different.

Oh God, not now, I thought. *Why on earth is he in my car now?*

The puppet strings pulled and I started to drive.

We rejoined the highway.

Silence.

I felt like a naughty child in his presence.

Did he know what I did last night?

I wanted to cry.

Daniel seemed distant, almost worried.

He was even more quiet than usual.

"Take this," he said, pointing to an offramp up ahead. We had only just come onto the highway, and now we were going off it.

He was never in my car for a lift in the first place, I thought.

No wonder we were already heading off the highway, this time to a notoriously dangerous area of the Cape. I put my left indicator on and drove up the offramp. *Oh dear,* I thought. *Where are we headed now? Maybe I'll get to drop him at home and finally put this mystery to rest.*

"Stop here," he mumbled. We were midway up the offramp.

I pulled over.

There were no other cars.

I reached for the ashtray in the dashboard's center console. I took out the two hundred rand note and gave it to him.

He methodically opened the door.

"Goodbye," he said.

The door closed.

Daniel walked to the grass and disappeared down an embankment.

He looked perplexed on this particular day—slightly confused or deep in thought. A sort of melancholic atmosphere of concern and sadness hovered in the air around him. I sensed feelings of disappointment.

He disappeared.

I waited to see if he would rise out the other side of the embankment.

He didn't.

I drove to the top of the road, my gaze constantly on my rear-view mirror, trying to look back and see him one last time. Would he appear out of the embankment? Walking toward where? Where did he live? Where had he gone? Where had he come from? Where was he going?

He didn't appear again.

He never would.

My heart dropped like a ton of led, sinking into a sea of tears.

LEAVING FOR DURBAN

I ARRIVED HOME, fell apart on my bed, and wept. I cried for my sins. For the pain I caused in the world. For Daniel. For all the things I was experiencing. I wept because I knew I had so much more to grow. I wept because I knew how terrible a person I could be. I tricked myself into believing I was a loving, caring, amazing person. On the odd occasion, it was true, but most of the other time I was also an angry, resentful, hurtful, pain-causing person. I was beginning to learn the truth about myself.

The truth hurt.

It wasn't long after this I completed my trip to Durban to fetch my mother's car. Durban is a city on the east coast of South Africa, far from my living quarters in Cape Town.

I was spending time with my family and sitting on the wooden deck one late afternoon when they suggested I move back to be closer to them. They thought it would be a good idea to settle near them, and I could build new relationships and communities. Something in their words touched me. I returned to my aunt's beachfront flat later, flopped on the bed, my mind in a turmoil. It was the last thing I could imagine, returning to the place I thought offered me nothing.

However, I knew it was the sign I had been waiting for—the ticket out of Cape Town.

As my mind wrestled with the bedroom pillows, something broke through the mental barriers and my heart opened to the possibility of the move. My mind softened into a new voice; *It's not only about career, it's not only about me and my path to success. It's not only about achieving goals.* The new voice spoke a changed tune; *it's time to rebuild relationships. It's time to establish trust and love. It's time to connect with family. It's time to grow into a new lifestyle. This will support you into the future.*

It frightened me, but my desperation had turned into inspiration before I knew it. I had a feeling in Cape Town months prior that I would need to leave. I didn't know where at the time, but now Life was presenting me with the answer.

Plot twist.

I never imagined moving back to Durban. I thought I was done there forever.

I had to surrender my thoughts. Durban would be a next step, a springboard to something else I couldn't see.

Soon I was back in Cape Town, telling my landlords I would be leaving. It also meant giving notice to the guinea fowl and Sheila the cat, explaining my time of healing was over, and I was moving on to new adventures.

God gave me the energy for all the extra effort. The packing, the saying goodbye, the route planning. I remember the final morning vividly, waking up and knowing it was all over—my experiences in this little magical place were done. My cocoon was broken. I reminisced about Little Ducky, the guinea fowl, the hawks, prayers on the mountains, and the beautiful nature… all over.

Lying in bed I felt this chapter coming to an end.

Tap, tap, tap. A sound on my front door.

Tap, tap, tap, TAP.

Close to my bed, a loud, sharp sound pulsed on the glass of my front door. *What is this?*

My reminiscing broken, I got up and drew back the curtain.

Lo and behold, they had come to say goodbye.

A group of guinea fowl, four of five of them in total, were standing outside my door. One of them was pecking at the glass door with its beak. *Tap, tap, tap.*

My heart swelled.

My eyes gleamed.

My spirit soared.

"They are saying goodbye!" My heart said.

"They are only here looking at their reflection in the glass", my mind said.

Their timing was impeccable. Moments ago, I was thinking of all the times they had safe kept me and accompanied me in my ramblings.

Tap tap tap, the leading guinea fowl went again.

I looked at them.

"Goodbye, guys. Thanks for helping me to spiritually awaken."

I closed the curtain and got back into bed.

The tapping stopped.

They had become a spirit animal to me. A small flock of angels directing me to comfort and safety.

Suddenly they began squawking outside.

A noisy, grinding, uncomfortable, and oh-so-African noise. They were singing their goodbye. I got up again and looked at them. I was touched. Their dawn chorus was sending me into my new life. They flew off into the bushes in a scatter of feathers. Tears and knowing-ness arose in me. It was the end of a chapter. I knew it. I was living in a movie.

I packed the last of my things. I had few belongings so I loaded the car quickly and prepared smoothies for the road trip. I was still very conscious about my health and asked, "Is this leading me towards more health or less health?"

Smoothies packed, I sat for a moment next to the little stream where I had spent much time falling apart and coming back together.

As I got to my favorite rocks, I was shocked to see Sheila the cat. It was not her usual spot—running water wasn't really her thing. I sat down and she looked at me. I knew she was saying a private goodbye. I wept. She had shown me so much love and companionship and was there for me during all my healing time. I wished I had given her more affection. She was a real friend.

As I petted her, I thought of the countless times she waited for me to get home. The countless times she comforted me on the deck. The countless times she meowed outside my room so I could speak with her. She had been my partner through it all, and now we were saying goodbye. "Thanks for everything Sheila," I said with a heavy heart. "I wish I let you sleep inside more often". It had taken her more than a year to be let inside my little room.

I left her sitting there in that stream bed.

She didn't move as I got up to walk away.

She just watched me.

Slowly I headed for the car.

Across the rocks and up the path I had walked hundreds of times. The little path which took me alongside the green hammock. The green hammock which had changed the way I listened to life.

I arrived at the car.

I mindfully started the engine, pausing to let the moment sink in. I slowly let out the clutch and drifted toward my infamous stop street at the beginning of the cul-de-sac.

This time, I wouldn't be back.

A RETURN TO JOY

ARRIVING IN PEACE

IT WAS A rather emotional trip across the country as I left behind some special relationships and fond memories of Cape Town. I decided to take a few nights extra on my journey so I could process the changing season of my life. My diary from that time is full of regrets, incredible experiences, and unfinished business.

I arrived in Durban a few days later. It was warm, hot, and sunny, even in the middle of winter. A deep sense of peace rested on me. Cycling along the beachfront on my first day, a stillness in my soul was so palpable I was touched. *Have I really listened to God and He is blessing me with this feeling?* I felt like I was on an amazing holiday experience. Everything slowed to perfect harmony and contentment.

Except this time I wasn't on holiday. It was another day in my normal life. My aunt was with me on the bicycle adventure, I was home.

I knew the peace wouldn't last forever so I relished the moment. I knew I had arrived. Where? I could not tell. The peace was not a calmness of mind, it was much deeper. My soul knew I had done a good thing. It could now rest. It was as if the deepest part of myself knew I had been obedient to the flow of life. I had given up resisting.

I knew no matter what happened in Durban, it was exactly where God wanted me. I was traveling in His will, not mine. I hadn't wanted to leave Cape Town which I thought would be the pinnacle of perfect existence. Now I was running on His time, His flow, His guidance. This was not exactly the plan I dreamed, but His path was lined with love, peace, joy, and abundance.

My previous path was stress, burnout, and disease.

I was embracing the new.

Laying my judgments down for something greater.

I was experiencing the inner gifts of love, peace, joy—for heeding His call.

I was finally listening to the music playing deep inside of me.

LITTLE APARTMENT, A LOT OF LOVE

THE APARTMENT WAS situated on the Durban beachfront with views of the ocean and lush green gardens beneath. It was idyllic in its location for my healing. Ocean. Walks. Gardens. It was also a big adjustment for me. A big adjustment for all of us in the little apartment.

Up to this point, I had lived in community houses and on my own. More often than not, I had been surrounded by people, parties, and oftentimes, peculiar behavior. Now my flatmates, friends, and confidants were my aunt and her friend, Khanyisile.

They welcomed me with open arms. It was incredible to receive the generosity of family again. Even though the apartment had very little space for me, the two older women made room. Khanyi chose to sleep on a mattress on the floor so I, the sick one, could have a bed. I was very moved by the gesture. If I sat up in bed and looked over the thin dividing wall, I could see Khanyi's feet sticking out on the mattress on the floor. I went to bed each night with the view of self-sacrifice – a typical characteristic of African women, their ability to keep giving, even when they have so little.

Initially I thought I would stay for a month or two. As time went by, two months became nearly two years. During this time, my aunt and Khanyi were extremely understanding of my situation and wellness practices. My aunt allowed her home to become a retreat space and joined in my outflow time, coloring-in time, cellphone curfews, and silence after 8 pm. I laugh when I recall this time. Khanyisile must have thought we were crazy when we stopped talking to each other as the clock chimed 8 pm. I still needed this quiet space, and she was content to watch her local soap operas on TV and play games on her phone. It was a miracle to live with people so supportive of my healing.

Living close to the beach, I picked up my previous routine of heading out for sunset walks. Sunset was a special, rejuvenating, healing, and spiritual time of the day for me. It topped me up to be outside at golden hour when the light changed from day to dusk, to eventide. After months of praying quietly on my own in the mountains in Cape Town, I now had a beach at my feet where I could sink my prayers into the sand. Not only this but when I headed down for my time with nature and God, I had companions there for similar reasons. On most days, many African men and women prayed out their hearts at the seaside.

This was not the "in the closet" kind of prayer I was used to. These people were often knee-deep in the water with their arms to the sky, pleading and begging with God. As I walked by, they didn't stop, slow down, or lower their voices. They were loud, raised, and animated. Some angry, some emotional. All in dialogue with Divine spark. It wasn't only typical "religious folk" on the beach speaking to their Maker. Sometimes men in suits appeared, looking like they had walked out of Wall Street, now staring at the horizon and speaking to the Big Boss. I wondered what they were praying for. Bigger businesses, better relationships, support for their families? Sometimes women carried their high heels in their hands as they walked to the water's edge. Each and all on the beach, in commune with their Creator.

This was faith in action. I was inspired. These people were not scared to show the world they had a relationship with God. It wasn't a secret. No ego to hold them back. No concerns about what others thought.

Personally, I wouldn't dare express my relationship with God so openly, especially in a public space. I was embarrassed. Yet here were multitudes of people unafraid to express themselves in public before the presence of the Almighty. It livened me. It encouraged my faith. It encouraged my prayers. I started talking out loud too. It took me out of my comfort zone. Whenever I passed someone and I was praying out loud, I would cringe inside. I wanted to keep silent but I purposefully pushed through my ego's judgments. No one cared. In Africa, on that stretch of beach, it was normal to be in dialogue with our Divine Provider.

THE HEART KEEPS KNOCKING

As time went by in the little apartment, something emerged from the depths of my heart. I started to hear a little whisper in the quiet time with myself, or in the evening walks, or the morning pages of diary writing. "It's time to take a break," my heart spoke softly.

I thought I was resting well and taking fairly good breaks already, but the voice was adamant…"You need a time out, proper time out!"

This was a calling for a bigger de-stress, to gain a proper perspective on my life, to celebrate what I had come through, to digest my new life, and to move to a new chapter.

One which didn't involve disease in its pages.

The whispers became more frequent and I started dreaming of a specific activity—a walking pilgrimage. When I played this long walk through my imagination, my body, and heart came alive. "This is what you need," my heart whispered with glee. "Can't wait!" Said my body. To my mind, it was impossible, "How will you cope? You are too unfit! You can't do that. It's too wild. Wait another year or two." This was true. I could barely manage a few hundred meters on the beach without worrying about overdoing it.

Regardless, my heart kept reminding me of an experience a few years earlier. I'd walked a famous route called the Camino de Santiago in northern Spain. My heart reminded me of the time; Freedom, lightness, simplicity, perspective, and space.

I was still working remotely, so between my business responsibilities and ongoing chronic fatigue sensitivities, I pushed the whispers aside more often than I'd like to admit. *Some other time, some other year. When I'm properly through this and settled, then I could take some time out.*

The whispers for the journey came and went over weeks and months. It ebbed and flowed like the tide of the ocean. Sometimes stronger on a full moon, sometimes softer and more forgotten. Hiding in the recesses of my heart it was sometimes enticed out by questions or prayer.

Mostly in my day-to-day stress of running a business and generally being alive, the feeling would go to hide until I created some quiet time for myself. Or, when I was reaching breaking point, it would gently remind me I could choose another way. I felt guilty for a moment for not listening, and then I would resume my old ways. I was stuck in this unhealthy cycle of ignoring the calling. When I rested a little, my doubting mind would return: "You see, you don't need a long break, you are fine. Take smaller breaks." Although true, my heart was playing a different tune.

The cycle of ignoring the whispers continued until a chance encounter with a great therapist.

A friend encouraged me to go for counseling and this time I willingly agreed. I was ready to speak, share and heal. I booked an appointment with happiness in my heart and scheduled our first session. The counselor lived an hour from my home, which proved an enjoyable adventure for me.

The day arrived for our connect. I was nervous about starting something new. As I neared the therapist's house for the first time— my heart full of prayers for healing and discovery—a hawk circled nearby. I watched it dance and dive on the hillside next to her home. *A good sign.* As I stopped at her front gate, a beautiful, small bird sat on the post. A kingfisher.

Another welcoming sign.

The birds were with me.

She met me at my car and guided me to the classic therapist couch. After some introductory questions, she looked at me with great care in her eyes and asked, "So, what do *you* feel you need to do to get better?"

Immediately the whispers of my heart became words in my mouth; "I feel like I need to take a long break—some proper time out."

"Of course you need a break," she said with compassion. "You've dealt with your mother's death, family challenges, business challenges, moving home, constant energy management problems, and a lot of change."

Butterflies fluttered in my chest—someone was agreeing with the voice of my heart.

The therapist gave me the perspective that I really did need a break. I couldn't see how much I had been through until I started expressing it. We also noted I didn't seem to value myself enough to give myself a rest. To do "nothing". To take time out. I was somehow having to "earn it". My mind was saying, "*when* you've done this, *when* you've done that." If I waited to get healthier, I might never go. It was the same when I burned out. I was waiting until I "got there", until *No Danger Diaries* was a success. It never happened. We still hadn't arrived. I realized it wasn't a case of "when I'm better, I can go walking", it was a case of "walking will make me better." My therapist was helping me win the battle of mind over heart on the pilgrimage of my wellbeing.

My heart was singing again and my mind was trying its best to ignore the music.

"What is holding you back?" she asked. I listened to the voice again in my head; "You don't have a real reason to go. You haven't earned it. You don't have the time, the money, or the health. Your business needs you. You've just moved to Durban and you can't up and leave now."

I was outwardly silent.

"My own mind is holding me back," I said.

It was the classical dance between my head and my heart. Even though I had won a few battles before this, I was still at war for a heart-led life. There were more consequences involved now. There were bigger odds at stake.

I needed to trust.

I needed to follow the whisper.

The small, still voice of my heart was calling me to freedom.

I needed to trust I would be given the energy and resources to complete the trip.

I needed to trust that whilst I was walking, all my responsibilities would also be looked after.

I needed to trust the Divine Parent watching over me now would take care of my whole life.

If I had truly surrendered my life to God, I needed to let Him control it.

"It's time for me to do a walking pilgrimage through Europe," I said. "I can feel it. That's where I need to be". My therapist was supportive. It made perfect sense to her, even though she knew I still had bad days without any energy.

"The Camino de Santiago," she said.

"Yes," I replied.

"I am also planning on going," she said.

What are the chances? My heart sang. *Has God led me here to give me another nudge?*

We reminisced about the beauty of walking for days with little else but a small backpack. We had both done long walks before.

She helped me identify some worst-case scenarios, and I spoke through any fears which welled up. She helped me get clarity on what I needed and be comforted I would be safe.

I decided I would be gone for 40 days.

As I was leaving, the topic of spirit animals came up, and I told her about the birds and hawks that had guided me.

She smiled as she looked at me, "Do you know what I consider to be my spirit bird?"

I shook my head.

"The kingfisher," she said.

When I left it was still perched outside.

A MEMORY OF ENCOURAGEMENT

I WENT HOME and wrote down more fears which arose. I made a list of solutions next to each one and dissolved fears which were extremely unrealistic. Sometimes I laughed at the irrational mind-stories.

F.E.A.R. False-Evidence-Appearing-Real.

I busted them one by one until peace returned about the upcoming journey.

There wasn't exactly an "aha" moment when I immediately decided to go—it took some time and patience. My mind still tried to bury me in a mountain of work whilst my heart reminded me of the necessity of the journey for my longer-term health benefits.

As I wrestled, the mind slowly came onboard.

One day I crossed the finish line.

A memory helped to carry me into action mode. It was an experience I had about three years prior.

The memory had lain dormant in my mind until this point.

It was a moment from my first Camino de Santiago. I had ended up on the trail unplanned. A friend had encouraged me to walk it while I was in Spain.

I was reminded of a morning when I woke at 5 am.

I was in a tiny village, staying in a pilgrim's hostel.

When my eyes snapped open it was still totally dark.

All the pilgrims were still sleeping or snoring. My usual routine was to wake nearer to 7 am, have coffee or tea, and head out onto the trail. This morning was different. An invisible force from beyond was tugging me into action right away. I was full of energy and purposeful.

I fumbled for my flashlight, slid out of bed, and walked hurriedly to the bathroom to brush my teeth. I suddenly had a mission to complete. I questioned the surprise of this early morning burst of inspiration, but I followed along because it felt right. I rolled my sleeping bag and carefully zipped my backpack, trying not to wake the roosting humans. Before exiting, I gave one last glance at the shadows of my sleeping companions. I was sad to leave alone. These folk had become my daily walking companions and friends.

Will I ever see them again? The thought flashed through my mind as I slipped out the slumbering dormitory.

I did another internal check. *Are you sure?* "Yes. Let's go."

As I walked outside, the air was crisp and fresh. The stars were out in full splendor.

I was immediately liberated and free to be on my own so early in the morning.

It was cold. The Spanish air brushed against my jacket, and my footsteps were the only sound wafting through the crunchy streets.

I kept walking. The streets and houses vanished as I switched on my headlamp to locate the yellow arrows to keep me on the trail.

Crunch, crunch, crunch, went my feet.

I was in awe at being under the beauty of the sparkling night sky before daybreak.

What a great time to be alive.

In the predawn darkness, I could see I was heading into an approaching forest. Although very dark already, the forest offered a deeper shade of black as I neared. One by one, the stars disappeared, shaded by the trees. To add extra spice to my solo venture, I decided to switch off my headlamp and walk by way of feeling. I listened to my footsteps to know I was still on the gravel. I figured the edge of the tree line would keep me in place.

Crunch, crunch, crunch, went my footsteps.

I was alive, elated, free, and wild. Alone in the forest at a strange hour. My eyes adjusted to all the different shades of dark. The trees. The night sky.

A bird made a sound. A flutter of wings.

I slowed down to concentrate on keeping on the road.

It became very silent. Eerie. I switched on my headlamp for a moment to get my bearings. Everything went white. A pure, foggy white. Low-hanging morning mist had moved in. The mist dimmed my headlight. I switched it off. Total darkness.

My mind started its games. *Is this forest dangerous? Could I be lost now? Are there wild animals or stray dogs? Are there things such as witches? Could I become a pilgrim statistic horror story?*

Then I heard a sound.

Crunch. Crunch.

It was not the sound of my footsteps.

I stopped walking.

Crunch.

Barely moving, I listened as intently as I could.

Crunch. Crunch. Crunch.

These crunches on the gravel were slow, about three seconds apart. Something was on the road ahead of me.

I switched on my headlight nervously.

White mist.

Crunch. Crunch. Crunch.

A wolf? A dog? A person?

I was unprepared for this moment.

There is no way this could be a person, I thought. *I was definitely the first person out of that nearest town this morning, and anyone who got up before me would have woken up at 4 am or sooner. No one would do that.*

Crunch. Crunch.

On full alert, I nervously proceeded. Fear rose inside me—I decided to keep my headlight trained on the spot I heard the sound coming from.

I was fully expecting to face a bear, or a dog, or a witch.

Then I saw it.

A figure about five feet tall in the middle of the road.

It was a hazy shadow outlined amongst the mist. I paused again, squinting my eyes to assess the danger. *Crunch.* It was definitely the thing making the sound and it was moving slowly away from me.

With my headlight trained on it, I slowly approached. I veered to the left to keep as much distance as possible between us. As I got within passing distance, the shape became clear.

It was an old lady.

She was completely hunched over.

She walked with a Zimmer frame to support her steps.

Each movement with the frame made a crunching sound on the gravel.

Crunch.

I stopped. I watched.

She picked up her frame, shuffled slightly forward, and put it down again.

Crunch.

One difficult step at a time.

I couldn't believe what I was seeing. In the middle of a small forest in Spain before dawn, an old lady was "walking" her pilgrimage. I stared. Transfixed. She was so slow it was painful to witness. Each step looked like a mammoth undertaking. She could only pick up the walking frame every three seconds or so as she shuffled her feet forward. *Crunch. Shuffle. Crunch. Shuffle.*

To be where she was at this hour, I wondered if she must have been up at 3 am. My mind raced. *How far would she get in a day before the sun becomes too hot? Is she only walking at night?* I had no idea. I couldn't fathom the scenario. It was the last thing I expected. The crunch I heard was the sound of the Zimmer frame hitting gravel. The sound of sheer perseverance. *Crunch. Shuffle.*

I shined the light of my headlamp near her and she didn't react. *Crunch. Shuffle.*

She appeared to be completely absorbed in her task. Her own world.

Crunch. Shuffle.

I stood motionless at a short distance, unsure of what to do.

Do I walk on by? Do I help? How do I even help? I wasn't sure if what I was seeing was real.

I decided to keep my distance on the left-hand side of the road as I passed. Close to her, I called out the familiar pilgrim greeting, "Buen camino!" which means "good path," but she didn't even raise her head. I leaned in a little nearer and said it again, "Buen camino!" She uttered something inaudible, still looking down at her feet. I tried to look at her face. I couldn't see it. Her head was bowed too low. She was very hunched. *Crunch. Shuffle.*

I walked further in front of her and looked back. I tried to get one more glance. The mist made it difficult. *What can I do?* I looked at the road in front of me. I wanted to help, but there was nothing I could do. She didn't speak English. I couldn't carry her.

We were simply two pilgrims in a forest on our own journeys to God.

I walked away.

Hesitantly at first.

I was profoundly impacted by the encounter.

Slowly I increased my pace, contemplating the meeting, and then, I returned to Daniel-speed. I heard one last *crunch-shuffle*, then she was gone.

An unexplainable meaningful encounter—awe and wonder filled my being.

This lady. Who is she? How far had she come? Where is she going? Why is she doing this? Is it a matter of faith that gives her the courage to achieve something seemingly impossible to me?

My heart cautiously explored the thought she was doing this for her God. I struggled to comprehend the notion she could be giving the last of her life to be on a pilgrimage for her belief system. *Why would she do this? What is driving her? Maybe I will read in the newspaper an old lady died on her last journey with the Lord?* I pictured the newspaper headline in Santiago; *'Last Steps with the Lord: 85-year-old lady dies of heart attack on pilgrimage'.*

I was moved by her determination.

Whatever was motivating her was real and inspiring.

I thought about those who had great excuses for never leaving their homes to adventure. I thought about the lies people believed—chains dragging us away from the life-changing possibility of heart inspired adventures. The missed opportunities for growth, perspective, healing, revelation, and insight.

I swore if I ever met another person with a moderate excuse for not setting out on their adventure, I would tell them this story.

The zimmer frame in the night.

A lady who had a thousand excuses to say no but said yes to the one good reason to go.

Faith.

It was nearly time to tell myself this story.

THE MIND SLAIN AGAIN

AS THE MEMORY finished playing, I knew what I had to do.

If she could do it, I could do it.

It was the ammunition I needed to win the war of the mind. Whenever the doubts came, I would shoot them down with this story. After all, I had experienced it myself.

I remembered the awe.

The struggle.

The feeling.

"My excuses are pitiful compared to that," I would tell myself, "She was in a much worse state than I am now."

I had seen her with my own eyes. I couldn't deny it. If I had chronic fatigue, this lady had chronic fatigue plus a dose of 90-years-old and a Zimmer frame.

The lady with the Zimmer frame was giving my heart the courage it needed to overcome the doubts of my mind.

Armed with the memory, the encouragement of my therapist, and my ever-believing-in-me aunt, I made up my mind. I would walk the Portuguese route to Santiago in Spain. I would give myself 40 days and 40 nights, like Jesus in the desert, and I would do my best to stay alive. I didn't know how I would do it, but I knew I needed God this time.

For the first time in my life I would not be walking alone. I would be walking with faith. It was also not about the end goal this time. It would be about the journey. If I got to the end, then I got to the end. If I didn't, then I had another tale to tell. If I needed to rest for five days in one place, I would. If I needed to walk only four kilometers in one day, I would. It would be a great test for me to listen to my body, heart, mind, and spirit. To God. To keep checking in. Only I would know what I could manage. Day by day.

Gone were the days of setting a goal and burning myself out along the way. It starkly contrasted the Daniel who had walked three years before. The Daniel who stubbornly set his mind to something and would damage himself and others in the process of achieving it. The Daniel who would walk 50 kilometers a day to quietly boast about the distance to fellow pilgrims at the dinner table. A Daniel who took pleasure in passing slower, struggling pilgrims on the path. This Daniel would be different. Restful. Mindful. Slow. Helpful. Courteous. Willing to surrender to what the path would bring.

I vouched I would help everyone I could and hopefully help myself in the process.

A Camino with God.

COMMITMENT TO HEAL

I STUBBORNLY DECIDED if God was in my heart and my heart was really calling me to do it, I would be given the energy to complete it. I still had chronic fatigue but I decided God would carry me through it. I decided while completing my walk, the same God would look after my businesses, finances, friendships, and everything else. The longest walks I had done in over two years were a mere kilometer or three along the mountain or beaches. Now I would be walking more than 800 kilometers across two countries, sleeping in strange beds with snorers, and eating foods that were not healthy smoothies. The journey would flip my world upside down. The journey would be a great surrender, to trust God would get me through somehow.

It was a final calling for faith. A final calling to let go of the stronghold which M.E. and chronic fatigue had on my life.

I knew if I held this trust it would shatter the chains of my illness forever. Or, it would leave me in a hospital somewhere in rural Portugal. Either way it would create a new chapter.

I walked over to my mobile phone where it lay on my bed. I was sweating. I was walking back and forward. My phone had the website open for booking my flight to Portugal. I had visited before and had failed to book it then. Even now I was delaying the process of committing. I picked up my phone. My thumb hovered over the 'book flight' button. Was it really this hard to click confirm? Was I really willing to change my life?

'Book flight'. Click.

'Confirm payment details'. Click.

'Enter credit card details'. Click.

'Confirmation email'. Received.

'Flight reference number'. Received.

Flights booked!

I fell to the bed from where I was standing. A fountain of energy poured over me. Like a waterfall, I was drenched by an invisible flow of life force. It tensed my body as if an electric current was flowing through me. Vibrant energy pulsed my heart and solar plexus from somewhere. Tears came to meet my eyelids. I was being given the energy to complete the task at hand. I was being Divinely supported. At this moment I knew wholeheartedly what God was calling me to do—go on a journey for Him. In doing so, I would overcome disease completely and begin to trust in a new way of living.

I lay there feeling like the Creator or His helpers had sent me this burst of energy. My soul was reconnecting to its highest purpose in a surrendered life, and knew what I was doing was for my greatest good and the good of others.

The energy experience gave me hope.

It was His will.

DANIEL IN PORTUGAL

THE DAY CAME in early October for me to head out. My bag was packed and my aunt and Khanyi sent me off with a small, meaningful farewell. My mission was to be as uncontactable as possible, but I promised to send updates via email when possible. I downloaded an app on my phone so I could send emails without having to open my inbox. No incoming messages, only outgoing ones. That was my plan and I stuck to it. At the same time I reached out to a friend in Spain. She had encouraged me she'd help if I got ill or stuck. This simple gesture brought me more comfort than I could imagine. Thank you, Veronica. She was the same person who had guided me onto a train years before for my first Camino experience. Our conversations gave me the confidence I needed at the right moment.

Deep down I knew this journey was a tipping point of getting better. It would be the fuel I needed to truly believe I was well. I knew my body had gotten rid of the disease, now I needed my mind to believe it too.

The proof would be in the pudding, or rather, the walking.

I arrived in Lisbon, Portugal, near midnight.

After collecting my luggage, I drew some cash from an ATM and caught a taxi directly to my hostel.

I arrived and minutes later headed to the bathroom to wash and get ready for sleep.

I unzipped my backpack for toiletries and clean clothes.

Surprise!

Everything was white.

I mean *everything*.

My foot powder had exploded during the flight and a fine, white dust coated the entire inside of my bag. Opening the zipper was like switching on a smoke machine. Instantly, the bathroom was filled with white mist.

I unzipped my toiletry bag to witness the foot powder making friends with my toothbrush.

Instead of relaxing and preparing for rest, I had to instead start de-powdering all my possessions.

Why is my trip starting like this?

I lifted one suspicious eyebrow to God.

My heart was pleading already… *don't leave me, and don't forsake me. You brought me here.*

After dusting, I got to bed well after 2 am.

I climbed into the quiet dormitory with extra doubt about the journey ahead of me.

At 6:30 am, the sound of the city awoke me.

I felt afraid.

New city. New sounds. New fears.

A voice whispered in me: *Let's start walking right away. There is no point in wallowing in fear. Get going!*

I salvaged a shirt from the evening "snowstorm" and repacked my bag.

I paused for a moment and looked around the room.

One last glance before the journey into the unknown.

I hoisted my pack onto my shoulders and headed for the reception.

I didn't expect to see anyone, I had paid online, so I didn't have the usual check-out formalities.

Slightly surprised, a set of eyes looked up at me from behind the reception desk.

We were both curious to see each other so bright and early.

"Bom dia," she said.

"Good morning," I replied.

I looked at her and smiled, "I'm walking to Spain now".

Considering I was in the middle of Lisbon, Portugal, it probably wasn't the most common over-the-counter statement.

She looked at me curiously, "Camino de Santiago?"

I paused for a second. Letting the gravity of it sink in.

"Yes," I said.

"Good luck," she said in an unfamiliar accent.

God luck, I thought.

I opened the heavy metal door and headed onto the cobbled street.

I looked to the left.

This way.

ME, GOD, AND YELLOW ARROWS

THE STREET WAS already alive.

People were setting out about their morning routines. A lady running with her dog. Partygoers from the night before draped like clothing on steps beneath a statue.

A peddler offered me illegal substances.

Around me was a mixture of morning air, cleaning up, and people activating.

I took out my map.

It was time to start navigating.

I had some experience from the Camino I had done years before. I checked the general direction and scanned the pavements and building corners for the infamous yellow arrows.

These arrows are a part of most European Camino's. They guide wearied pilgrims toward their end destination and span thousands of kilometers.

No sooner had I walked a couple of hundred meters, I saw the first one. I was elated. A little yellow arrow painted on the bottom of a wall. It was so inconspicuous, nestled amongst the city's jargon, posters, and media, yet it lit my heart from the inside out. These innocent and clumsy waymarkers would guide me from the center of Lisbon in Portugal to the Cathedral of Santiago de Compostela in Spain.

If God allowed me to get that far.

I'm running on His breath.

After several more minutes of walking, I arrived at a beautiful, old church. It was already bustling. Onlookers admired the architecture, doing their Hail Marys and taking selfies with Jesus. I looked at the receptionist behind a small desk. I took out my pilgrim passport and handed it to him, hoping he would know what to do. He opened a drawer and pulled out an old stamp pad. Without saying a word, *thud* went the stamp into my book.

The moment was surreal.

It was really happening.

I was qualified for a journey of a lifetime.

I was now Camino official.

The stamps in my Camino passport would allow me to receive a certificate of completion if I made it to Santiago. I looked at the book. Empty pages. There were still so many stamps to be collected. So many experiences to be had. Which places? Which names? Which towns? Which people? What adventures would I have?

I walked out of the church and scanned for the waymarkers. A clumsy yellow arrow showed the way. It pointed to the left, and off I went.

I rounded the corner and below me was the next arrow, painted high on a cobbled wall. I asked a passerby to take a photo of me under the arrow. It would be my *before and after* picture. As she gladly agreed, she looked truly excited to be standing with a real live pilgrim.

"Santiago?" she asked.

"Yes," I replied. Both of us silently contemplated the gravity of the hundreds of kilometers still to be trodden. She seemed in awe while I was in secret speculation. She snapped some pics and asked if she could pray for my journey. I was touched. A heartfelt prayer from God to bless my journey. She prayed earnestly and honestly, and her simple prayer cemented the sacredness of the moment. I was deeply blessed. Already my morning had been fruitful. I thanked her and put my phone back into my pocket. I turned. I knew this was the official send-off.

It was now me, God, and the yellow arrows.

CAMINO OF THE HEART

THAT FIRST DAY was tough. Up and down the steep steps of Lisbon. My physical body hurt and my mental body doubted. My backpack cut into my shoulders. It was too heavy. I wondered what all I was carrying in there. The nagging doubt was forcing me to believe I wouldn't make it.

I found my way to a youth hostel on the outskirts of the city. My whole system was in shock from exertion. To a normal person it would not have been much of a challenging walk, but to my mind and state of being, it was an adventure of Himalayan proportions. I wondered how quickly I would be able to adapt. I wondered if I would already need to take rest days before continuing.

I made dinner in a big open-plan communal kitchen. One or two people were dotted around the space. I wondered if they were pilgrims. I returned to my bunk bed.

What will the morning bring?

When I flicked my eyes open to the first rays of sunlight, I first scanned my body.

Severe fatigue.

Stiff and sore muscles.

I felt sluggish.

I was low on energy.

Even worse, my mind was foggy.

I wanted to lie in bed and sleep.

My hope dissolved like disprin in a lake.

Nightmares from past M.E. days came back to torment me.

You will never make it, they whispered.

I lay in bed, not knowing what to do.

Should I push on or should I rest?

I was already at a tipping point. I had to make my first decision concerning my health, wellbeing, and the journey ahead.

My thoughts spun like a merry-go-round.

Fear clutched at me.

What is the worst that can happen? I asked myself.

Rest. Go slow.

I continued to console myself: *Stay in bed. Recover. Remember—as long as it takes.*

Whatever happens, I said to comfort myself, *I can always rely on rest.*

And that's what I decided to do.

To be still for the moment and let my body and mind recover.

When you don't know what to do, do nothing!

I prayed; *God, help me. What can I do? What do you need me to do? This is your journey.*

I put the pillow on my head. I lay very still and quiet, listening for any incoming messages in my inner world.

Suddenly, a response, "You are carrying too much stuff, Daniel".

It emerged from the quiet depths of my being.

I had positioned myself to receive a response of support, I had got one.

"What stuff?" I replied.

I thought about my backpack, but the voice indicated there was something more.

I stretched my listening for a further answer.

I lay under the pillow, searching for feelings and thoughts.

Suddenly, from out of nowhere, pain regarding my mother surfaced. I remembered her face, her care, her nurturing. My heart became an emotional soup.

Stuff.

This was followed by waves of anxiety. My thoughts went to the vitamins, supplements, precautions, and supportive wellbeing accessories I had in my bag.

The penny dropped.

I was carrying too much weight because I still had ties to my mother's mortality and strings to my illness.

Now that God had brought me to the trail, I knew I would have to let even more go. I could hang onto the past in the comfort of my home, but on the Pilgrimage, these things were exposed, and I had to move on to get on.

There was no more space for them here.

I crawled out from my duvet-pity-party and headed first to my backpack. I would start with the physical baggage. *Get the kilograms off your back,* said the voice. I reached into my pack and pulled out a pair of jeans. *What on earth would I need these for? I'm not going out and have no one to impress.* Out they went. Next was a beautiful, warm jacket my aunt had given me, a present she had received many years before. "Sorry, Aunty," I said aloud as they joined the jeans. I rifled through all my items. No need for rope or extra water bottles or other accessories, which I had originally deemed as absolute essentials. The Camino had already taught me what was absolutely essential… travel lightly.

After shedding a couple more kilo's, I climbed back into bed.

I would leave these items here for a fellow pilgrim to pick up. Maybe someone else would be blessed by my excess.

Shed the mental load, was the next impulse.

A major thing weighing me down was my own expectations. The expectation to have walked farther on the first day. The expectation of not being tired. The expectation of getting "somewhere" on any particular day. The expectation of "completing" the Camino. The expectation to "be better". I was doing the best I could, so I went through the mental list of affirmations again;

I do not need to 'finish' anything. I do not have an end goal. I do not have anywhere to be other than here. Being in Portugal is a total wonder in itself. Enjoy each day for what it is.

Letting go of these expectations began a beautiful practice to surrender each day. Take it as it comes.

Calmness returned to me after the inner pep talk.

Inches Daniel, Inches. A few small steps every day.

Things were already looking up for me from my own pillow talks.

Physical baggage… released.

Mental baggage… released.

I scanned my heart.

Emotional baggage next, came the answer.

Feelings of my mom and her death welled up again. I realized an important part of this journey was also for her. To remember her and commemorate her. I had brought with me a treasured stone of hers to Portugal. An actual physical slab of rock was sitting at the bottom of my backpack. It had an inscription on it; *It is here with the wind that I hear my soul.*

I had planned to carry it with me and release it on a beautiful mountaintop to say my final goodbyes.

Thinking about the size of the rock, I thought to myself, *will you even make it to a mountain top with so much extra weight?*

Why do I want to suffer carrying this darn thing? Why are you waiting for some perfect moment in the future that you might never realize?

The time is now.

What was once a good idea to my mind was now causing me suffering.

I will not carry this for one more day, I said to myself.

I sat up in bed and returned to my backpack. I dug to the bottom of my bag and hoisted it out. It was flat and moderately thick. It took two hands to hold it.

I knew what to do.

I would begin the ceremony right now. I would lay this down on only my second day. There was no need to drag it around with me. I was to face my emotions today.

I packed a few things in my carry bag and exited the hostel.

I meandered down a few roads as I flowed toward the Tagus river, a mighty river that runs through Portugal and grazes Lisbon.

Sorry mom, I can't take you where I wanted to, sorry I've got to say goodbye here.

I sat down on the grass next to a few manicured shrubs and small trees close to the river. I looked across the mighty Rio Tejo river. It was wide and impressive.

As I gazed into the power of nature, something else was building in my heart.

It was a source of its own powerful flow.

Not now. I can't break down now.

Without consent, grief poured from my heart. Tears flowed down my cheeks. I was sobbing. It felt like yesterday my mother had passed. My heart memories were so fresh.

I wondered in which little box this grief had been stored. I thought I had emptied all the boxes labeled 'mom'. I thought I had faced the pain and grieved healthily. It showed me I couldn't empty the well of grief, it simply changed form, each month and year bringing fresh feelings and new thoughts to seal the tomb of sweet mortal memories.

My well of grief was deeper than I thought.

I surrendered. It was part of my *no-expectation* and *nowhere to be but here* philosophy.

When the tears slowed, I took out my notebook and wrote a letter to my mom. I wrote about all the things I was grateful to her for. I wrote about all the things she taught me. I wrote about the things I was disappointed in her for. I addressed the letter directly to her. I wrote about things I needed to ask for forgiveness for. I told her about the things I forgave her for. I said goodbye. I suggested it was time for us to both move on.

I tied the letter to the 'soul stone' I was carrying. I finished it with a neat little bowtie. My mom would have liked that present. I stood up and walked to the end of a nearby jetty protruding out into the river. My emotional state was part guilty and part relieved. Guilty and disappointed because I didn't make it to the big picturesque mountains I had planned. Relieved I was facing uncomfortable moments now and could continue lighter. I walked to the end of the pier. My eyes misted. I looked at the nearby birds in the water. My mom loved birds. I scanned the surrounding sights and atmosphere, soaking the very moment into the pores of my being.

It's time.

I threw that stone as hard as I could.

It sailed through the air and splashed into the mighty Tagus river. The flock of nearby birds took flight as the stone landed. I stood there, watching the birds.

The flock did a big loop and flew close to my head.

My mom's moment.

My heart sang to God.

It wasn't the moment I wanted to choose, but it was perfect. The letting go.

I said some last words and walked back to my belongings on the grass. I lay down, concealed myself from passersby, and allowed more tears to flow. Drop by drop. More healing gold for my heart. I knew it was part of the reason I was on this trip. Without the distractions and the stress and strain of being always on the go, I could finally take the lid off some of the emotions that were keeping me ill.

I looked at the beautiful flowers. My mother seemed to be everywhere. I felt more peace. My heart was happier. I began packing my things—less ill than before. I was less fatigued, more clear-headed, less sick, and more vibrant. Something had cleared.

It wasn't rest that I had needed. It was to let down my baggage. To release. No amount of days in bed would have created the lightness I felt of more healing.

I walked back to my hostel room with a slight spring in my step. The morning's impending doom and duvet party had disappeared.

I might actually be able to do this, I thought.

Hope returned.

Step by step, Daniel.

Breath by breath.

One day at a time.

TO WALK AND RELEASE

THE NEXT DAY I woke up shining like a new person. My confidence returned and my body strengthened. I was now ready to meet the remaining days moment by moment, allowing God's plan, setting my own agendas aside, receiving the Camino as it would arrive to meet me.

A new prayer edged its way in; *God, may I use my energy to be of service to this planet.*

I prayed this prayer day after day.

If you give my energy back, may you direct it to those who need it most.

A small bit of my selfishness was being burned off.

One stormy night, many days from the Tagus River, I was alone in a small hut. Thunder and lightning pelted the dark, milky sky. As I sat at a small kitchen table eating dinner, memories of my sister's traumatic episode reappeared. They forcefully came marching in as the storm broke overhead. One minute I was eating dinner—the next—I could not take another bite. The memories were vivid. I relived the moments of coaxing her to the hospital, trying to keep her in the car from running away at random traffic lights, telling her we were going to get ice cream when we were headed for the psychiatric ward. The memories tore open my heart. I suppose I hadn't faced the trauma as I thought I had. With each scene, I felt it all over again. I remembered as she screamed obscenities at me whilst she was strapped to a hospital bed. As the thunder clapped, my heart opened. Like sand pouring through an hourglass, memories moved through my heart. As each grain touched my heart, they were transformed into something else. I was crying loudly. Shuddering. Sobbing. The storm intensified.

No one could hear my sobs.

Alone in the dark, I surrendered to the emotions volcano.

The power of the storm masked the sound of the sobbing emanating from my body.

Tears rolled as rain arrived. Fears came as flashes lit the sky. As the wind lashed the small house, it blew away emotional tension from the invisible holds in my body.

I never chose the time or the hour. I simply walked into spaciousness to allow it. By giving myself time, processes like this arrived naturally. No medicines, no therapists, no one to talk to. A natural process of grieving and transformation of trauma to love occurred in Divine timing. God knew the time and the hour. I never tried to hide anything inside me. I thought I had grieved and processed, yet I realized there were chambers in me I couldn't access in the daily routine of normal living. To break open new parts of myself required me to break my routine.

The moments came when they chose to come. I didn't know when they would. Often a little discomfort would be a warning, and when it hit, I didn't always know what I was releasing. I stopped worrying about it too. I let it flow like a soothing waterfall. Sometimes the timing was inconvenient. Sometimes I walked and cried and laughed. Sometimes I walked and sang. Sometimes I skipped with joy. Sometimes I floated with ideas. Sometimes I slowed with sorrow, and sometimes I stopped in total revelation. Sometimes I paused to scribble ideas in my journal as they came to meet me mid-stride. Each day was a fresh song. People came and went. Loneliness came and went. The full spectrum of being human was knitted into the jersey of my very own Camino. I noticed after each week, I was more like a helium balloon, getting lighter and lighter.

I laughed more and spoke out loud. I voiced my troubles to the trees and to others.

My challenges. My past. My future.

I listened to others.

I processed alone.

I processed with friends.

I processed with God.

This ancient technology of walking was food for my soul.

I walked into a freedom that would last a lifetime.

I remembered what Claudia had once told me, *Solvitur ambulando.*

"Do you know what that means, Daniel?" she asked.

"It is solved by walking."

BEYOND EXPECTATIONS

WITHIN THE FIRST week I had already experienced what I considered a miracle. On average I walked around 15km a day. I thought this was the maximum distance I could manage without over-exerting myself. On this particular day, I got caught in a trap. I was 12km down a rural dirt road when I checked the map and discovered I wasn't even halfway. Miscalculating, I realized there were still another 17km to go. This was more than double my usual distance. I frantically scanned the map for any means of roadside assistance. Nothing. No train, no taxi, no lifts. Most of the upcoming kilometers would be amongst the farmlands.

Standing in the middle of a hot, rural Portuguese road, I started to worry. *Would I make it? What would be the cost of this? Two or three days in bed?*

I kneeled on the dirt road for a moment and prayed to the heavens; *God, if you brought me to this, you will have to carry me through this. I can't do this alone. I need you. I need your Divine energy.*

I didn't want to go back. I wanted to go forward.

I wanted to walk with God.

I repeated this prayer again and again.

I eventually stood up and started walking.

Even as a healthy person, I knew this would be hard on my body.

I pressed on.

Hours slipped by.

I finally exited the farmlands and stepped onto tar roads again.

The sun was setting.

I took out an old beaded necklace.

I prayed.

As I touched each bead, I told God something I was grateful for.

There must have been at least 30 beads on the necklace, but I kept going.

Each step was an answered prayer.

I was grateful I was alive.

I was grateful that whatever happened, I was getting close to completing this day of walking.

I was grateful I was in Portugal.

I was grateful I had the courage to give myself a pilgrimage of time and space.

I was grateful to be me.

Some hours later I strode into a town, having completed 30 kilometers. I walked to a Bombeiros (fire station) to inquire about accommodation. They referred me to a hostel another kilometer away.

I arrived at the check-in counter and was still standing.

This was a miracle in itself.

What will be the cost of today's exertion? I thought.

I walked to town to find food and returned to my room for rest.

The morning will tell.

As my eyes flickered open the following morning, I scanned my body.

Using all the practice from my green hammock days, I searched for signs of oncoming M.E.

I moved my body around a bit. I flexed my feet, scanned my calf muscles, and felt the general condition of my body.

I am ok! Hallelujah!

I felt slight stiffness but no energy-less or fatigue!

I scanned my mind.

Clear!

I couldn't believe it.

I walked further than I could imagine, and I was fresher than I'd ever been. It was a pure gift from God.

I was reminded again—I didn't choose the time or the hour.

When He brought me to it, He carried me through it.

It was Divine energy all over again.

When I partnered with God, anything was possible.

When I followed God's plan, I was provided for.

As my inner world delighted and I continued my morning routine, I reflected on my walk thus far. I thought of when I was on my feet most of the day helping other pilgrims. Although we covered little distance, we were on our feet for long hours, and I had the energy for it. Not when I went out of my way to do it because I thought I had to, but when the moment felt right and natural to serve, when I put my plans aside, I was propped up by the provision of God. I thought of the times I had pushed for a destination, I was tired, flat. It was Personal energy vs. Infinite energy all over again—which one would I serve? It was an easy answer. Put myself aside and ride with the flow of Divinity. What an adventure!

As I brushed my teeth, I recommitted to being obedient to my heart in all moments. To play in the sea of endless energy. If it could help me on the Camino, then I knew it could surpass any thoughts or physical limitations.

It would all happen whilst I followed my heart.

I forgot I was ill.

LITTLE DOGGY: AN ACCIDENT OR A MEETING

OVER HALFWAY AND looking likely I would make it to Spain, I remember a morning filled with Divine timing. Crunching my way along yet another gravel road, I was particularly uncomfortable in my emotional body again. I was edgy, possibly on the verge of tears or about to snap angrily at somebody. Not for any reason other than I woke up feeling "prickly". Luckily there was no one around to receive Mr. grumpy. I was alone on the road. Lost in thoughts as I floated along the road, my mind-ventures were interrupted by sounds approaching from behind. I turned around to witness a group of four. Three dogs and a man on a bicycle. The dogs were bounding recklessly and playfully along the left shoulder of the road. I watched their carefree fun in motion, a contrast to my inner grumpiness. The dogs were playing about 15 meters in front of their owner on the bicycle. Suddenly, from the opposite direction, a car emerged on the horizon. A shock of nerves rattled me. The dogs were not paying attention. They were lost in their world of dog games. I looked at the bicycle man. He appeared unphased and nonchalant.

I looked back at the car and back to the dogs. The gap between the two was closing considerably. In my calculation the dogs were safe enough on the shoulder of the road, but close enough to have an accident if something startled them to change direction. I stood between the two worlds—the oncoming metallic monster and the innocently playing dogs. Seconds before the worlds collided, the smallest dog veered into the road. I shut my eyes. I heard the sound of dog-meets-car. A limp body washed up at my feet. I froze in horror. The worlds had collided.

The little dog was motionless.

The long open road was now a mortal melodrama at the tip of my toes.

Oh God.

I didn't know what to do. My first instinct was to walk away. I didn't want to participate in something I had not created. I tried to go but my feet were stuck. I was frozen.

Within seconds the man on the bicycle was on the scene.

He hunched over his little dog.

He cried out in Portuguese.

He stroked the little dog along the full length of its body.

He spoke to it.

The dog was in one piece but motionless.

Maybe it will get up? I thought.

Get up, little doggy, get up.

I watched.

Why, Lord, Why this?

The driver came running over.

Shouting loudly, the two men tensely exchanged words. They both hunched over the little dog. I seemed invisible to them. No one gave me the slightest attention. The driver was apologizing profusely. The bicycle man was angry. The air was charged.

Why have you brought me here, God? Why am I involved in this? What should I do?

"Pray," came the answer inside.

I stretched my hands out over the trio and started praying. I prayed for peace for the man who lost his dog. I prayed for the release of guilt the driver was sure to carry. I prayed for forgiveness on all parts. I prayed the little dog was on its way to doggy heaven and would be received joyously.

The two men didn't notice my outstretched hands over their heads.

Peace replaced the trauma and fear in me.

The air settled.

The bicycle man picked up his dog. He walked to the other side of the road and laid the little doggy in the bushes. The driver went back to his car. The bicycle man had tears running down his face. He looked shell-shocked. The other two dogs looked confused. The bicycle man cycled down the road. I was still standing motionless. I looked on. I was simply the observer. First there were four, now three.

Like that, life had happened.

What would the bicycle man tell his family?

Did he have a family?

Why was I involved in all of this?

Grief purchased on the ledge of my heart. The previous bad mood inside turned to tears. The road was suddenly as empty as before. My heart felt empty too. I shuffled to the other side of the road.

Near to the little doggy I made a cross out of sticks and sat down.

Salty tears streaked long lines on my face.

I said goodbyes and cried. I didn't know if I was crying for the dog or crying out my own pain. The hurt was so real and tangible. The little dog had triggered a deeper well of pain I was already carrying. My pain of loss, abandonment, grief. The little doggy was a catalyst for my own release.

As I squinted into the distance through teary eyes, I noticed a pair of pilgrims approaching. I could see by their walking sticks and backpacks they were on their Camino.

As they came closer, I didn't have the motivation to stand up. The weight of grief and confusion was like rocks in my pockets. I didn't bother wiping the tears from my eyes.

I'm crying and so what.

If they asked me I would tell them about the little doggy, who moments before, was living his happiest life.

As the pilgrims approached me, I sensed this was God's timing.

Pay attention, a voice inside me said.

Moments before, I was talking to God about the little dog. Now, somehow, my full attention was focused on the incoming duo.

It was as if God himself was arriving to meet me.

The pilgrims arrived.

The woman spoke first.

With little to no introduction she simply said, "Hi, we saw you yesterday walking fast through the forest. We thought we'd never see you again."

There are hundreds of pilgrims on this trail. Why would they want to see me again? I thought.

"What do you do for a living?" the man asked.

The automatic puppet took over my words.

"I'm a dance teacher," I said, slowly standing up. "I have a global movement of people who come together at sunrise to dance, share joy, and experience something deeper and more connected".

"That's it," he said with a sense of authority, like he had been contemplating this for ages. "The church is losing the young people. You need to keep doing what you are doing and take it to the youth".

My soul jolted as if a lightning bolt set itself off inside me.

Whatever he said penetrated a deep part of me. God was near.

The dog. The tears. The people. The words.

I said nothing.

I walked in step with the duo for a while, feeling like I was on 'level deep' while wrestling for words in my inner world.

Was God answering the question I had been asking for ages—"What do you want me to do with my life?"

Was He really speaking purpose into me?

I searched deep within myself for a reply, *Help young people connect to themselves, each other, Creation. Share this joy with the world so they may know themselves and their Divinity.*

The three of us walked silently until I slowly trailed off, never to see them again.

I will never forget how I felt when that man spoke.

"Do it for the young people".

His words stuck like velcro to my soul.

I started thinking *maybe this was how Secret Sunrise was already becoming an international movement? Not by our hands, but because the Creator has given us something special... born from pure intention—to share joy.*

The man was a pastor. He didn't know me from a bar of soap. Yet he commanded me with such authority I felt absolutely necessary to take joy to the young people.

This wasn't an idle stroll through the Portuguese countryside. It was walking with God in the garden.

I thought about the small dog.

Had he intervened?

Had he laid down his life?

If it weren't for the dog, I wouldn't have met the people carrying the truth of my purpose.

I was humbled by death, life, God, coincidences, and miracles.

Each day on the Camino unraveled more of who I was to become.

SEW GRATEFUL

A FEW DAYS later, I met Mohammed sitting outside a village. As a fellow pilgrim, he looked bedraggled and forlorn on this day. *Not too different from my intense doggy day,* I thought. He told me some of his woes, which included a ripped backpack he was holding. His only backpack. It was evident his belongings might plop out at any moment. In his hunched-over posture on the low cobbled wall, we briefly chatted and soon headed our own ways. Little did we know, in true Camino fashion, we would meet a few hours later in a forest.

As I meandered up a section of the trail he suddenly appeared through some trees on the edge of the woods. I instantly recognized him by how he carried his little "bag baby". Cradling it in his arms he was still trying to avoid the precious contents falling out. In typical pilgrim style, we began chatting, heading deep into conversation as though we were long-time friends. He was mind-meandering about the infinite possibilities of accessible miracles from the universe, and as we exchanged thoughts on *how to send emails to God,* I had this impulse to pray for him and his bag.

If you don't ask, you don't get.

I asked him if I could pray, and he appeared excited at the prospect.

I was new at this whole *faith on the outside* thing, so I tentatively began a prayer:

"God, please help Mohammed. You know his bag is torn and you know what he needs. Please help him to fix it, or bring him a new one, or let him find one. You have all the solutions in your hand. You have the whole world in your hand. Help us please."

When I finished, we both earnestly contemplated the prayer in silence.

Little did we know, God had something in mind.

I felt a pull to the left as we walked only a few paces further.

I slowed.

I paused.

Mohammed looked back at me.

"Do you mind if I check this out?" I said.

"Sure," he replied.

I walked back a few paces, having no idea where I was heading.

A stump of a felled pine tree appeared in front of me.

I bent down and looked closer.

In the center of the pine rings lay the treasure.

A needle and thread.

An answer to Mohammed's torn bag.

I couldn't believe it, and yet I could.

"I think this is for you," I said.

He walked over to see what I had in my hands.

His eyes looked to the needle and thread, then to mine.

It can't be.

Coincidence is one thing, but a needle and thread lying on a fallen pine in the middle of a forest wins the lottery, especially when you need to sew your bag.

I watched Mohammed's inner world doing a topsy-turvy.

I knew the feeling well.

When God arrives, you cannot believe He has actually arrived for you.

He knows me personally and cares for me!

What a Divine revelation!

Mohammed's mind was fighting the miracle, trying to solve the puzzle of "perfect coincidence". He spilled some scenarios about how this moment could have happened.

I had by now experienced too many of these to fight the Divine reality.

I enjoyed God's humor.

Our Great God is beyond our mind.

I thought to myself as I watched him: *How can the Creator of it all fit into the story of our limited minds?*

I was learning to expect and accept answered prayers.

God-incidence, not coincidence.

Mohammed told the next people we met that I had special prayers.

I wished him to realize he had special prayers.

We all do.

God is always listening.

He can fix a lot more than our broken bags.

"Therefore I tell you, whatever you ask for in prayer,
believe that you have received it, and it will be yours".

- JESUS.

A CATHEDRAL CONNECTION

I WALKED INTO Santiago de Compostela, the capital of northwest Spain's Galicia region, by myself. Most pilgrims consider this to be the end of their Camino. You can hand in your stamped pilgrim passport at the office and collect your certificate of completion. These pieces of paper are beautiful and personalized, a precious reminder of the time committed and courage it takes to journey for days or weeks. In my own journey, I made many friends along the way, but I completed the journey as I had started, alone.

I walked up to the famous cathedral and lay down on my back. I sprawled out on the cobbled paving and relished the deep surrender which carried me through it all. I sailed through on the breath of God's mighty wind, releasing my expectations to allow His daily plans. As I looked up at the blue sky and the unfinished cathedral architecture, my heart swelled with thanksgiving.

By letting go of the goal of arriving, I was here.

I stood up and headed for the front door of the church. I was in time for the special pilgrim service. During this service, the priests swing a giant ball of incense (over the heads of the congregation) to bless the pilgrims who have completed their journey. Allegedly, it is a ritual of old designed to quell the smell of the dirty pilgrims as they filled the pews. There were hundreds of people entering the church to receive the blessing.

As I walked under the arch of the big doorway to the church, my shoulder bumped into a man. I turned to look. His face lit up. It was the generous stranger-friend who had given me his jacket days before when I was freezing. I was wearing it. We recognized each other immediately, even though our previous exchange at the border had been brief. Without a word, our arms instinctually lifted and rested around each other's shoulders. Old friends on a pilgrimage through life. His words at the time of the gift exchange were, "So that's why I've been carrying this spare jacket with me! My son gave it to me at the start and I've carried it this whole time for you!" Of all the hundreds of people entering the service, I bumped into the man who had treated me like a son. We were immediately friends by spirit. A special connection formed by Grace which language needn't explain. We felt the instant love of God. We found a place to enjoy the pilgrim service. Our arms remained in an embrace like father and son receiving a blessing. My mind was confused, yet it felt so natural. Tears watered the corners of our eyes as something spiritual moved with us.

What an end to a journey.

God with us..

The service ended and we had lunch together. He shared some deep and meaningful events happening in his life. He told me he had not shared it with anyone.

My heart was full.

He had a flight to catch, so he paid for our lunch and we shared our final hugs goodbye.

Thank you, Gerd, for sharing your story with me.

I remember it as it was yesterday.

I trust your life unfolded with the fullness of His love.

I walked slowly back to the monastery I was staying in.

It was beautiful.

The simplicity lent itself to closeness with God.

I lay on my small, single bed in my room.

I contemplated all the synchronicities, coincidences, conversations, and Camino magic.

Could everyday life be like this?

END OF THE EARTH

AFTER NEARLY A month of walking (without digital contact to my 'outside world'), I finally switched on my phone to receive messages. I contacted my aunt to let her know I was complete with the Camino journey. I also reached out to a new Camino friend. Her name was Agatha. We had met weeks earlier and had spent many days on the trail together.

If you want to know someone, walk with them for a week.

Agatha and I became close friends on the trail.

We had parted several days earlier when our Camino journeys carried us on slightly different paths. I thought she might still be around Santiago before her flight.

To my delight, she replied to my message within minutes.

She was nearby!

I suggested one last journey together.

My idea was to head to Finisterre—*the end of the earth*—a Latin translation describing a small town on the northwest Spanish coast. I was tired of walking, so I suggested we rent a car. We agreed to go the next day. By God's grace, the last VW polo waited for us in the parking lot of the rental place. We booked it and set off.

It felt different to be driving after so much walking! I was also delighted to be reunited with my Camino friend. We shared so many precious memories.

As we meandered along well-maintained roads and beautiful green scenery toward Finisterre and Muxia, we both sat in the silence of the inevitable goodbye to soon follow.

Every journey must come to an end.

Abruptly we arrived at a fork in the road.

There was an option to turn right and head to Muxia or proceed straight to Finisterre. Both were considered 'Camino end points'. I wondered if we had enough time to do both or if we should choose one?

Agatha appeared unconcerned, so I consulted my heart.

Which way should we go, heart?

I waited for any familiar internal signs. I had been following my heart daily on the Camino. I felt a gentle pull toward the direction of Muxia. Very subtle, yet distinctly in that direction.

I trusted.

I had long since surrendered to the wisdom of the heart.

I indicated and turned right.

Off we went to Muxia.

As we neared the town we came upon a beach. It was a beautiful white sand, windswept beach. The serenity tantalized our senses so I stopped the car to explore. We jumped out and wandered the sand stretch like hermit crabs in our own happy worlds. The gravity of the moment tugged on me.

This is really the end.

Living the Camino life is over.

I may never see Agatha again.

We absorbed the special atmosphere of Muxia. A mixture of serenity, peace, and wildness stirred by the undulating Atlantic ocean. It was a soul-stirring place. Coming out of our own worlds and reconvening near the car, we kept driving to find a lunch spot with a view.

Our final picnic. Our last supper.

I parked in another spot near the ocean.

We got out of the car to set up for lunch.

Agatha and I knew the daily Camino routine well:

Choose a spot. Lay down yoga mat for seating. Get out ingredients. Chop ingredients. Serve in two plastic tupperware containers. Eat. Wash. Rest.

Agatha chose a spot close to the ocean.

I rustled in my bag for supplies (rice, leafy greens, tomato, tuna).

We dished.

We ate in silence as we often did.

I appreciated Agatha immensely. After my struggle with disease, she had been a joyous ray of sunshine who returned laughter, ease, love, and friendship back to my world.

The sound of the ocean echoed around us as we washed our plates.

As was her custom, she reached for her book and quietly began reading.

My innerworld had other plans.

Something inside was calling me to explore.

I noticed a beautiful church nearby and thought I'd take a closer look. Leaving Agatha engrossed in her book, I walked over the rocks to the entrance of the church. It was enchanting. Perched on the rocks at the edge of the ocean it looked like an old seagull waiting to take flight. I had no idea how the church had endured the wicked ways of the icy Atlantic all these years. Admiring it, I climbed a little higher to get a better view of the surrounding area.

I rounded to the right of the church and climbed a small hillside. Strolling along I was in a deep state of contemplation. I was experiencing the end of the journey. The end of Agatha's companionship. The end of the simplicity of walking every day. The end of my time in Portugal and Spain.

I knew I was standing there by Grace. It wasn't my energy, fitness, or planning which carried me along the hundreds of miles. It wasn't my strength. It was a gift from heaven to be where I was. It was trust which carried me to this state of health, happiness, and holiness. I reflected on the many friends I had met along the way and the conversations which shaped my life and understanding. I thought about days when I had to rely on divine strength rather than personal strength. I remembered miraculously answered prayers. I witnessed the presence of God every day, and I wanted to live a life like this. Not only for a moment in time but a lifestyle of living in His presence.

The Great Giver was always giving, and I was ever receiving.

I continued to climb up the hillside.

And that's when it happened.

LIGHTNING STRIKES TWICE

LOST IN THOUGHT, I stumbled into a large, solid shape, rising up above me in the landscape.

A giant, square-shaped rock.

About four times my height and about five meters wide.

In the middle of the rock was a crack.

Not just any crack.

Running down the center was a split, in the shape of lightning.

A zigzag splitting the rock in two halves.

I stared at the rock.

My spirit melted.

Lightning rock.

I instantly recognized I had arrived at the place I had seen in my dream many months before.

It was the dream of the Stonehenge-shaped rock. A memory resuscitated when I was searching passionately online for this lightning-shaped rock that meant so much to me.

I couldn't figure it out at the time.

Now I was standing in front of it.

The search was over.

I fell to my knees.

I was engulfed by Presence.

Stirred by the hand of our Creator.

Awe poured onto me like honey.

While my mind figured out if this was really happening, my spirit soared with the angelic.

I was now living the dream.

Walking the dream.

God's dream.

He sent the dream to me when I was living in Hout Bay. It was so clear, so meaningful. I knew it had to be important. Now it wasn't a dream anymore, it was my life.

As I experienced a closeness to God—my heart contracted and pushed tears from my eyes.

Something deep inside me stirred, shifted, melted, joined.

My consciousness grew, my very idea of life expanded.

I changed in a way I couldn't see.

Total revelation swirled around me—I cannot easily find the words.

I am fully known.

This idea entered the empty recesses of my heart.

I am fully loved.

My Great Creator came here before me.

He gave me my dreams.

He goes ahead of me.

He never forsakes me.

Everything is good because He genuinely loves me and never leaves.

I felt tiny, big, loved, connected, and overwhelmed.

I was curled in a little ball beneath the rock in my dream—a meeting with lightning rock.

It was clear God held the master plan and guided me to lightning rock. The same rock I could not find on the internet a year before.

It was real in my dream, now it was physically and materially real. God had been with me through all of it. He was with me during my illness, during the 800 km of trail, and he would be with me after it. I felt fully connected to the Master Dreamer. My soul stirred.

Recovering my senses slightly I reached for my phone and took some pictures. I wanted to remember lightning rock forever. More than this, I wanted to remember the closeness to My Creator forever.

If you want to see where I had my encounter with the Divine, you can search for a church called Virxe da Barca (near a town called Muxia). You will see the lightning, zigzag shaped rock-of-dreams in the background. It was here I was touched by the Maker's hand. It was here I became known.

I looked around. The place exuded a special and sacred atmosphere. I imagined many humans had searched that hillside looking for the Divine. Searching for truth. I imagined people for centuries laying their hearts down at the edge of the earth, waiting to hear from their Great Lover. I was told this path had been walked for millennia before. I wondered how many had completed their pilgrimages and been stirred by revelations like mine? How many people had God led to union?

The Master Guide.

I arrived to meet a new part of myself—remembering a truth I already knew. Whoever sent me the dream of lightning rock knew my future. God knew me by name. He knew I would meet the cracked rock. Knew I needed an old lady on a Zimmer frame to motivate me to a journey of a lifetime.

It was His story, and I was the canvas of His love.

To realize God knew me was life-changing. To be known personally by God!

As I walked around the green hillside at the edge of the ocean, a tide of overwhelm washed over me. Awe filled my soul whilst liquid kissed my cheeks in streaks.

Challenging memories surfaced in my mind—Suicide, depression, breakdowns, trauma, anxiety, incurable illness, an untamed mind, and a worldwide dance movement. God had carried me through it all. He was my savior. The reason I was still standing. It was His spirit operating in me which carried me through it.

I needn't worry anymore.

He was always present.

I could surrender to trust.

Words cannot describe this ancient memory impressed into our beings when we realize another layer of who we truly are.

Coming out of total awe, my mind reactivated with memories of the doctors who said I would be lucky to jog around the neighborhood. Well, that block was now 800 km and growing.

When I had composed myself and landed back on earth, I started the slow life-changing walk back to Agatha. Each step was a precious moment in time. A kiss from Creation. Each step I knew belonged to both myself and God.

Agatha was still reading. I didn't say a word. I picked up my walking sticks and went to the edge of the rocks. I watched the waves crash and spray tiny pieces of the Atlantic Ocean into the atmosphere like glitter. I stood looking into the horizon, on the edge of the earth, my heart open to the gates of heaven.

I lifted the bamboo walking sticks I had carried for hundreds of kilometers. I didn't need crutches to get me through the journey of life anymore. I only needed God.

To partner with Divinity.

No more pity party.

From where does my help come? It comes from the Creator of heaven and earth.

I threw the bamboo sticks into the ocean.

I watched them float momentarily before a big wave splintered them onto the rocks.

They were gone.

My mind wouldn't hold onto any more crutches. It wouldn't hold me back by having me believe in limitations. It would be fixed on the Infinite, with infinite possibilities.

I had discovered the divinity in my heart again, and we would soar.

I was returning to joy.

The Camino of my life had put down the baggage within me to finally allow me to take a tiny step closer to Truth. It was momentous for me.

I was listening to Divine music.

I was dancing with Daniel.

I was moving closer to true joy.

I was healing.

I was healed.

THE LAST HAWK

RETURNING FROM THE Camino de Santiago to Durban in South Africa, I was renewed in mind, body, soul, and spirit. There were no more excuses for things I couldn't do. Lightning rock had struck huge bits of unbelief from me. Now I could trust that I was well and held by the caring hand of our Creator.

God existed.

God cared.

Something bigger was within and outside me.

Guiding me.

Soon after I returned, I was asked to participate in and facilitate a Secret Sunrise dance retreat in the Drakensberg mountains. I gladly agreed. I felt my calling now to help others heal as I had been healed. During my journey, I had processed a lot, refined a lot, and mined a lot of my own inner gold. I was now willing to share that with the world—as difficult as it was to speak about it.

I arrived at the retreat venue high up in the Drakensberg mountains.

It is a stunning place.

The atmosphere is so pure you can effortlessly dial into creation.

My spirit soared.

Our venue was perched on a mountain overlooking a wide valley.

As I stared over the vista, moments before the retreat was due to begin, an internal urge nagged me to go for a walk.

"Not the best timing," my mind chimed.

I agreed.

The final guests were due to arrive any minute. After all the listening to my inner world, I knew what I had to do. *If God has brought me this far, He will take me onwards. He knows what is best.* I had long ago learned to trust the subtle "pull" to do something. I knew if God needed me out there, I had to do it, no matter what others thought.

At this moment a subtle magnetic pull tugged on me to take a walk to the nearby cliff edges. I looked across the plateau. The scenery was breathtaking. I loved being on top of the mountains. I was home. As I perched on the cliff edge, surveying the natural beauty, I realized I'd arrived in a place I'd longed for years—to feel somewhat "normal" again. I was in awe that I could do a full week's work for Secret Sunrise, surrounded by dozens of people—dancing, playing, healing, processing—and I would still have energy for more. This was astounding. For the Daniel who had lain in bed for months, who had longed for the mountains, sat in the green hammock on his own, hour after hour, day after day, this was landing in paradise.

I no longer had a fear of failing or flaking out halfway. I knew I was strong enough. I had done the Camino, I had the mental, physical, and spiritual fitness. I had learned some important lessons.

I knew if I partnered with God, I would always have energy to complete His tasks.

By God's grace I was standing and fit right now. After years of longing to be a part of a normal functioning tribe again, here I was. I had changed from riding spiritually solo to sharing the tandem bicycle of life. It was "we"—Me and God—God and me. I had a partner, and He would never leave me or forsake me. I would never be alone again.

I knew it was also time to surrender my healthy life, as I had surrendered my sick life. Being well again didn't mean it was time to "take control of the things I had lost", being well again meant there was more of me available to serve Divinity.

If I continued to surrender, I would be carried into the fullness of life. A life of joy I couldn't imagine. A life not only without disease but a life so completely fulfilling I would become a well of living water which others could also drink from.

I knew the next step I had to take.

I had to give up my life all over again.

Another deep surrender.

To give back what I had been given. I had given my life in death, now it was time to give my life in life.

My handover wasn't done now from a place of desperation, it was from a place of strength. A handover to my Savior from my own willingness and consent and knowing. I chose to give up my life, not because I had to but because I wanted to. It was the best way for me, the highest way.

I stopped and stood motionless on the cliff edge, staring into the distance. Emotions stirred within me. The wind buffeted against my jacket and face. I remembered my mother's favorite rock with the inscription: *It is here with the wind that I hear my soul.* I knew what my spirit was calling me to do. With a deep knowing, a deep connection, I prayed to surrender my life again.

My prayers reached out from my heart. On the cliff edge, I tuned into all-that-is. I connected with mother nature and Father Creator. I was divinely held and surrendered. I knew I was safe. I knew I would be guided to a joy I couldn't imagine. A plan which wasn't figured out by me, a painting painted by the Master Painter.

Time passed.

As I finished soaring in the spirit, I suddenly remembered the retreat was starting and decided to head back. I was going to be late and I was concerned others would be thinking, *typical Dan, doing his own thing as usual.*

This time I let it go. No one was me. It was my unique journey of the heart, and I was committed to it. With or without human support, I would do it. How could I explain everything that had brought me closer to God? I was serving only one Master now, the Divine Creator of the Universe. It was by His hand whether I would rise or fall. I was working for someone else now. I had a new boss. God. I was running on His time, His leave, His provision. I knew deep inside this kind of surrender—serving Divinity over human desire—would be how I got there. Wherever "there" actually was. I knew this surrender would help me arrive at a place where my restless spirit would find peace. I was committed to my calling—a heart-surrendered life—God had designed this for me, and I was following.

I felt the moving parts of my soul fitting together like a grand puzzle.

My heart reached out in prayer again. "God, if you are out there, show yourself to me. Reveal yourself to me so I know you are with me now. Remove all doubts. Let me know you exist. Let me never doubt again."

The prayer rose from me like a bird lifting up on thermal air currents. I sensed I had been prayed rather than trying to pray.

My heart reached out to the heart of life.

God reaching out to God.

Not knowing what to expect, I stretched both my arms wide open to the skies. My heart was turned to the heavens. My heart was roaring. The wind continued to buffet.

I waited.

Nothing spectacular happened, except for a feeling of completion.

I guessed God might come another day.

What would I expect to see anyway?

How does the Master of Creation reveal himself to an insignificant dot like me in His creation?

"Really," my mind chipped in, "What sign would He even show you?"

And then I saw it.

A dot.

It was moving fast.

I watched a tiny speck of brown, soaring quickly above the ground. It was below me, at the bottom far left of the cliff faces, increasing in speed.

Is it moving toward me?

My heartbeat quickened. I knew what it was.

My spirit animal.

A hawk.

I knew it was coming to meet me.

My soul melted as I realized what was actually happening.

Was this God?

Before I could catch my breath, the hawk was behind me.

I looked over my left shoulder, it was hovering mere meters above my head.

Instantly my left arm raised itself.

The Puppet Master was at it again.

I wanted to bring my arm in but it was fuelled by an internal energy.

It was straight out at my side.

Is this really happening?

Is this God?

Revelation burst from a deep place in my soul—the entire scene was an act of surrender. *Can I hold my arm out and actually let a wild hawk land on me?*

Can I trust?

"You might fall over the edge," my mind chimed in.

I could see the hawk's every detail. It was magnificent. Sharp beak. Piercing eyes. Talons reaching out. I could hear the buffering wind flicking its feathers.

It had all come to this.

Suddenly my mind, in a final act of defense, pierced through the awe of the moment, "Maybe it's a tame hawk, Daniel? Maybe it's someone's pet?" I surveyed the scene again. There was nobody around. Nobody living out here. There was simply no way this was someone's pet. My mind was trying to edge God out. Edge the miracle out.

"Maybe someone hand-raised it, and it's looking for food now?" I looked around at the vast wilderness surrounding me. There was nothing but wide open skies, valleys, and mountains.

I couldn't move. The Puppet Master still had me in His dance.

A feeling of surreal flow rippled through me—the same as meeting African Daniel on the roadside.

The hawk was moving in.

Closer. Closer.

I was frozen.

The hawk used the wind blowing off the cliff face to keep itself extremely steady. I watched its every move as it made micro-adjustments to try another landing on my outstretched arm. At times it appeared completely still and suspended in midair.

I was suspended in awe and terror.

It was about 1.5 meters from my outstretched arm now. Maybe less. My mind panicked. I was suddenly aware I was standing dangerously close to the cliff. My mind spoke, "If that hawk hits you with force, you will fall over the edge."

Fear surged inside me.

My heart replied, "Do you trust me?"

My spirit soared, "This is God."

The hawk was mere feet from me now. The sound of wind in its wings mesmerized me—even to this day. It was a buffeting sound, like air rippling against a grocery packet. I could see the detail on its talons clearly. They were stretched slightly forward, ready to grab my arm.

Centimeters from my outstretched arm, in the final seconds before talon touchdown, I snapped my arm back to my body. The hawk whipped a few feet back to its original hovering position over my left shoulder. Terror and fear rose in me. *Can I actually do this? Can I let a wild hawk land on me?* The cliff edge was close. The talons were sharp. *Hasn't God brought me to this? Isn't this my Divine encounter of a lifetime?*

I thought about the owl which had once tried to land on me, now, after all these years of growth, could I not surrender to this moment?

As the hawk resumed its position, I put my arm out again.

Slowly the beautiful bird of prey lowered in again. It wasn't done with me. Mesmerized like prey, I was motionless in front of it. As it neared my arm, I panicked again. My mind jostled up another memory. It reminded me of a woman I'd met at a Birds of Prey sanctuary. Her arm was broken and in a plaster cast. One of the bigger birds of prey had snapped her bone when it tried to take off with her.

I looked down at the cliff.

Fear had me in its grip; "This is dangerous, I could lose my life."

When I pulled in my arm at the last second the hawk diverted again and was back up in an instant.

One last time, I tentatively outstretched my arm again.

I felt I was personally lifting my arm this time. It wasn't automatic like the involuntary lift of the Puppet Master. I was somehow now in the game—playing with the limit of our understanding of creation.

Fear and hesitation coursed through my veins. *How long can this game last?* I stared at the hawk. *Who are you?* I could still hear the wind flickering in its plumage. Every feather was rustling as if it were in a hurricane. It was magnificent.

For a moment, awe returned. It gave me enough confidence to hold my arm still this time. *God, is this You? God, is this You? God, is this You?* The question stormed through me as I tried to steady myself.

The hawk slowly lowered. *This is it.* It would be its last dive. It approached in slow motion. The talons reached out. My fear of going over the cliff gripped me. I cried out suddenly. I fell to the ground. It was too much. I pulled my arm in against my body for protection. I couldn't comprehend it. I couldn't grapple with what was going on. I huddled in a ball with my eyes closed.

Amongst the cold stones and rocks of the mountaintop, I sobbed, "I can't do it, I can't do it. I'm so sorry, I'm so sorry, I'm so sorry."

I was sorry to God.

I was sorry to the hawk.

I was sorry to myself.

I felt like a failure.

Disappointment swirled in me.

Tears fell from my eyes as I lay in the fetal position. I was only a child. I couldn't do it. I couldn't surrender completely.

The wind still gusted around me.

It is here with the wind that I hear my soul.

I opened my eyes to see if the hawk was still there.

Gone.

I hadn't fully surrendered.

I hadn't fully trusted.

If I really trusted God, I would have allowed that hawk to land on me.

There was still unbelief in me.

I scanned the sky, hoping desperately to see my feathered friend. To feel closeness again.

A closeness to nature, a doorway to divinity. Mine was gone.

The door closed.

The hawk had left.

I lifted myself up and looked at the horizon.

I wanted to beg for more forgiveness and somehow try again, and then I remembered the retreat!

Whilst I was dancing with hawks, the Secret Sunrise dance retreat was surely on its way, without me.

I had no idea how long I had been gone for. It felt like an eternity. Time had stretched.

I needed to return to the people.

God, why do you do this to me? Why do you make me an outlier? A person who is so different. Why do you have me on this deep spiritual journey? Now not only will I be late, but how can I tell anyone about what has just happened?!

I headed back to the center.

I hesitantly approached the back door expecting the *where-have-you-been* glares.

I could see people milling outside. It was a good sign. The retreat hadn't started. "Thank You, God, thank You for holding time."

As I got to the entrance door, my best friend and business partner Sebastian came bounding out. His usual flamboyant, larger-than-life-buzz greeted me. Of all the people I was bumping into first, it was him. If anybody in the world could remotely understand my encounter, it could be him. I felt to share, but I had a mixture of resistance and pressure to speak. I knew I had to start sharing my stories and spirit encounters. "Get it out of your head and into the hearts of others, Daniel," a whisper encouraged me. "Start grounding your stories," said the voice inside. "When you share something, you make it real".

"Howzit, my bru!" Bast said with a big smile. "What's up?" He could sense I was in one of my deep spaces and going through something.

I looked at him. His joyousness, his aliveness. His energy. Tears welled up as I searched for the words. Speaking about them was akin to speaking about God. It was challenging.

"A hawk just tried to land on me," I said. My voice was strained with tears trying to squeeze themselves from my eyes.I waited for the reaction. The judgment. The disbelief.

He looked at me with a glint in his eye, and excitement exuded from his pores. His face lit up. "What! That's incredible!" He beamed. "I just saw a hawk diving and hovering over there by the cliff edge." He pointed in the direction I had come from. He continued talking excitedly. "I was standing inside and through the window I could see it moving up and down near the cliffs. I didn't see anyone below because of the trees. It must have been you there!"

I was stunned. This is not what I was expecting. I was prepared for unbelief, and instead, I received comforting and encouraging words. God was still holding me. More moments of divine connection. Sebastian. The hawk. Me. God. We had somehow shared the experience together. My heart expanded. God was with us. His fingerprints were on all of it. God had allowed me to share this experience so I wouldn't feel alone. So I wouldn't doubt it. So I knew it was real. So I could start telling my stories. His stories.

God knew my every need. I had His support. Now and forever.

Sebastian was still smiling.

He hugged me.

It was so good to have someone who understood.

All I needed to do now was to continue to surrender my life into God's hands.

Continue letting go of control.

Soften to resistance.

Allow.

Surrender to joy.

I am learning this journey is continuous, an ever unfolding string of moments to give over to God.

When I think I have surrendered an area of my life, I often have another "hawk moment".

He knows my weak areas.

This hawk was a teacher, asking me, "Have you really surrendered?"

Surrender leads to greater contentment.

To inner fulfillment.

To deeper peace.

To more joy.

I trust my obedience will lead me to true love.

EPILOGUE

Years have passed since this "hawk moment".

I'm still learning to surrender.

More moments arise that test my trust in the Heart of God.

Always another layer to peel back.

Whenever I thought I was completely healed, another moment of healing arose.

Every time I thought I surrendered, I was called deeper.

After M.E I began healing the other broken bits of myself.

Insecurity. Dependence. Control.

Through suffering comes wholeness.

Even in a higher state of wholeness I have suffered much.

And continue to.

More layers. More completed relationships, more deceased family members, more exploring a path through the maze of main-stream identities.

The closer I move to God, the more I see my brokenness.

In a way, I will always be healing.

I must heal to unravel my true identity.

The only one who knows the way is my heart.

Great joy arrives by heart-living.

I often have moments when I step back and say, "How is this happening?" or, "What am I even doing right now?"

This is how I know it's right.

I couldn't plan it.

It's beyond my mind.

It's the journey of my heart.

It's obedience to our great and loving Creator.

It is the best place to be.

Surrendered.

Joyfully.

CLOSING PRAYER

As you stand on the threshold of your own surrender,
or witness people going through theirs,
I pray you would look into the flames with joy.
That you would count it all joy.
Suffering will leave you lacking nothing.
Complete and whole.
By suffering, you are moving toward higher love.
The scriptures say; "If you cling to your life, you will lose
it; but if you give up your life… you will find it."
I pray you give your life to God and find His joy.
True Joy.
May you meet Him full on, as He met me.
He is running after you right now.
Turn around and say hello.

Dear God,
I give you my heart.
I choose to surrender to Your will.
Help me let go of control and let in Your
everlasting, unconditional love.
Please forgive me for what I've done in fear and lack of love.
Show me Your love.
Help me lay down my life for an exciting journey of discovery.
Help me follow my heart.
Help me to see the light.
Guide me.
I give myself over to you and Highest Love.

May the presence of God's love bless you into abundance.
May the sacrifice of His Love fill your Spirit.
Go forth now and shine.
And watch your world transform.

You are the light of the world.
People do not light a lamp
and put it under a basket,
but in the middle of the room,
and it gives light to all who are in the house.
Let your light so shine before others,
that people may see your good works,
and glorify God in heaven.

- CHRIST

As you read these final words I'm sitting on a small
wooden chair in an apartment in Egypt. The shadow
of Mount Sinai simmers in the distance.
The water of the red sea mirrors the afternoon sky.
As the last sentences make their way to my eyes, my
life story catches up to the present moment. I look
out the window and see the unkept tops of palm
trees swaying gently in the afternoon breeze.
Egypt has called out to me from the depths of my heart.
I have responded.
Here I am.
Why?
I don't know.
It isn't for me to know.
I'm on assignment.
For the King of our hearts.

Thank you for reading my story.
I am deeply touched that you have taken the time to know me.
Please share your stories with me.
Your encounters.
Your revelations.
Feedback.

We are all one.

www.danielcameronbecker.com